Presidents Can't Punt

THE OU FOOTBALL TRADITION

The OU Football Tradition

Presidents Can't Punt

by George Lynn Cross

University of Oklahoma Press : *Norman*

Also by George Lynn Cross

Blacks in White Colleges: Oklahoma's Landmark Cases (Norman, 1975)
The World of Ideas: Essays on the Past and Future (with others)
(Norman, 1968)

Library of Congress Cataloging in Publication Data

Cross, George Lynn.
   Presidents can't punt.

   1. Oklahoma. University—Football—History.   2. Football—History.
I. Title.
GV958.04C76   796.33'263'0976631   77-8867

Publication of this book has been aided by a grant from the Wallace
C. Thompson Fund of the University of Oklahoma Foundation.

To Harold V. Keith,

who, while achieving status as one of the premier sports-information directors of the country, always kept collegiate athletics in proper perspective—games to be played by boys and girls.

Preface

THE great football tradition at the University of Oklahoma has been the subject of much discussion, both oral and written. In the following pages I give my impressions of why and how it all came about and, perhaps, raise the question of whether it should have come about. My confidence in attempting the account is bolstered by the fact that for nearly twenty-five years I was president of the university, during a time when the institution soared to a football zenith through the coaching genius of Bud Wilkinson and Gomer Jones, subsided somewhat for a brief period, and then regained national prominence under Chuck Fairbanks.

It may be of interest to the reader to know how I became involved with football at OU. After four years as head of the Department of Botany at the University of South Dakota, I came to the University of Oklahoma as assistant professor of botany and microbiology in September, 1934. Paul B. Sears, a distinguished plant ecologist, was head of the department at the time. In the late 1930's, Sears accepted a position at Oberlin College, and I succeeded him as head of the department. Soon after the bombing of Pearl Harbor, Homer Dodge, dean of the Graduate College, was called to Washington, D.C., to aid in the war effort, and I became acting dean of the college. In 1943, Joseph A. Brandt, president of the university, resigned to become director of the University of Chicago Press, and I was named acting president of OU. In 1944, I was named to the presidency, a post that I held until my retirement on June 30, 1968.

During my tenure as president I was occasionally asked why I appeared to have such an intense interest in intercollegiate athletics. Occasionally the questions seemed to imply that such interest on the part of a university president was unseemly and that his attention might better be directed toward what was happening in the areas of his academic responsibilities. From my point of view the explanation was simple. I had participated in track, baseball, and football in high school. Because of my high school record, I was offered a "football scholarship" at South Dakota State College, Brookings, South Dakota. The scholarship consisted of a job washing dishes in a women's dining hall and a job with a construction company wheeling concrete during the summer months. I had always enjoyed sports, both as a participant and as a spectator. At the time I became president of OU, intercollegiate athletics seemed to provide wholesome and exciting extracurricular activities that could be enjoyed by participants and spectators alike—and might attract the favorable attention of the state's citizenry. Thus my interest in athletics.

Source materials for the following account include a scrapbook of newspaper clippings, minutes of the meetings of the regents of the University of Oklahoma, Bud Wilkinson's weekly newsletters, and *Thirteen Years of Winning Oklahoma Football,* by Volney Meece and Bill Bryan, printed by the Globe Color Press of Oklahoma City.

It is a pleasure to acknowledge the assistance of several who gave help during the preparation of the manuscript. Ms. Barbara James, secretary to the Board of Regents of the University of Oklahoma, was most gracious and patient in helping me find items of interest in the regents' records. The staff of the Office of Sports Publicity at the university, especially Addie Lee Barker, Harold Keith, and John Keith, were most helpful in providing information and many of the illustrations. Harold Keith made invaluable suggestions concerning revision of the original manuscript. Kenneth E. Farris, associate athletic director and business manager of athletics, was most cooperative in supplying information. David Swank, professor of law and faculty representative to the Big Eight Conference, supplied copies of the minutes of the faculty representatives of the conference that were missing from my files. Jim Weeks, sports editor of the *Norman Transcript,* provided source materials concerning the history of the Big Eight Conference. Charles Bennett, managing editor of the *Daily Oklahoman* and the *Oklahoma City Times,* gave helpful suggestions and supplied several illustrations from the files of the Oklahoma Publishing Company. I warmly appreciate his cooperation. I am indebted also to my wife, Cleo S. Cross, who made many helpful suggestions concerning grammar and punctuation. I am most indebted of all to my secretary, Ms. Robbye Meaders, not only for a superb job of typing and retyping but also for splendid editorial assistance as the final copy of the manuscript was prepared.

GEORGE LYNN CROSS

Norman, Oklahoma

Contents

Illustrations

Presidents Can't Punt

THE OU FOOTBALL TRADITION

CHAPTER 1

The First Fifty Years
1895–1945

FOOTBALL got under way at the University of Oklahoma in the fall of 1895 with John A. Harts as coach. The first season was not impressive. The team played only one game, against the town team of Oklahoma City; the university was defeated, 34–0.

Apparently OU did not have a coach during the 1896 season, although the records indicate that the team won two games from Norman High School that year.

In 1897, Vernon Louis Parrington, a graduate of Harvard University, who came to the University of Oklahoma from Emporia College in Kansas to teach English and modern languages, was induced to take over football (and baseball) coaching as an extracurricular activity. During the next four seasons his teams played twelve games, winning nine, losing two, and tying one. Parrington remained at the university until June, 1908, when he was dismissed as a result of the political shakeup that took place at the university with the advent of statehood in 1907. The Republicans had been in power during territorial days, but in the first state election Democrats swept into office. The new administration thought that some changes should be made at the state university, and Parrington was one of the casualties. (Later, as a member of the faculty of the University of Washington at Seattle, Parrington won a Pulitzer Prize for his three-volume *Main Currents in American Thought.*)

From Parrington's time football was an established program at the University of Oklahoma, although it did not produce any championship teams until Bennie Owen took over the coaching duties in 1905. According to the university catalogue of that year, the university had become a member of the Southwestern Intercollegiate Athletic Association, which included Texas, Arkansas, Colorado, and New Mexico universities.[1] Teams coached

[1]Roy Gittinger, *The University of Oklahoma: A History of Fifty Years, 1892–1942* (Norman, University of Oklahoma Press, 1942), 49.

by Owen won conference championships in 1910 and 1911.

Before the 1915 season Oklahoma became a member of the Southwest Conference, along with the University of Texas, Oklahoma Agricultural and Mechanical College, Texas Agricultural and Mechanical College, the University of Arkansas, Baylor University, and Southwestern University, of Georgetown, Texas. OU won a Southwest Conference championship in 1915 and tied for another in 1918.

In December, 1919, the University of Oklahoma shifted its membership to the Missouri Valley Conference, which consisted of the University of Missouri, the University of Kansas, Kansas State Agricultural College, Iowa State College, Drake University, Grinnell College, and Washington University, at St. Louis.[2] Oklahoma A&M College was admitted to the conference in 1925. Oklahoma's football team, coached by Owen, won the Missouri Valley Conference crown in the first season the university held membership, 1920. There were no other championships during Owen's tenure as coach (through 1926), but his teams compiled a creditable over-all record: 128 wins, 52 losses, and 13 ties.

After the 1927 season an extensive reorganization occurred within the Missouri Valley Conference. Grinnell College, Drake University, Oklahoma A&M, and Washington University discontinued their memberships, and the remaining institutions, with the addition of the University of Nebraska, organized the Missouri Valley Intercollegiate Athletic Association; the new association became known unofficially as the Big Six Conference.

After OU won the Missouri Valley Conference championship in 1920, football fortunes at the university waned for several years. The upturn that led to the prestige now enjoyed by the university probably dates back to 1935, when Lawrence N. ("Biff") Jones was lured to Oklahoma from Louisiana State University. Jones did not produce any championship teams during his two-year tenure as coach and director of athletics, but he did establish good business management in the Athletic Department, and his teams were reasonably successful.

Jones was succeeded by Tom Stidham in 1937. Stidham coached four years and won the Big Six championship in 1938. His cham-

[2] *Ibid.*, 116.

Coach Dewey ("Snorter") Luster. He coached at OU for five years, producing two Big Six championship teams. None of his teams ever placed lower than second in the Big Six. Sports Information Department, University of Oklahoma.

pionship team played in the Orange Bowl in 1939 against the University of Tennessee, and, although the team lost the game, 0–17, Stidham's over-all record gave Oklahomans a renewed taste for big-time football.

Dewey ("Snorter") Luster became head football coach at OU in 1941, with Lawrence E. ("Jap") Haskell as athletic director. The eleventh coach to serve the university, Luster coached five years, won two Big Six championships, and never finished lower than second place in the conference. His record in conference play was 18–4–3, the best of any Oklahoma coach in Big Six competition. His teams were never able to defeat the University

5

of Texas, however, and during the final two years of his tenure they lost to Oklahoma A&M by lopsided scores. The losses to Texas and Oklahoma A&M overshadowed an otherwise excellent record, and Luster was subjected to a great deal of undeserved criticism during the final two years of his coaching career, a period that coincided with the first two years of my presidency of the University of Oklahoma. In addition, Luster was handicapped by ill-health; his doctor did not permit him to attend the game with Oklahoma A&M in 1944. He came to my office one day during the 1945 season and said that he wanted to be relieved of his coaching duties at the end of the season. His resignation was announced to the newspapers on Friday, November 9, 1945. The search for a new coach began immediately.

CHAPTER 2

On Hiring a Football Coach—Jim Tatum

1945-46

NEWS of Luster's resignation brought a barrage of suggestions and applications to the president's office during the following weeks, and, naturally, there were many rumors about his successor. The Board of Regents of the university took careful stock of the situation at their first meeting following the resignation. The regents were E. C. Hopper, Jr., Eufaula; Don Emery, Bartlesville; Lloyd Noble, Ardmore; Erl Deacon, Cushing; William R. Wallace, Oklahoma City; Ned Shepler, Lawton; and Joe W. McBride, Anadarko. Hopper was president of the board.

While discussing what to do about a new football coach, the board somehow became involved with the social and psychological problems of the citizens of the state. One member reminded the group that John Steinbeck's *Grapes of Wrath* had all but destroyed the morale of Oklahomans. He thought that many of them actually felt a little apologetic about living in Oklahoma. What, if anything, could the university do to improve the situation and help develop pride in the state? At that point, Lloyd Noble, sandy-haired, tan-jacketed oil driller from Ardmore, leaned back in his chair and observed that the university might have an unusual opportunity to help in that it was looking for a football coach at that particular time. He went on to say that, with the war ending, a four-year supply of high-school athletes would be returning from the armed services, most of them with four years of athletic eligibility remaining. If the university could recruit a sufficient number of these athletes and come up with the right coach, it might be able to field a great football team almost immediately.

Then came the inevitable question: How could the University of Oklahoma get information about returning athletes and attract them to the institution? One of the regents—Erl Deacon, as I recall—reminded his fellow board members that each branch of the armed services had sponsored football teams during the war

The University of Oklahoma Board of Regents, 1945–46. STANDING, LEFT TO RIGHT: Erl Deacon, Joe McBride, Ned Shepler, Don Emery, Lloyd Noble. SEATED: George Lynn Cross, president of the university; E. C. Hopper, president of the board, William R. Wallace, and Emil Kraettli, secretary of the board. Courtesy Board of Regents, University of Oklahoma.

and those teams had had coaches. If one of the service coaches could be hired by the university, he certainly would know the names of the outstanding football players being discharged from the armed forces.

This seemed a good possibility, because OU's athletic director, Jap Haskell, had been on leave of absence serving with the United States Navy during the war. He had visited the campus briefly while on leave during the preceding summer. He and I had discussed the probability that Luster's health would not permit him to coach beyond the 1945 season, and he had given his views about a possible successor. Haskell thought that the most promising prospect likely to be interested in the job was Jim Tatum, a graduate of the University of North Carolina and head coach there in 1942. Haskell was acquainted with Tatum and had seen him in action as coach of a navy team at Jacksonville, Florida.

After spending a few minutes discussing procedures to be followed in hunting for a new football coach, the regents wound up their session by agreeing that it should be the responsibility of the president of the university to bring to the board the names of two promising prospects to be chosen with the cooperation of the Athletic Council and the director of athletics. The board would select one of the two.

During the following weeks the names of several outstanding coaches were sent to university authorities from several sources. When Haskell resumed his duties as athletic director on December 1, he was given the list of prospects to be screened with the help of the Athletic Council. Haskell and the council finally came up with the names of six individuals whom they thought should be brought to the university for interviews. Tatum's name was fifth on the list.

Four of the prospects were brought to the campus, but it was agreed that none quite fit the requirements at OU. The only additional possibilities were Jim Tatum and "Red" Drew, coach at the University of Alabama.

It was agreed that Tatum and Drew should be invited to the university for conferences. Tatum accepted and agreed to be present for the next monthly meeting of the Board of Regents on January 9, 1946. He asked if he could bring with him a prospective assistant coach with whom he had worked in the navy's recreational program. The man he had in mind was Charles B. ("Bud") Wilkinson, who had played football at Minnesota and had served as an assistant coach at Syracuse University, where he had worked for and received a master's degree in English. It was agreed that Wilkinson could come with Tatum at university expense.

Tatum and Wilkinson appeared at my office on the morning of January 9, a few minutes before the regents were scheduled to begin their session. The two men, each well over six feet tall and weighing about two hundred pounds, presented an impressive appearance as they entered the office. They visited with the regents for perhaps an hour and a half. The discussion centered mainly on the chain of events that had brought the pair to Norman—their experiences together in the navy and their acquaintance with Jap Haskell. Then the discussion turned to the function of intercollegiate athletics in an institution of higher learning. Tatum gave his views, stressing the need for high standards of scholarship for athletes and for cooperation between the athletic department and the rest of the university. He spoke in a very earnest manner, but I had an uneasy feeling that he was saying what he thought the regents wanted to hear.

Tatum did most of the talking, but the regents directed a few questions to Wilkinson, who responded with a great deal of poise and a smile that one of the regents later described as "winsome." The two men finally withdrew, explaining that they had to be on their way to St. Louis to attend a meeting of the National Football Coaches Association. As they left, Tatum suggested that any additional negotiations could be carried on by telegram or telephone.

After the two men had gone, Regent Hopper asked for comments from the board. There was a great deal of favorable discussion, and it was agreed that the pair would make an excellent beginning for a new football coaching staff. Regent Noble, however, remarked that, while he had been favorably impressed by Tatum, he had been even more impressed by Wilkinson. He wished that the situation had been reversed—that Wilkinson had been the applicant for the head coaching position and Tatum the prospective assistant coach. Other members of the board agreed, and there was serious discussion of the possibility of offering the head coaching job to Wilkinson. After a time I was asked to give my opinion. I told the board: "Under the circumstances, I think institutional ethics might be compromised in offering the head coaching job to Wilkinson. But of equal importance, if Wilkinson should be willing to consider such an offer, he would not possess the personal ethics I hope to have in a football coach." The board agreed that this was "probably right" and that they should think about the matter during the noon hour and make a decision later in the day.

That afternoon, the board resumed its discussion. It seemed apparent that two or three members had worked out a solution during the noon break. Regent Deacon promptly offered the following motion:

I move that the president of the university be authorized to contact Jim Tatum relative to the coaching position and ascertain what length of time he will give us to make up our mind; and if time is available to interview "Red" Drew, we'll try to arrange for an interview. That if Mr. Tatum cannot give President Cross time to interview Mr. Drew, he be authorized to hire Mr. Tatum on a three-year contract at $8,000— $9,000— and $10,000, with three assistants, one at $6,000 and two at $5,000; and that he be hired with the condition that he bring "Bud" Wilkinson as assistant coach. In the event he interviews Mr. Drew, and it is still President Cross's desire to employ Mr. Tatum, he be authorized to do so.

The motion was passed unanimously.

The next day I got in touch with Tatum by telephone. He did agree, though with some reluctance, that he could wait until we had had an opportunity to visit with Red Drew. Drew later visited the campus. Although he made a good impression, the Athletic Council, after consultation with Haskell, expressed a preference for Tatum and recommended that the position be offered to him. I then sent Tatum a telegram offering him the position under the terms outlined by the regents, including the requirement that Wilkinson come as assistant coach.

A day or two later I had a long-distance call from Tatum. He objected vigorously to the requirement that Wilkinson be brought

11

as assistant coach, pointing out that a head coach should have complete freedom to choose his assistant coaches and that it was a reflection on his judgment and ability to require him to bring with him any specific individual. Moreover, he said, after attending the meetings in St. Louis, Wilkinson had decided not to go into coaching but instead would return to Minneapolis and enter the real-estate business with his brother and father. After we talked for thirty minutes or so, I finally told Tatum bluntly that I had no authority to do anything other than offer the position under the terms set forth by the regents and that I would not ask the regents to reconsider their action.

A few days later Tatum called me again to report that he had discussed the matter with Wilkinson and that the two of them were inclined to accept the appointment as a team. He told me, however, that he was not entirely satisfied with the terms of the offer I had made. He had hoped that the contract would be written for a five-year period. In view of the fact that it provided for only three years, he thought that his salary should be $10,000 a year. I explained to him that I had been authorized only to offer three years at $8,000, $9,000, and $10,000. As a compromise, I said that I would be willing to recommend to the Athletic Council and the regents at their next meetings that a clause be inserted into his contract providing that in the event that he was not retained beyond three years he would be paid an additional $3,000, which would bring his total salary to the equivalent of ten thousand dollars a year for the three years. He agreed to this, and on January 19 I received a telegram from him:

YOU MAY ANNOUNCE MY ACCEPTANCE OF POSITION AS HEAD COACH OF FOOTBALL OKLAHOMA UNIVERSITY ON BASIS OF THREE YEAR CONTRACT FOR $8,000 1946 $9,000 1947 AND $10,000 1948 STOP WITH CLAUSE FOR A $3,000 BONUS IN CASE MY CONTRACT HAS NOT BEEN CHANGED OR IS NOT RENEWED AT END OF 1948 STOP   WILKINSON WILL JOIN ME

JIM TATUM

P.S. $8,000 1946 $9,000 1947 $10,000 1948 $3,000 1948 BONUS

The Athletic Council and the regents agreed to go along with those terms.

In a later conversation Tatum admitted that he had talked Wilkinson into coming to Oklahoma as assistant coach with the understanding that he would be free to resign after the first football season and return to Minneapolis. Apparently Wilkinson had agreed to help his friend get the job.

CHAPTER 3

The First Postwar Season

1946

TATUM lost no time getting started in his new responsibilities. He arrived in Norman late in January and stayed at Jap Haskell's home until he could find a house of his own for his wife and their baby daughter, Rebecca. He called me soon after his arrival and said that he had found a second assistant coach, Walter Driskell, who had been a line coach at Colorado and Wyoming before the war and later had served in the navy's B-5 physical-fitness program and as a damage-control officer on the aircraft carrier *Wasp*. After a long-distance telephone conversation with the president of the Board of Regents I got informal clearance to approve Driskell's appointment and release the news to the press.

Tatum still had to pick a third assistant, as well as a freshman coach, but he indicated that he wanted to talk with members of Luster's coaching staff before making additional selections. Dale Arbuckle, assistant to Snorter Luster and acting director of athletics during Haskell's absence, was still on duty at the university. He and Orville Tuttle, another assistant coach, were possibilities for consideration.

Tatum, Wilkinson, and Driskell were on the job during the final days of January, 1946, busily planning for the months ahead. Of paramount concern was spring practice, which Tatum predicted might begin as early as February 9. The university was still on an accelerated schedule adopted during the war, and the spring semester would end the first week in May, nearly a month earlier than usual.

Actually Tatum did not get spring practice started quite that early. Instead, he decided that it would be better first to spend some time getting acquainted with football fans throughout the state. With the help of Harold Keith and Jap Haskell he organized an itinerary of appearances that took him and Wilkinson to twenty-three Oklahoma cities in the two-week period from February 4 to February 17. The three huge young men made quite an impression wherever they appeared.

Head Coach Jim Tatum (below) and Assistant Coach Charles ("Bud") Wilkinson,
February, 1946. Courtesy *Oklahoman and Times*.

L. E. ("Jap") Haskell, director of athletics, University of Oklahoma, February, 1946. Courtesy *Oklahoman and Times*.

After returning to Norman, Tatum spent a week with his staff preparing for spring practice, which he launched on February 25.

I attended several of the practice sessions and was much impressed by the businesslike way the coaches conducted the drills. It was obvious that meticulous planning had gone into the preparation for each practice; not a minute was wasted.

Even as he was busy getting the spring drills under way, Tatum moved rapidly to complete his coaching staff. Two members of the professional Washington Redskins team, George Radman, former North Carolina University back, and Dick Todd, who had played in the backfield for the Texas Aggies, were added to the staff early in March. William ("Dutch") Fehring, who had played his college ball at Purdue, was also added, and Frank Crider, OU freshman coach in 1941 and 1942 was retained. Todd was hired to help only through the spring practice sessions. He was under contract to play with the Redskins that fall. The coaching staff as a whole received the enthusiastic approval of the football fans in the area. Many of them came to watch the practice sessions.

Several athletes who had played under Luster before the war or who had been recruited for the fine freshman team he assembled just before the war got under way, were on hand for the spring workouts. Outstanding among them were Dave Wallace, Plato Andros, Joe Golding, Don Fauble, LeRoy Neher, Max Fischer, Wendell Sullivan, William O'Dea, John Osmond, Albert Downs, Clyde Chancellor, George Kerbo, Tommy Tallchief, Boyd Bibb, and Otis McCrary.

Tatum had four intrasquad practice games during the spring drills, and he experimented with both single-wing and T formations. He had announced in one of his earlier press conferences that he hoped to use the T formation a good bit because of its more colorful and explosive results, but he sought proficiency with the single wing because it provided greater power inside the 10-yard line.

The backfield situation looked promising, with Jack Mitchell, Dave Wallace, Bill Remy, Johnny Allsup, Joe Golding, Leroy Neher, Don Fauble, Laddie Harp, and Charles Sarratt receiving considerable attention in releases from Harold Keith's Publicity Office.

In the line there seemed to be a lack of depth. The center position was in reasonably good shape with John Rapacz, Max Fischer, and Pete Tillman. Three of the guards—Paul Burris, Ben Stout, and Tom Harrell—appeared to be outstanding. There was lack of depth at tackle, although Plato Andros and Norman McNabb looked good. Gene Heape and Joe Harrell worked effectively at end.

As spring practice neared a close, Tatum announced that a four-week summer practice would be held from June 15 through July 15 for high-school graduates, recently discharged service-

17

men, and others who had not taken part in spring practice. It was hoped that end Jim Tyree and back Eddie Davis, members of the prewar football squad, would be back from service in time to take part in summer practice.

After completing spring practice, Tatum returned to his program of getting acquainted in the state and persuading as many good high-school athletes as possible to attend summer practice. He was able also to make an amazing number of contacts with athletes in the armed services who were about to be discharged and arrange for them to come to summer practice. He was unusually effective in persuading returning servicemen to transfer from other institutions: Jack Mitchell came from the University of Texas; Warren Giese, from Western Michigan; Nute Trotter, from Texas A&M; Wade Walker, from North Carolina; Paul ("Buddy") Burris, from Tulsa University; and Homer Paine, also from Tulsa University.

The result of all of this recruiting was that scores of football players came to the University of Oklahoma that summer for what really amounted to tryouts for athletic scholarships. The less capable athletes were screened promptly and sent on their way. The good ones continued practice, and if they qualified, they were promised scholarships. The net effect of the summer's work, as one sports writer pointed out, was that Tatum was able to pack about four years of effective recruiting into one season's effort.

Tatum screened his athletes very skillfully. He was an excellent judge of athletic potential and also of coaching ability, as he demonstrated in assembling his coaching staff. He had unusual organizational talent, which became increasingly apparent as I watched him manage the large number of athletes that he brought in for summer practice. I got the impression, however, from watching him on the field and attending an occasional staff meeting that he was not an outstanding football coach. He called on Wilkinson to do much of the actual teaching during the squad meetings. His genius appeared to lie in his ability to select personnel, players, and coaches, induce them to join his team, and then effectively organize their efforts.

When practice finally ended late in July, the turf in the stadium

18

and adjacent practice fields was badly worn, and it took real effort to bring the grass back in time for the autumn activities, scheduled to begin in late August. In truth we did not have good turf on Owen Field that fall. The grass had taken too much of a beating from the "auditions" that had been conducted over it for so many weeks.

The season's opener was with Army at West Point on September 28, 1946—about the most uninviting prospect that a young coaching staff could have had for its first game. The Army team had completely dominated collegiate football during the two previous years. In 1944 it had won all its games by a margin of at least two touchdowns, and in 1945 it had won all of them by a margin of at least three touchdowns. So impressive was the 1945 Army team that Harry Grayson, sports editor of the NEA Service, selected the entire starting lineup as his All-America eleven that year. Most of the personnel of the 1945 squad were returning in 1946.

Oklahoma was given little chance to win the ball game or even to make a good showing. As I read the sports pages that fall, the consensus of the sports writers seemed to be that the Oklahoma team would lose by at least four touchdowns. Hal Middlesworth, sports editor for the *Daily Oklahoman,* predicted 33 points for Army and 0 for the University of Oklahoma.

Two of the big names in the Army lineup were Glenn Davis, a fleet halfback, and Felix ("Doc") Blanchard, who was known for his powerful inside running. Army fans referred to Davis as "Mr. Outside" and Blanchard as "Mr. Inside." Both were superb football players, and, playing behind a line that averaged 200 pounds, they provided a threat for which it was difficult to plan an effective defense. To add interest to the coming battle, Blanchard was a cousin of Jim Tatum.

The already apprehensive Oklahoma fans were not reassured by the fact that the Army would open its schedule a week ahead of its engagement with the University of Oklahoma, an obvious advantage over the Oklahoma team, which would not play until the encounter. Army's opening game was against Villanova, and Wilkinson was sent east to scout the contest. Army crushed Villanova 30–0, and about the only comfort Oklahoma fans could take

19

from it was that Blanchard had been taken from the game with what appeared to be a slightly injured leg.

It was announced that the OU team would fly to West Point in two DC-3's, which would take off from Norman's Max Westheimer Field. A few hours before departure weather conditions convinced Braniff officials that the planes should take off from Oklahoma City Municipal Airport instead. It was the first time an athletic team representing the University of Oklahoma had used air transportation. Tatum was somewhat concerned about the safety factor, and he decided that he would place a complete team and half the coaching staff in each of the DC-3's. If one of the planes crashed, there would be enough players and coaches left to fulfill the engagement with Army. (Apparently it never occurred to him that the game might well be canceled if half of the OU squad and staff was killed in a plane accident.)

The thirty-seven members of the squad and their coaches boarded the two planes at 8:30 on the morning of September 27, for the eight-hour flight to West Point; I was in one of the planes. Both arrived safely at West Point that afternoon, and the Oklahomans went immediately to the Thayer Hotel. The following day was a memorable one for me. Several weeks before, Major General Maxwell D. Taylor, superintendent of West Point Academy, had invited me to be his guest for the day's activities—to review the cadets in the morning, join him for lunch, see the game with him, and attend a reception in his home after the game.

The day began with a tour of some of the facilities of West Point with General Taylor and other military personnel. After the tour President Harry S Truman joined our group to review the West Point cadets as they marched on the huge parade ground under a bright morning sun. Later President Truman spoke informally to the approximately two thousand young men who comprised the West Point student body. He then left the group to take care of other matters, although it was understood that he would join us later at the football game. The rest of General Taylor's party had lunch in the mess hall with the cadets and then were taken to Michie Stadium and conducted to the superintendent's box. I was seated at General Taylor's left, and a space was kept for President Truman on his right. Oklahoma Congress-

President Harry S Truman joins President Cross and Major General Maxwell
D. Taylor for morning activities preceding the OU-Army game.

men Jed Johnson, Ross Rizley, and Lyle H. Boren were also in
the box as guests of the general. Admiral William D. Leahy was
seated at my left, and the other military personnel who had
attended the morning review were sitting elsewhere in the box.
I remember a curious feeling of nervous tension as we sat waiting
for the game to get under way.

The Sooner squad that came onto the field for the pregame

21

Some members of the 1946 team. FRONT, LEFT TO RIGHT: Wade Walker, Plato Andros, John Rapacz, Buddy Burris, Homer Paine. BACK: Merle Dinkins, Joe Golding, Eddie Davis, Jack Mitchell, Dave Wallace, Jim Tyree. Apparently no picture of the entire 1946 squad was taken. When he was asked about this oversight, Tatum assembled the squad for a picture but became impatient when the cameraman was slow setting up his equipment. When he said that he had to return to his car for a missing item, Tatum allegedly said, "To hell with the picture! We're gonna scrimmage." Courtesy Ken Rawlinson.

warmup included some individuals who later were to become well known to football fans: Jim Owens, Homer Paine, Wade Walker, Buddy Burris, Plato Andros, Norman McNabb, Stanley West, John Rapacz, Darrell Royal, Joe Golding, Jack Mitchell, and others. As the two teams warmed up, someone asked me what kind of showing I thought the Oklahoma team would make. I replied cautiously, "I don't think the Army backs will run against the Oklahoma line as well as they have against other opponents."

I added that "Oklahoma had a pretty fair line." I thought I detected veiled amusement on the faces of some of my new friends in the box.

As game time approached, President Truman had not appeared. Time for kickoff arrived, and still no President. After the game had been delayed for several minutes, the President finally appeared, the "Star-spangled Banner" was played, and the game began.

The first quarter was scoreless. Both teams appeared to be jittery, and the backs had trouble handling the ball. The Army backfield was handicapped by the absence of Blanchard, out because of the injury he had received in the Villanova game. But the two great lines staged a bruising battle before the crowd of 25,500, including an estimated 1,500 Oklahoma fans. Ferocious blocking and tackling caused several fumbles by both teams; alert opposing backs were quick to pounce on the loose balls. About the middle of the quarter, General Taylor leaned over to me and said, "You know, Oklahoma does have a pretty fair line."

Shortly after the beginning of the second quarter Oklahoma held Army for downs near the Army goal line. Joe Green, punter for Army, received the pass from center in the end zone and fumbled it for a moment. Before he could get the kick away, Stanley West and Norman McNabb blocked the punt; McNabb and Joe Morrison covered the ball, one on top of the other, for an OU touchdown. Dave Wallace completed the conversion, and OU led 7–0.

There was no more scoring until the closing moments of the first half. Then, as the final seconds ticked by, Arnold Tucker, Army's superb T-formation quarterback, completed three passes, two to Glenn Davis and the third to Henry Foldberg, for the tying touchdown. The conversion attempt, by Jack Mackmull, was successful, and the score was 7–7.

As the half ended and the teams trotted to their dressing rooms, I remember someone turning to me and saying, "By golly, Doctor, you've got a better line than we have!" President Truman and General Taylor made similar complimentary remarks about the OU line, and Taylor mentioned, almost in awe, that the Army

23

team had been able to make only two first downs during the entire first half.

After colorful halftime ceremonies, the two teams resumed their even battle, Army striving to preserve a nineteen-game winning streak that had established it as the nation's best, and OU hoping to upset the nation's number-one team and bring itself into national prominence.

Army took the lead early in the third quarter, 7–14, after Oklahoma's punt was blocked on its own 15-yard line. It seemed, at the beginning of the final quarter, that Oklahoma had an excellent chance to tie the score. The Sooners had a first on the Army 8 1/2-yard line. But on the first scrimmage a much disputed series of events took place. According to one version—the way the officials saw it—Wallace, the OU quarterback, swinging wide with the ball on an option play, attempted a lateral to Darrell Royal. He was tackled before he could get the lateral off, and the ball squirted into the air. The alert Army quarterback, Tucker, grabbed the ball and ran with it the length of the field for a touchdown. As Tatum and his assistant coaches saw the play, Wallace managed to get the ball to Royal, who knocked it or dropped it to the ground momentarily, regained it, and then lost it to Tucker. If the ball did touch the ground, it would be dead at that point, and Tucker's scoring run would be nullified. It would be Army's ball deep in Army territory. Moreover, with the great playing of the Oklahoma line, it was likely that the Sooners would regain possession of the ball early in the fourth quarter and make a successful assault on the goal line. From where I sat, it looked as if the ball might have hit the ground and bounced into Tucker's arms, but I was a biased observer.

In any event, Army was ahead by 14 points, 7–21. The Sooners were unable to do anything constructive on offense during the rest of the fourth quarter, and the game ended with no change in score.

Statistics revealed that the two teams had tied in number of first downs, 7 and 7. The OU team had outrushed Army, 129 yards to 83. The best of the Army backs had had little success getting through the Sooner line. In seven attempts Tucker wound up with a net loss of 6 yards. Davis did a little better, carrying eleven times for 11 yards.

Quarterback errors had made the difference—understandably so, because the Army team had been using the T formation for four years, while the game that day was Oklahoma's first experience with the tricky offense. The Sooners received excellent treatment from the eastern press; the consensus was that the Oklahomans had contributed two touchdowns to the Army cause and that, except for these errors, the final score might well have been a tie.

I did not return to Norman with the team but went to Washington to attend to a few matters of business there, including a talk to the Oklahoma State Society. When I got back to Oklahoma, I found the OU fans very enthusiastic about the Army game despite the score. Later in the week I went to the stadium to see how the football team was progressing. I found that Tatum, though disappointed about the loss to Army, was on the whole well pleased with his team's performance—especially the performance of the line. From locker-room conversation, I gathered the impression that the game had been quite an emotional experience for him. The players reported that he had been very much irritated by the delay caused by President Truman's late arrival. He said he thought that Army had arranged for the President to delay the game in an effort to get the OU team mentally off balance.

Tatum had been greatly excited throughout the contest and had exhibited his excitement in an extraordinary way. According to the story, Charles Sarratt, one of the OU backs, who had been injured during the third period of the game, was sitting by the trainer on a side-line bench soaking a swollen ankle in a pail of ice water. When Tucker intercepted Wallace's lateral to Royal and ran the length of the field for Army's third touchdown, Tatum removed Sarratt's foot from the pail, lifted the pail to his lips, and took a long swig of water. He then put the pail back on the ground and put Sarratt's foot back into it. I was skeptical of this story, but a half-dozen or so witnesses declared that it was true. As the season wore on and I had several opportunities to observe firsthand his excitable behavior, the incident seemed less surprising.

The following weekend the Sooners barely edged the Texas Aggies by a score of 10 to 7, although they outgained their opponents in net yards, rushing 205 to –8. By the end of the game it seemed apparent that OU did indeed have one of the best lines in the country. If the offense could improve, Tatum's debut might be a great success.

The third opponent of the season was the University of Texas, a long-time, traditional foe. The Longhorns defeated the Sooners 20–13, although the Oklahomans outgained Texas on the ground, 143 yards to 81. The difference was in the aerial game, where Texas excelled, 87 yards to 21.

A week later, OU defeated Kansas State handily, 28–7, in a game characterized by the extraordinary running of halfback Joe Golding, who carried the ball 43 yards to a touchdown on his first play of the game and traveled 81 yards to score again on his last play. The Sooners gained 329 yards on the ground to their opponents' 46 but once again showed little promise in the air—18 yards to Kansas State's 59.

Next on the schedule was Iowa State College, in those days never much of a threat in football. The game was played at Ames on a sunny day and on a firm turf. The Sooners won by a score of 63–0, although the starting players stayed in the game only the first seventeen minutes.

It has often been said that rain and mud are football's greatest equalizers. The sixth and seventh games of the 1946 season demonstrated the truth of the saying. The week after the victory over Iowa State the Sooners went to Fort Worth, Texas, to play the Horned Frogs of Texas Christian University, coached by Leo ("Dutch") Myer. It was raining in Fort Worth the day of the game, and the Frogs took full advantage of the aquatic environment. OU managed to win, 14–12, only because the TCU team was unable to convert after either of their touchdowns.

The weather was even worse the following week at Lawrence, where the Sooners met the Kansas Jayhawks. The field was almost completely bare of grass, and rain poured onto the playing surface throughout the game. The undermanned Kansas team,

26

very well prepared by Coach George Sauer, carried the game to the Sooners throughout the contest. OU outgained the Jayhawks on the ground (192 yards to 81), but lost by a score of 13–16 because of an almost unbelievable field goal kicked by Kansas through the rain in the waning moments of the game.

Next on the schedule was the Homecoming game at Norman. The opponent was the University of Missouri, powerhouse of the conference in the preceding year and, despite OU's rather impressive record at mid-season, favored by the sports world to win handily over the Sooners. But the game was regarded of sufficient importance that Bill Stern, the nationally known sportscaster, came to Norman to broadcast the details of the action by radio.

But there was another event scheduled for that week; one that, for me, transcended in importance everything related to Homecoming, including the football game on Saturday. A third child was on its way to join the Cross family, and was expected before the weekend. My wife, Cleo, was already in the hospital in Oklahoma City. On Thursday evening, shortly before dinner, our two children (Mary-Lynn, age fifteen, and George William, age ten) and I were talking in the kitchen when the phone rang. Dr. Gerald Rogers, at St. Anthony Hospital, was on the line. He told me that the baby might arrive that evening and suggested that I come to the hospital.

I quickly got ready to leave, left by the rear door, and started to the garage. As I walked across the back yard, I could hear shouting. I thought it was a crowd of students on Boyd Street east of the house. I got into the car and drove out of the east entrance behind the house just in time to see the first of a large group of students coming past what was then the Masonic dormitory, now Whitehand Hall. They were obviously headed for the president's home and I knew I had to disperse them before I dared to go on to Oklahoma City. I drove my car across the street and parked on the east side of University Boulevard, got out and walked leisurely south toward the group, who were chanting, "No school tomorrow!" Unrecognized, I joined the fifteen hundred to two thousand students and proceeded with them to the columned front entrance of the big white house. As I walked with them, I soon learned that they felt they needed a holiday on Friday to prepare floats and house decorations for Homecoming on Saturday. Bad weather had handicapped them during the week, and they had got behind in their preparations.

I edged my way toward the front of the group as we approached the house but kept sufficiently in the background. A student rang the doorbell, and shortly Mary-Lynn appeared and, in response to the students' request to see President Cross, explained, "Daddy isn't home. He went to Oklahoma City to see mother at the hospital."

By this time the entire front yard of the house and Boyd Street as well were filled with students and onlookers, most of whom were shouting, "No school tomorrow! We want a holiday! We want to see President Cross!"

After Mary-Lynn's report the leaders of the group withdrew to discuss further strategy. They were gathered on the lower steps leading up to the entrance of the house. Keeping my face in the shadow of one of the columns as best I could, I suggested that we visit Dr. Royden Dangerfield's home. Since he was assistant to the president, he might be able to do something in the president's absence. The suggestion was received with enthusiasm, and I was asked where Dangerfield lived. I said that I thought he lived somewhere on Lahoma Street—but they could get the address from a telephone directory. One of the boys returned to the front door for additional conversation with Mary-Lynn, who agreed to bring the telephone directory to the door. Then, to keep them out of the house, she offered to call Dr. Dangerfield to find out if he was home and available to talk with them. This seemed a fine suggestion, and so Mary-Lynn called Dangerfield and told him that "some boys" were there, and she wondered if it would be all right for them to come over and see him. He thought the "boys" were a small group who had talked with him earlier in the day about some matter, and he readily agreed that they could come to his house. The word spread, and the assemblage moved west on Boyd Street toward Lahoma. Satisfied that the problem was solved for the moment, I left the crowd, returned to my automobile, and resumed my interrupted trip to Oklahoma City.

Dr. Rogers' call turned out to be premature. Our third child was not scheduled for arrival that night after all. But while I was visiting with my wife in her room, I received a phone call from Dangerfield. He told me in obvious agitation that there was a "howling mob" of two or three thousand students in front of his house demanding a holiday on Friday. He said that students were driving up and down Lahoma honking their horns, and he wondered what to do about it. I asked him what he thought we ought to do, and he said he thought we ought to dismiss classes. After some discussion we agreed that he should try to negotiate with the students for a half day off—no school Friday afternoon. I learned the next day that the students had agreed and had left singing "For He's a Jolly Good Fellow." They marched for several minutes around the campus, spreading the word.

I spent Friday in a state of some tension and anxiety. A regents' meeting was scheduled for that evening; I was expected to ride in the Homecoming parade the next morning, to be followed by a football game with what was regarded as the strongest team in the conference—all of this and a baby due to arrive any minute.

Friday morning and afternoon passed without incident, and the regents arrived late in the afternoon for dinner in the Union Building, followed by their regular monthly meeting.

The meeting got underway about 7:30 P.M. in my office. Shortly after eight o'clock Dr. Rogers called to tell me that if I wanted to be present to greet the new member of my family I had better start for Oklahoma City. I arrived at St. Anthony Hospital a half hour later, and after a wait of only five minutes or so a nurse came out and told me that I was the father of a fine-looking boy. We named him Braden Riehl.

Saturday morning I rode in the Homecoming parade, had lunch with the regents, and then joined the crowd on its way to the stadium to see how the Sooners would fare in their contest with the Missouri Tigers.

The game was a sellout, and a huge radio audience waited to hear Bill Stern's description of the play. Later I heard that Stern had given the Missouri team a tremendous buildup during the pregame activities, obviously thinking that Oklahoma had very little chance of making it a close contest. He was so sure

Coach Jim Tatum watches as quarterback Jack Mitchell gets his instructions from coaches on top of the OU press box during the OU-Missouri game, November, 1946. Courtesy *Oklahoman and Times.*

of it that apparently he did not pay much attention to what actually happened after the kickoff, because when OU scored a touchdown, kicked the extra point, and took a seven-point lead, he reported that Missouri had scored and was leading by seven points. In a few minutes someone straightened him out, and he corrected his error.

Actually, the game was not very close. The OU defense, a 7-2 formation with the ends dropping off like corner backs, held their opponents to 54 rushing yards and 99 yards through the air. The final score was 27–6 in favor of OU. At the close of the game the fans realized that the University of Oklahoma finally had a great football team on the ground. (The passing game had been unimpressive—thirteen attempts with four completions for 36 yards that day.)

Tatum was understandably elated by the win over Missouri,

and he approached the remaining two games on the schedule, Nebraska and Oklahoma A&M, with obviously increased confidence. He gave evidence of that confidence one day when I visited practice as he was preparing for Nebraska. He indicated that he was not entirely satisfied with his situation at the University of Oklahoma and said that he might consider making a move unless certain arrangements could be worked out. One source of his dissatisfaction was the way Harold Keith had handled publicity. I did not understand what he meant by this complaint. It seemed to me that Keith had done a fine job of publicizing the football program at OU, and certainly he had given more than adequate attention to publicity for all members of the coaching staff.

Tatum was also dissatisfied with the director of athletics; he thought that Jap Haskell should be removed from the post. When I asked him who he thought should replace Haskell, he said that Neil Johnson, the chairman of the Athletic Council, would be his choice. He believed that an athletic director should not be closely involved with football affairs—only to the extent of approving schedules, purchases, and so on, on a more or less routine basis. He did not think that athletic aid for football at OU was adequate, and he suggested that he would be able to have a larger and better squad if counseling jobs in university housing could be given to his football players. He also wanted a revised contract—a longer term and a salary increase. He told me that he would talk more about these matters later.

That weekend the Sooner football team had little difficulty defeating the Cornhuskers from Nebraska, 27–6, the same score as the one in the Missouri game. The superiority of OU's running game was demonstrated once again: 262 yards on the ground to Nebraska's 62. The Sooners also showed some improvement in their aerial game: 116 yards to Nebraska's 69.

There now remained only one game on OU's schedule for 1946, but in the minds of many OU alumni it was the most important game of all—the annual clash with the Oklahoma Aggies, scheduled to be played at Stillwater. Before 1944 no one at OU was greatly concerned about the outcome of this game because the University of Oklahoma had almost completely dominated

31

the series from the time of the first contest back in 1904 (OU 75, Aggies 0). Its winning habit had been interrupted only briefly from 1929 through 1933, when Lynn Waldorf coached at Stillwater.

With the advent of Head Coach Jim Lookabaugh a new era in football fortunes had apparently dawned at A&M. During the final two years of the war he had assembled a remarkable group of deferred athletes, headed by Bob Fenimore, a two-time All-America triple-threat back from Woodward, Oklahoma. Under Lookabaugh's tutelage the Aggies had defeated the Sooners at Taft Stadium (in Oklahoma City) in 1944 by a score of 28–6. In 1945 they humiliated the Sooners on Owen Field by a score of 47–0.

Mindful of what had happened in 1944 and 1945, Tatum took the 1946 game with the Aggies very seriously. He invited me to come to a practice session and say a few words to the squad about the importance of the game. I went to practice Friday evening, and explained, as plaintively as I could, my chagrin that the OU teams had not won a ball game of any kind from A&M during my term as president. I concluded my remarks by expressing the hope that the present football squad would be able to do something about the situation the following day. Later, while I was visiting with a small group of players, George Brewer said to me, "Don't worry about the game tomorrow, President Cross. We're going to get that situation all straightened out."

A&M President and Mrs. Henry Bennett had invited the Cross family to come to Stillwater for lunch the day of the game, but Mrs. Cross and Mary-Lynn decided to stay home with Braden. My son Bill and I drove to the A&M campus that morning, had lunch with other guests at the president's home, and then went to the stadium to see what the afternoon had in store for us.

The first few moments of the game were not reassuring. The temporarily inept Sooners yielded two touchdowns early in the first quarter, but the Aggies missed both attempts for extra points. Bill and I, seated in the box with President Bennett, were much impressed by the intensity of the Aggie fans. We could hear shouts: "Where's that All-America center Rapacz?" "Where is the great Joe Golding?" "Poor Sooners!" and so on. The official guests in the president's box were more restrained but were obviously happy with what appeared to be happening.

I learned later that my good friend Ray Parr, seated amid a group of Aggie fans, finally could stand the jeering remarks no longer. He rose to his feet and offered to bet twenty dollars that OU would win the game by 50 points. He had no trouble getting a taker, and he profited handsomely when OU finally came through with a 73–12 win. He could have given sixty points and come out on top.

When the OU team finally got down to business, the game quickly turned into a shambles. The great Fenimore, handicapped by an injured knee, was far from his usual form and watched most of the game from the sidelines. As a matter of fact, no one on the Aggie team played very well. The Sooners rushed for an amazing 415 yards, while the Aggies gained only 7 yards on the ground; they passed for an even more amazing 249 yards, while their opponents were able to gain only 174. The total yardage gained rushing and passing was a record-setting 664 yards for the Sooners, compared to 181 yards for the Aggies.

As the afternoon wore on, the disappointed A&M fans started leaving the stadium. The box in which Bill and I sat emptied gradually, and at length President Bennett excused himself to make a radio talk. Finally Bill and I were left by ourselves near the center of the large box. Feeling a little conspicuous, we went down to the side lines to watch the action of the final moments.

After the game Bill and I visited the OU dressing room. The team and coaches were celebrating the victory. Tatum was so excited that he could scarcely speak coherently to the sports writers. Wilkinson and the other assistant coaches seemed less emotional, but all agreed that it had been a wonderful afternoon for OU.

Most fans thought the season a successful one despite losses to the Army, Texas, and Kansas, the last of which pulled Oklahoma into a tie for the conference championship. When the final figures were in, OU's powerful line led the nation in defense against rushing. It had blocked the backs to sixth place nationally in yards gained rushing.

There had been some talk toward the end of the season about

John Rapacz, Plato Andros, and Paul ("Buddy") Burris were the first postwar University of Oklahoma football players to receive All-America recognition, 1946.

the possibility of OU playing in a bowl game. Speculation ended shortly after the A&M game, when officials of the Gator Bowl, at Jacksonville, Florida, extended an invitation to the Sooners. The members of the football squad promptly voted to accept, and the Big Six Conference gave its approval. The game was to be played in Jacksonville on January 1, 1947, with North Carolina State (Raleigh) as the opponent.

The Gator Bowl was a very recent addition to the bowl family, established only the year before by Jacksonville businessmen as a local Lions Club project to benefit the blind. After learning something of the size of the undertaking and the financial problems involved, the Lions Club withdrew from sponsorship, and the Gator Bowl Association was organized, with forty of Jacksonville's leading citizens as charter members. The new association did not sign teams for play in the bowl until December 13, 1945, when Wake Forest and South Carolina finally were matched, with a guarantee of ten thousand dollars to each team. The Gator Bowl seated only twenty-two thousand spectators, and so it was necessary to set a fairly high price for each seat (six dollars) to realize a sum large enough to attract good teams.

Tatum was tremendously excited about the prospect of playing in a bowl so early in his career at OU. He prepared for the game with energy and determination that I have seldom seen devoted to any project. He visited my office frequently to discuss various matters having to do with the future of football at OU. On one occasion he told me that he thought his squad's interest in the approaching game could be deepened if he could tell them that each would receive a present of some kind after the game—a shotgun, golf clubs, or some other valuable item. I reminded him that the regulations of the Big Six Conference prohibited gifts of any kind to athletes for any purpose except for financial aid that had been approved by the conference. He seemed to accept this decision, though with reluctance and disappointment.

During one of our conversations he told me of overtures that had been made to him by President H. C. "Curly" Byrd, of the University of Maryland, who was eager to rebuild the football program there. Byrd had been head coach at Maryland for twenty-one years before he was promoted (or demoted) to president of the university. Byrd had asked Tatum if he would be interested in the head coaching position at Maryland. Tatum hinted, though he did not say so outright, that Byrd's experience as a football coach might mean that Tatum would receive somewhat better cooperation at the University of Maryland than he was likely to receive at the University of Oklahoma in coming years. However, he indicated that he did not plan to do anything about the Maryland offer until after the Gator Bowl game.

The football team practiced during early December, and disbanded for Christmas on December 20. Members of the squad reassembled on the twenty-sixth and flew to Jacksonville.

CHAPTER 4

More on Hiring a Coach—Bud Wilkinson

1946-47

I did not accompany the team. I had not been greatly impressed by what I thought a relatively minor postseason contest, and I decided that I would use the holidays to clear my desk and get some personal affairs in order.

But on December 29, Regent Lloyd Noble called me from Ardmore and told me he had heard on good authority that Tatum planned to visit the University of Maryland immediately after the Gator Bowl game and take his coaching staff with him—that a package deal was to be considered whereby the entire staff would transfer to Maryland, and with it, perhaps, some of OU's better athletes. He asked me if I had ever told Wilkinson of our interest in him as a head coach for OU. I replied that I had not. He asked me if I would be willing to fly to Jacksonville the following day, have a talk with Wilkinson before the game, and offer him the head coaching job in the event Tatum decided to leave Oklahoma. I expressed willingness to do so but suggested that airline reservations to Florida might be difficult to get because of the two bowl games to be played there (the other game, of course, being the Orange Bowl). Noble offered to send his company plane and pilot, Ben Scott, who would take me to Jacksonville and bring me back after the game. He suggested that I might want to take a couple of additional passengers; there would be room in the plane for four in addition to the pilot. I agreed and invited Robert Landsaw, owner of a Norman furniture store, and Ray Fischer, head of the Fischer Plumbing Company, to make the trip with me. I invited Landsaw because he was a friend who had supported me during a fuss over whether the Navy (South Base) should remain active in Norman after the war ended, a proposal that I had opposed. I asked Fischer because he had been bitterly critical of my attitude in the Navy matter, and I thought that the trip might give me an opportunity to change his thinking. It was agreed that the three of us would meet the next morning at Max Westheimer Field and leave for Jacksonville at 8:00 A.M.

Occasional flakes of snow were drifting from the sky as I drove to the airport that morning. The plane, the pilot, and my two copassengers were waiting when I arrived. We took off promptly, although Scott did mention, rather casually, that we might have some trouble with the weather.

The plane was a single-engine, staggered-wing biplane. We had been in the air for only a few minutes, flying southeast from Norman, when the snowflakes gave way to sleet, and ice began forming on the wings and body of the little plane. Looking through the window on my right, I could see the icy glaze gradually extend over all the plane's surfaces. I knew enough about aerodynamics to realize that the plane could not stay in the air indefinitely under such conditions, even with the best efforts of the 450-horsepower Pratt-Whitney engine out in front. Unhappily the oak and hickory landscape, which I could see only dimly below, did not appear to offer much hope for a successful emergency landing.

It seemed to me that we were in a difficult situation, but I did not feel that I should ask any questions. The pilot was having his problems and had no time for conversation. As a matter of fact, no one seemed inclined to do any talking. The three passengers agreed later that we had been extremely frightened. The pilot was noncommittal.

Having little else to do, I studied the instrument panel. When I looked at the airspeed indicator, I saw that, instead of showing an airspeed of 180 or more miles an hour as it should have, it registered zero. Knowing that we could not remain aloft at zero air speed, I nudged the pilot and pointed to the indicator. Scott glanced at it and nodded. After a few moments he leaned over and explained that the airspeed indicator operated in response to the speed with which air was passing through an opening on a wing, and the opening had become plugged with ice. This information was helpful, though not completely reassuring. Scott went on to tell me that he was trying various altitudes, probing for air where there was no sleet.

After what seemed an interminable period of time but was probably only a few minutes, Scott leaned over and said, "It's

OK. We're out of it." As I looked out at the sleet-coated wings, I could not see that the situation had changed very much, but finally I could tell that no more ice was forming.

After perhaps another five or ten minutes I noticed a crack in the ice encasing the lower surface of the upper wing just outside my window. Suddenly a chunk came loose and hit the tail of the plane with a crack that sounded like a rifle shot. A series of chunks followed, and the resulting clatter shook the nerves of the three passengers. As we agreed when we discussed the trip later, we did not see how the tail stood up under such abuse.

The plane was soon free of its shackling load, and, to my great relief, the airspeed indicator began working once again. But the problems of the day were by no means over.

The whole southeastern part of the country was overcast with a mixture of thunderstorms, fog, and ice. We had flown on instruments since leaving Norman, and we were destined for instrument flight all day long. We were able to land for refueling and lunch, somewhere in Mississippi as I recall, but the ceiling was extremely low. We were scarcely five hundred feet above the ground when we sighted the runway on our final approach.

We flew under similar conditions the rest of the day and arrived at the Jacksonville airport late in the afternoon. When we established contact with the Jacksonville radio, the operator gave us the dismaying news that we could not land there, that there had been no landings since about eleven o'clock that morning, and that we were to proceed to our alternate destination. I overheard Scott reply that our alternate destination was also closed in and that we had no choice but to land at Jacksonville because we did not have enough fuel to reach any airport that was open. Hearing these words caused a slight shiver in my spine, and I wondered why I had agreed to make the trip in the first place, merely to hire a football coach. In the meantime, one of our passengers, Fischer, had become violently airsick, perhaps in reaction to the apprehension and turbulence of our journey. I wondered whether his occasional audible retching in the back seat was interfering with our pilot's concentration.

Jacksonville radio agreed, though with obvious reluctance, that it would be necessary for us to attempt a landing there; the

operator cautioned us, however, that there was virtually no ceiling at times—fog and mist on the runway. Using what by modern
standards was very primitive navigational equipment, Scott made
some computations and then attempted to land. Proceeding on
final approach, he descended until the altimeter indicated an
altitude of about 150 feet, but none of us in the plane could see
any sign of a lighted runway. He did not dare probe lower because
some Florida pine trees reach heights greater than 100 feet, and
he could not be sure of the accuracy of the altimeter.

With one failure behind him, Scott leveled the plane, flew
out over the Atlantic and, after working for a few moments with
his little disk-shaped calculator, announced that he would make
a second attempt to land. He flew the usual pattern—downwind
leg, base leg, and then the final approach. He dropped to minimum altitude, but once again there was no sign of runway lights.

Scott seemed unperturbed by two failures and remarked cheer-
fully, "Well, we'll just have to try it again." This meant another
trip out over the ocean, more computing, and then a third attempt
to find the good earth. As we were on our downwind leg for the
third time, we suddenly noticed to the left of the plane a yellowish
streak in the mist below. Scott remarked, "That must be the runway," and then, applying aileron in opposition to rudder, he
slipped the plane vigorously to the left and lost enough altitude
so that we could see two shimmering yellow lines below and
slightly behind us. He continued with a rather more gentle slip
as we curled around to the left and approached the end of the
runway—perhaps the shortest approach that he had ever made
to any runway. But he timed everything perfectly, and when we
leveled off fifty feet or so in the air, the runway was immediately
in front of us, visible throughout its length because of a temporary
local thinning of the fog and mist above the field. We had no
sooner landed and taxied to the terminal when the fog settled in
once again. It was as if the door had been opened, so to speak,
to let us in.

Scott's ashen-faced passengers were a little weak and trembly
as we crawled from the plane, but all of us, even Fischer, felt
better in a few minutes. We caught a cab to our hotel and had a
light supper, and I went to bed early.

The next day I had a talk with Wilkinson and told him about our interest in him as head coach at OU if Tatum should go to Maryland. I asked him if he would take the job if it should become vacant, and he said that he would be interested. I offered him a three-year contract at ten thousand dollars a year. He replied that he would prefer a four-year contract so that he could bring at least one crop of freshmen whom he had recruited through their senior year of competition. I told him that, while the regents had not authorized me to make a commitment beyond three years, the length of Tatum's contract, I would agree that his contract should be for four years and I did not doubt that the regents would approve the additional year. He then told me that the rumor that Noble had reported was based on fact—that the coaching staff had planned to go to Maryland following the Gator Bowl game. However, he assured me that, under the circumstances, he would not go to Maryland with Tatum but would return to Norman with the team. Vastly relieved by the success of my mission and somewhat recovered from the strain of the trip, I settled down to enjoy my brief holiday in Jacksonville.

There was good weather and a good turf at the Gator Bowl stadium on New Year's Day, and the twenty-two thousand seats were filled at kickoff time. During the early portion of the game the two teams played more or less evenly, but the Sooner coaches were able to come up with a defense that effectively contained the North Carolinians after they had scored a couple of touchdowns, and the final score was 34–14—an impressive victory for the University of Oklahoma and a fitting climax to the first year's efforts of a young coaching staff and team.

The squad was scheduled to return home the following day, and I learned that there would be some empty seats on the plane. Deciding that I had had enough of flying in bad weather in a single-engine plane, I arranged to return with the team. I did this with some feeling of guilt about my fellow passengers on the flight to Jacksonville, but they agreed readily that it would be a good idea to fly home with the team. It would give me an opportunity to become better acquainted with the boys.

When I boarded the plane, I found to my surprise that Tatum had decided to return to Norman with the team rather than go to Maryland. Wilkinson had reported our conversation to him and told him about his decision to accept the OU coaching job if it became vacant. When Wilkinson told him that he was no longer interested in going to Maryland, Tatum apparently realized that he might not be able to move the rest of the coaching staff and that perhaps it would be best to return to Oklahoma and try to better his situation there.

When I saw Tatum on board, I had momentary regret that I had abandoned the little plane. I had no desire to spend several hours on the flight with him; I had learned from past encounters that he could talk endlessly, with exhausting intensity. Hoping to avoid him, I walked to the front end of the DC-4 and took a seat on the right side next to the window; but I had scarcely sat down when Tatum plumped down beside me.

He spent the first few minutes telling me how unethical he thought I had been to offer one of his assistant coaches the head coaching job at OU before he had resigned and only hours before his team was to compete in a bowl game. He was offended and hurt, he said, by such treatment. I listened patiently, with the unhappy thought that there would be several hours of such conversation before I could find relief at the journey's end.

However, shortly after takeoff we ran into turbulent air. The plane rose over a series of updrafts and dropped violently between them. Tatum, who was not a good air traveler, soon began to feel the effects. When he stopped talking for a moment, I glanced at him and noticed that he had begun to turn a little pale. The paleness soon turned to a greenish cast, and I had a feeling that my problem might be solved. Finally, when he became noticeably ill, I signaled for a hostess and suggested to my sick friend that we remove the armrest between the two seats so that he could lie down. I would find a seat elsewhere. He accepted the suggestion, and when I left him he was in a semireclining position with his head on a pillow, holding a sick sack.

We soon got out of the rough air, and I enjoyed most of the rest of the trip, visiting with as many members of the squad as I could. I say "most," because as we approached Houston, Texas, our pilot announced that one of the four engines had gone bad and that we would have to stop at the airport for repairs. But we were delayed there for only a couple of hours.

Back in my office on January 2, I found myself very much

41

in the dark about what should be done about the coaching situation. Tatum had given no indication to the public that he planned to take another job. The football fans were very enthusiastic about the record he had compiled during his first year as head coach at OU, and I knew they would be quite upset if he was permitted to leave without a serious effort to keep him. Yet I thought that it would be much better for the university to have Wilkinson as head coach. I finally decided that I should make an apparent effort to hold him at OU but keep my recommendation to the regents short of what I figured would be needed to keep him.

A special meeting of the regents had been scheduled for January 8, 1947, to consider a proposal for an addition, or additions, to the Oklahoma Memorial Student Union Building. I decided that a recommendation for an increase in salary for Tatum and his assistant coaches would be in order for the special meeting, and I discussed the possibility with Jap Haskell and the members of the Athletic Council. We agreed together on the amount of the increases that would be recommended. We agreed also that the clause in Tatum's contract providing that he would be paid a bonus of three thousand dollars in case his contract was not renewed should be stricken if he did not accept our offer.

The board assembled for its special meeting on January 8, with President Wallace, and Regents Noble, Emery, White, Shepler, and McBride in attendance; Regent Deacon was absent. At the beginning of the meeting I asked permission to bring up the question of remuneration for the football coaching staff because of certain developments that had occurred since the agenda had been mailed out. My request was granted by the unanimous consent of the board.

I then explained all that had happened—the rumors of Tatum's negotiations with Maryland, my trip to Jacksonville to visit with Wilkinson, and my conversations with Athletic Director Haskell and the Athletic Council. I recommended that I be authorized to negotiate with Tatum for a salary of twelve thousand dollars a year for the two remaining years of his present contract, with the provision that the clause providing for a three-thousand-dollar bonus be stricken from the contract. I recommended also

42

that I be authorized to adjust the salaries of the assistant coaches to provide a maximum increase of one thousand dollars each. The regents approved the recommendation unanimously. They then adjourned, after agreeing to meet again on January 17.

After the members of the board left my office, I notified Tatum by telephone and letter of the action taken. I was quite sure, however, that the salary increase alone would not hold him. From my conversations with him I had become convinced that he would leave Oklahoma unless he could have a much longer contract, with the added provisions that Harold Keith be replaced as director of sports information and Jap Haskell replaced as director of athletics. Tatum had denied that he wanted the latter job for himself; he insisted that he had no ambition or desire to be bothered with the administration of other sports, he wanted complete independence in operating his football program. He thought that this could best be achieved by naming someone off campus, such as Neil Johnson, director of athletics.

It appeared that I might have been wrong about Tatum because during the following few days he talked as if he had no intention of changing coaching jobs and would remain at OU. In a special release to the *Tulsa World* on January 10, he was quoted as saying:

> The administration of the university has been so generous with myself and the staff at the end of our first year at OU that I don't believe there is a chance of our losing any of our staff.
>
> Several of the coaches have had attractive offers but none have asked to be released from duties here, even before the administration let us know of their splendid gesture in readjusting our contracts.

But Tatum's apparent satisfaction with what had been done for him and his coaching staff was short-lived. Within a day or two after his release to the *Tulsa World,* he was in my office expressing doubts about the situation at the University of Oklahoma—the length of his contract, Harold Keith's fitness for his job, the athletic directorship, and other problems that might need to be remedied if he was to remain at OU. He told me that he had been approached again by Maryland with a written offer that he considered much more attractive than the one he had received from Oklahoma.

After talking with him for an hour or so, I finally told him that I could not recommend to the regents that his situation be improved beyond what had been agreed to. He left my office, and a day or so later I received a letter from him in which he submitted his resignation as head football coach, effective February 1, 1947. He requested that he be released from his contract, which was to expire January 1, 1949.

The Athletic Council met Wednesday, January 15, and voted to recommend that Tatum be offered a five-year contract at twelve thousand dollars a year. When I received the council's recommendation, I got in touch with Tatum by telephone and told him that I would make this my recommendation to the board of regents. Tatum told me that he could not accept because he had made certain commitments to officials at the University of Maryland that he thought he should honor. To keep the door open, he hinted that if his situation could be improved to the extent that it would be readily apparent to the people at Maryland that in his own best interest he should stay at OU, he was sure that they would understand his decision to remain.

When the regents assembled on Friday, January 17, I reported all that had happened since their last meeting, including of course, Tatum's statement that he would not accept a five-year contract at twelve thousand dollars a year.

Regent Deacon then moved that "the resignation of Jim Tatum be accepted and that he be released from his contract." But during discussion of the motion, Regents Wallace and Noble reported that they had heard from what they regarded as reliable sources that Tatum would be willing to remain at the University of Oklahoma with a five-year contract. I told the board members that I did not believe this to be true and suggested that they talk with Tatum themselves. They agreed to do so, and a few minutes later Tatum joined the board. After making several conciliatory statements of appreciation for the good treatment he had received at OU, he told the board that he would not accept a five-year contract at twelve thousand dollars a year. He said that he would accept a ten-year contract at an annual salary of twelve thousand dollars, providing the salaries of Coach Driskell and Coach Wilkinson were raised to sixty-five hundred dollars each, with a four-hundred-dollar annual raise for Coach Fehring. But, as a further condition, he added that it would be necessary for him to have a replacement for Coach Radman and one additional coach on a part-time basis at a salary of twenty-four hundred dollars. To my very great surprise he expressed general satisfaction with the administration of the Athletic Department. He said that he thought it would be a good idea to combine intercollegiate athletics, intramural sports, and physical education for men under one director, who would thus be in a position to coordinate use of the personnel and equipment of the three divisions.

Regent Noble then asked Tatum about rumors concerning his dissatisfaction with sports reporting for the institution. Tatum said he did not think Harold Keith would "do as a publicity man for the football team," and he described several incidents in which Keith allegedly had failed to handle the publicity effectively.

Tatum then left the meeting, and the board took under consideration some resolutions concerning the expansion of the Oklahoma Memorial Union. After this business had been transacted, I reminded the group that the coaching situation had been left hanging in the air and asked that some positive action be taken concerning Tatum's resignation. Regent Shepler asked if I had a recommendation. My response, recorded in the minutes of that meeting, was as follows:

Before I care to make a recommendation I should like to hear the members of the board discuss the role of football at the university and if possible come to a decision in regard to what I consider a matter of basic policy.

If our objective is to be that of winning games, regardless of all other considerations, I am ready to make what I consider to be an appropriate recommendation. If, on the other hand, we are to regard football as an activity of the university subordinate in importance to the institution's welfare as a whole, I have another recommendation. It may be the feelings of some members of the board that it is possible to achieve both of these objectives at the same time. In my opinion this is impossible.

If the objective is the winning of football games at any cost, the only factor to be considered in selecting or retaining a head coach is his ability to win games. His methods of winning need not be scrutinized

45

too closely. His relations with other agencies of the university will not be of great concern as long as he is winning. Therefore, the amount of his salary and other features of his contract need not be considered in light of what can be done for others. The impact of his personality on the members of his squad may be ignored. He will, in actual practice, be responsible to no one on the campus—only to the board of regents.

If, on the other hand, football in the university is to be a part of an educational and public relations program in a more genuine sense, many factors must be considered in the selection or retention of a head coach. His integrity, loyalty and personality must be taken into consideration in addition to his ability to win football games. His relation to his associates and the faculty become of paramount importance. Therefore, his salary and the other features of his contract must be considered in the light of the university's general problem. His influence as a man upon the members of his squad becomes important. His ability to view the sport in its proper perspective must be considered.

I should like to request that the board determine this issue before I make my recommendation today.

Apparently, my statement to the board was not very effective, because the minutes indicate that almost immediately Regent Wallace offered a substitute for Deacon's earlier motion to accept Tatum's resignation and release him from his contract. Wallace moved that "we employ Jim Tatum for a period of ten years on the basis he said he would stay this morning and is outlined in his proposal."

Regent Emery then inquired whether the motion was a recommendation of the president. Wallace replied that his substitute motion had been made in the absence of a recommendation by the president—that the records would show that the president had not made a recommendation.

Wallace stated further that the determination of policy by the board with reference to athletics that the president had requested was inconsequential as far as he was concerned in the disposition of the problem before the board at the moment. He followed this statement with an expression of appreciation of the "president's intellectual and academic qualifications" and stressed that he was not antagonistic to the president in any way.

At this point Regent Deacon withdrew his earlier motion, and then Regent Emery asked, "Does the record show that the motion before the board is made prior to the determination of policy requested by President Cross?" To this Regent Wallace replied, "Yes." The question was then called and the voting recorded. Regents Wallace and McBride voted in favor of the motion. Regents Shepler, White, Deacon, Noble, and Emery voted in the negative. The motion was declared lost.

Regent Noble then moved that "the board offer Mr. Tatum a five-year contract at twelve thousand dollars annually, and in event that Mr. Tatum will not accept the offer, the board accept his resignation." Regent Emery inquired if this motion reflected the recommendation of the president. I replied that I was willing to make this recommendation. The motion carried unanimously, and I was asked to call Tatum and tell him of the board's action. But wishing to avoid any misunderstanding, I asked my secretary to invite him to the office once again.

While we were awaiting Tatum's arrival, Regent McBride moved that "we make it six years instead of five. If he does not accept, then accept his resignation." Once again, Regent Emery asked if there was a recommendation from the president on the pending motion. I replied that I could see no basis for making a change in my original recommendation but that I had no objections to a six-year contract if the board saw fit to offer it. In making this concession, I felt reasonably sure, although I did not say so, that Tatum would not accept. The motion passed.

Within a few minutes my secretary reported that Tatum was in the outer office. I left the meeting and joined him there. On behalf of the board I offered him a six-year contract at twelve thousand dollars a year, and he said that he would not accept. As he left the office, he passed a group of reporters who were waiting to hear the outcome of the negotiations. He remarked to the group, "It surely takes a long time to resign from this institution."

I returned to the meeting of the board and recommended that Charles ("Bud") Wilkinson, assistant football coach, be named head coach with a four-year contract providing for an annual salary of ten thousand dollars for the first two years and eleven thousand dollars for the third and fourth years. Some members of the board wanted to talk with Wilkinson before taking action on my recommendation, and he was invited to appear. After a brief conference the board approved his appointment and gave him the privilege of selecting his own staff of assistants.

In the meantime, Tatum and Wilkinson had got together and agreed that the regents and administration should be asked not to issue a press release on the coaching situation until each of them had had a chance to talk with the football team and the assistant coaches. The request was granted, and the regents adjourned that afternoon without issuing a release, much to the disappointment of the several members of the press who had been waiting most of the day.

My session with the regents that day had been a disappointing and frustrating experience. Why had things not gone more smoothly? Why had action been contemplated by the board without recommendation from the president? Why had my request for determination of policy concerning the role of athletics in the university been ignored?

Finally it occurred to me that the fault had been my own. I had asked the board to determine policy when I should have recommended policy and recommended it firmly. I had tried to give the problem to others without offering my own solution. To use a football analogy loosely, I had tried to punt out of trouble when I should have kept possession of the ball.

After reflecting on this for a time, I realized that a university president cannot punt, cannot pass problems to someone else. He must run with the ball and try not to fumble. Once possession is lost, the ball may bounce in any direction. I resolved to keep this in mind for future use, not only in dealing with athletic problems but also in handling all matters having to do with the responsibilities of my office. I found later that this course would not be easy.

Tatum's actions during the early weeks of January were puzzling to sports writers and sports fans. It was soon learned that his Maryland contract was for five years at an annual salary of twelve thousand dollars. No one could understand why he had first expressed such great satisfaction with the situation at Oklahoma and then taken the Maryland position for the same salary with a contract one year less than he would have had at OU. A possible explanation was that, almost immediately after he had indicated that he would stay in Oklahoma, Maryland came through with an offer that he felt that he could not turn down. But to give himself a way out he accepted the offer subject to securing a release from his contract at OU. Thus, if OU should come through with something better than the Maryland offer, he would be able to say that he could not get a release. He really wanted to go to Maryland, but, on the other hand, if he could get a ten-year contract at twelve thousand dollars a year at OU, an unbelievably lucrative arrangement for that time, he would be in a position either to stay at Oklahoma or to renegotiate with Maryland on the grounds that OU would not release him to accept a lesser offer elsewhere.

It was announced on January 19 that Tatum would leave Oklahoma to take up his new duties at Maryland effective February 1 and that Walter Driskell would go with him. It was announced also that Wilkinson and Dutch Fehring would form the nucleus of a new coaching staff at Oklahoma. In leaving, Tatum had kind words for the University of Oklahoma as reported in the *Norman Transcript* on January 19: "It is with a great deal of regret that I leave the University of Oklahoma. OU has been mighty good to me. I hope I have done something good for her."

He scoffed at rumors that he had demanded a change of athletic directors at OU: "Jap Haskell, the athletic director, is my friend. He brought me here. I would never consider staying at the university unless Jap Haskell was the athletic director."

CHAPTER 5

Wilkinson Takes Over—More About Tatum—Control of Athletics

1947

WILKINSON took over his new responsibilities without experience as a head coach but with impressive credentials otherwise. He had played college football at the University of Minnesota under Coach Bernie Bierman during the 1934, 1935, and 1936 seasons. The Golden Gophers of Minnesota were national champions in each of these years, and there could be no doubt about the quality of the football taught by Bierman—or about the effectiveness of the single-wing offense he used.

Moreover, Wilkinson had had the unusual experience of playing both in the line and in the backfield; he played guard in 1934 and 1935, but at the beginning of the 1936 season he was switched to the backfield, where he played blocking back and called signals. Thus as a player he had had opportunities to become familiar with all phases of the single-wing system, an offense based on power, drive, and precision of execution.

He was an All-Big Ten and All-America guard in 1936. In the national All-Star game in August of 1937, he quarterbacked the All-Stars to a 6–0 win over the professional Green Bay Packers, the first time the collegians had ever defeated the pros.

In addition to playing football, Wilkinson lettered in ice hockey and golf. He was goalie on the Big Ten championship ice-hockey teams of 1934 and 1935 and was team captain the second season. He was awarded the Big Ten Conference Medal as the graduating senior with the best record in both athletics and scholarship. He received a degree in English with a business-management minor at Minnesota in 1937.

After graduation he went on to Syracuse University, where he served as assistant coach for five years and completed work leading to a master's degree in English and education. There, as assistant to Ossie Solem, he picked up experience with the A formation, which Syracuse used during the 1941 season.

He returned to Minnesota as an assistant to George Hauser

in 1942, but when the war broke out, he entered the service as first lieutenant in the Navy. He coached the quarterbacks and centers on Don Faurot's Iowa Preflight Sea Hawks team of 1943. In this assignment he gained experience with Faurot's T, an attack based on deception and a run-pass option. Later he worked on Coach Jack Meagher's Sea Hawks staff until he was assigned to the aircraft carrier *Enterprise* as hangar-deck officer in September, 1944. On the *Enterprise* he participated in naval engagements at Iwo Jima, Tokyo, Kyushu, and Okinawa. In September, 1945, he became athletic director on the staff of the chief of Naval Air Training at Pensacola, Florida. One month later he was discharged from the Navy and within a few weeks was hired as backfield coach at the University of Oklahoma.

Wilkinson was only thirty-one years old when he took the head coaching reins at OU. Except for his size (an erect six-foot two-inch frame—195 pounds of well-shaped bone and muscle), there was little about him to suggest the profession of coaching. He was a handsome man, with wavy hair that showed just a hint of the thinning that would come in later years. He was quiet, soft-spoken, and quick with a disarming smile that helped influence people. All in all, he gave the impression of an executive on his way up in business or industry or a member of one of the professions, perhaps a young college professor. His facility with language and excellent enunciation made him very articulate and persuasive in conversation.

His methods of coaching were quite different from those I had seen used by other coaches. I never heard him shout or raise his voice in reprimand. When a player made a mistake on the field, he would call the boy to him, put his arm around the boy's shoulder and explain privately what he had done wrong. All in all, I was pleased that Wilkinson had become head football coach at OU. I had great confidence in his ability. I did have a slight feeling of uncertainty about how he would get along with a squad that had become accustomed to the forceful, intense methods of his predecessor.

Wilkinson and his charming wife, Mary, were the parents of two boys, Pat, aged six, and Jay, aged four. Pat had undergone an emergency appendectomy on Thursday of the week his father

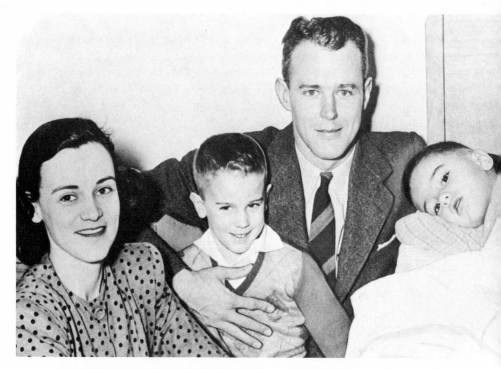

The Wilkinson family: Mary, Jay, Bud, and Pat. Pat's appendectomy delayed for one day the announcement that Wilkinson would succeed Jim Tatum as head football coach at OU. Courtesy *Oklahoman and Times*.

was named head football coach. Wilkinson stayed at his son's bedside, which delayed for a day the release of his acceptance statement to the press.

A few days after his appointment Wilkinson came to my office for a talk. He was impeccably dressed and, noticing just a slight tinge of gray in his hair, I remember silently agreeing with someone who had written in a newspaper article that "he could well pose for a Lord Calvert ad."

He told me that he needed a good line coach as a first addition to his staff. He went on to say that in his opinion the Nebraska Cornhusker line was the toughest and best-coached forward wall the Sooners had played against the previous season. It had been coached, he said, by a young two-time All-America center from Ohio State University named Gomer Jones. Wilkinson wanted very much to hire Jones. He thought that Nebraska was paying

Wilkinson and Line Coach Gomer Jones during a practice session. Courtesy *Oklahoman and Times.*

him forty-five hundred dollars a year and that possibly he could be moved for five thousand dollars. I told him to go ahead and explore the possibility. A few days later Oklahoma had a new line coach, but not at five thousand dollars a year. It took fifty-five hundred dollars to hire Jones away from Nebraska.

As winter ended and spring arrived, much of my time continued to be devoted to problems relating to the athletic program. A meeting of the regents of the university was scheduled for March 20. I did not look forward to this meeting with any relish because I knew that it would involve some unpleasantries having to do with the finances of the Department of Intercollegiate Athletics and the ability of the athletic director, Jap Haskell, to administer the athletic budget.

The problem had emerged during the latter portion of the football season, and came to a head after the close of the season on January 1, 1947. For weeks I had been hearing rumors of heavy spending on football activities, and, while I did not want to make an issue of the matter during the season, I resolved to check into it as soon as possible after the turn of the year.

As things turned out, this took a bit of doing. The Athletic Council at OU was then a separate corporate body that collected and disbursed the monies involved in intercollegiate athletics. The corporation had been established in 1928 to handle funds raised for the construction of the stadium. I was told by a member of the council that the corporate structure had been continued to allow greater flexibility in the use of athletic funds—that occasionally expenditures might need to be made that should not be scrutinized too closely by university officials. The university received periodic reports from the treasurer of the council, Bill Cross (no relation to me), but they were not as detailed as I would have liked.

Immediately after the Gator Bowl game, I asked Cross for a report covering receipts and expenditures. He immediately sent a preliminary report, with the promise of a final statement to come later. After careful study of the preliminary document, Roscoe Cate, financial assistant to the president, and I were unable to account for six thousand dollars listed under "expenditures." All necessary expenses of the trip appeared to have been paid, and it seemed unlikely that miscellaneous items could total six thousand dollars.

Then it occurred to me that Tatum might have bought gifts for the players who made the trip, even though I had reminded him of the conference rule prohibiting such gifts. A day or so later, while walking on the campus, I ran into Joe Golding. After chatting with him for a few minutes, I said, "Joe, how were the gifts to players handled at the Gator Bowl? Did all who made the trip receive presents or were they given only to those who actually played in the game?"

Joe replied, "President Cross, the squad voted on that. We voted that all who made the trip would be treated alike."

I asked, "What was the gift? Tatum was talking about the possibility of shotguns or sets of golf clubs."

Joe replied, "We voted on that, too. We decided to take cash— $120 apiece." This cleared up the mystery of the missing money. Fifty boys at $120 apiece would total $6,000.

Tatum was still on the campus, and I invited him to come to my office. During our session I asked him if he had given presents to the members of the football squad during their visit to Jacksonville. He admitted that he had. I reminded him of our earlier conversation about the conference regulation prohibiting gifts of any kind to athletes, and I reminded him also of my specific request that no gifts be given in connection with the Gator Bowl game. He replied that after he had talked to me he had visited with the "boss man," who had told him that it would be all right to give the boys something. I asked him whom he meant by the "boss man" and he replied, "Neil Johnson, the chairman of the Athletic Council." He reminded me, in what seemed a somewhat triumphant manner, that the Athletic Council was a corporation that operated independently of the university and that the head man in athletic affairs was the chairman of the Athletic Council. He seemed unconcerned that a violation of conference regulations had occurred that, if it became known, could make all involved members of the squad ineligible for future competition.

Knowledge of this violation placed me in a most uncomfortable quandary. From a strictly ethical point of view, I realized that I should report the violation to the conference and the National

Collegiate Athletic Association, but, on the other hand, to do that would mean that the athletes involved, who had received the gifts in good faith without knowledge that they were violating regulations, would lose their eligibility for further competition and perhaps lose the opportunity to continue their college education. It would mean also the ruin of the university's football program for the next few years. I finally decided to tell the regents of the university and let them decide what should be done. I telephoned the president of the board and recommended that we report the violation to the conference and to the NCAA and that with the report should go a statement that the coach and the athletic director were being dismissed from the university. I believed that if this were done the disciplinary action the conference and the association might take would not include loss of eligibility for the athletes. My suggestion apparently was not considered seriously by the board; the unrecorded decision was to "keep quiet" about what had happened but to take every precaution to see that it did not happen again.

In the midst of it all, of course, Tatum resigned to take the Maryland position, and I was left to dig more deeply into the finances of the Athletic Department with Haskell. I requested and received a report from Bill Cross covering the receipts and expenditures of the department during the first half of the fiscal year. Cross's statement showed that the receipts for the six-month period had been $341,078.95, with expenditures of $292,821.34, which would have represented a nice improvement in the department's cash position. However, I noticed that $25,899.94 of the receipts had come from bonds that had been cashed during December—in other words, taken from athletic reserves. Delving deeper, I found also that, far from being in a better cash position than at the beginning of the fiscal year, the Department of Athletics was actually running a deficit in excess of $60,000 by midyear, although its ticket receipts had been the largest in the history of the university.

I found Haskell frank and cooperative, but since he was uninformed and somewhat naïve about athletic expenditures, I had a series of conferences with Bill Cross. From him I learned that the department had been paying the coaches seven cents a mile for travel by personal automobile, while the state law covering

56

travel by state employees had set the rate at five cents a mile. Haskell later explained this by saying that the state laws did not apply to the Department of Intercollegiate Athletics, because the Athletic Council was a corporation and its employees were not employees of the state.

I made a complete report of the confused situation to the regents of the university at the meeting on March 20, and they decided to talk with Haskell immediately. After conferring with him for a couple of hours, it was clearly the consensus of the regents that, although he was genial, honest, and extremely well-liked, an individual with better business and managerial ability was needed to fill the post of athletic director. As one regent put it, he was disturbed "not so much because Haskell had permitted Tatum to spend money in such profligate fashion but because he apparently did not know that the money was being spent." A motion was passed to instruct me to give Haskell an opportunity to resign from his post. If he refused, I was to notify him that he would be relieved of his duties effective June 30. I wrote to Haskell telling him of this action and saying that I would see him the following Monday to learn his decision. When I talked with Haskell, he refused to resign. I gave him oral notice that he would be relieved of his duties as of June 30. I also called in reporters and gave them a brief statement: "The regents considered carefully the activities and finances of the athletic department during the past year and came to the conclusion that Mr. Haskell should not have charge of the department after June 30."

News of Haskell's dismissal was, of course, featured on the front pages of the state's daily newspapers, and there was much speculation about why it had happened.

Haskell attempted an explanation in a four-and-a-half-page statement. He claimed that part of his difficulty had arisen because he had recommended hiring a football coach whom the president and regents of the university did not wish to employ; they had someone else in mind. He admitted that his budget had been overspent, but, he said, that had happened because the administration had placed on his department financial responsibilities for travel and for the employment of coaches that he had not foreseen at the time the budget was prepared. He stated also

57

that he believed he had incurred the enmity of influential regents by not adding Tulsa University to the football schedule.

After I had studied carefully a copy of Haskell's lengthy statement to the press, I concluded that his usefulness as director of athletics had ended—that it would be wise to place the department under different management immediately rather than wait until June 30. I called Lloyd Noble, who had been elected president of the Board of Regents at the March 20 meeting and suggested that Wilkinson be asked to assume the duties of athletic director on an interim basis until a permanent director could be selected. Noble agreed, and I got in touch with Wilkinson, asking him to assume the extra responsibility temporarily without additional compensation. Wilkinson was agreeable, and he took charge of the department on April 1.

During the month of March, Roscoe Cate, vice-president of the university, and I had frequently discussed the problem of bringing the athletic program under the control of the president's office. We were interested not only in maintaining a balanced athletic budget but also in correcting or investigating several other matters, especially the possibility that OU had been providing illegal financial aid to athletes. Under the regulations of the conference aid could be given to athletes only as payment for services performed for the institution and at rates no higher than those paid to nonathletes. The schools of the Big Six Conference were handicapped by this rule because the Southwest Conference had adopted a plan which involved the granting of scholarships amounting to fifty or sixty dollars a month plus tuition and fees. The NCAA code of 1946 provided that an employed athlete should work 160 hours a year, but was not clear concerning the hourly rate of pay for such service. It was difficult to compete for athletes with this discrepancy in regulations, and it was perhaps understandable, or at least inevitable, that some of the schools of the Big Six Conference would find ways of evading the more stringent regulations of their organization.

Cate and I were convinced that the University of Oklahoma had been guilty of violating conference regulations during the 1946 season. From a careful examination of Athletic Department expenditures, Cate learned that an average of $4,518.95 had been expended monthly from January 1 to November 30, 1946, for direct payments to football players and for payment of room-and-board bills. The total of the eleven-month period was $49,-708.51. It seemed obvious that the football players could not have earned that much money at the prevailing campus rates which were 50 to 60 cents an hour.

From the records available to us it appeared that the basis for payment to the members of the football squad had been $15.00 a month plus room and board for single men and $75.00 a month for married men. But there were no records of work performed by athletes, and it seemed clear that the year's operation had been in violation of the regulations of the conference—in violation also of the 1946 NCAA code.

We were convinced that several other schools in the conference were similarly guilty of violating conference regulations, and we had evidence that Oklahoma A&M College and the University of Tulsa, not subject to our conference regulations, provided substantial financial support to promising athletes. In addition to the illegal aid provided by the institutions themselves, inducements from private sources were rumored to be commonplace in OU's area of competition. A wide variety of benefits, including clothing, groceries, automobiles, and employment for the parents of athletes, were allegedly provided, with or without the knowledge and cooperation of the institutions involved. It was an unsavory situation. Cate and I often discussed the impact that it must be having on the athletes, who could not fail to know that the aid they were receiving was in violation of conference regulations.

The over-all problem apparently attracted the attention of the NCAA. At a meeting held on January 8, 1947, the association revised Article III of its constitution to provide a set of principles for the conduct of intercollegiate athletics in their member institutions—with special attention to recruiting and financial aid to athletes. The statement of principles provided that responsibility for the conduct of intercollegiate athletics should be vested in the institution itself. It provided also that aid for athletes should be awarded on a basis of need, by the regular agency established in the institution for that purpose and should be awarded on the same basis as aid given to nonathletes. The aid could not exceed tuition for instruction and/or stated incidental

59

fees, except when the total aid involved a government grant or a scholarship not based on athletic ability. With respect to recruiting, the principles provided that coaches could not operate beyond the boundaries of their own institutions and could not, under any circumstances, offer financial aid or equivalent inducements to any prospective athlete. Coaches were permitted to appear as speakers at banquets and other functions throughout the recruiting area, but they could not visit with individual athletes on such occasions.

Because practices in the Big Six Conference were known to differ so markedly from the statement of principles of the NCAA, the presidents of the six institutions decided that a joint meeting with their faculty representatives to the conference would be in order; there was need for a general discussion of the problem. The meeting was scheduled for March 1, 1947, in Kansas City, Missouri.

It was decided at this joint session that the conference could live with the new regulations of the NCAA, except for the provision that an athlete could not receive aid in excess of tuition and fees. It was agreed that the six schools would follow the policies of the conference with respect to aid, but I suspect that no one at the meeting knew exactly what the policies of the conference were.

After the combined meeting of the presidents and faculty representatives the latter group continued with their own meeting and took up several matters of more than usual interest. On the agenda were requests from the University of Colorado and Oklahoma A&M College for admission to the conference. The admission of Colorado was approved by unanimous vote, but action on the application from Oklahoma A&M was deferred, despite Walter Kraft's argument for the admission of OU's sister institution. It was reported later that one of the faculty representatives had remarked that, in his opinion, "one institution from the state of Oklahoma was about all the conference could handle at the moment."

With the number of schools in the conference changed to seven a change of name seemed necessary. Forgetting that the official name of the league was still the Missouri Valley Intercollegiate Athletic Association (the Big Six tag had been merely a nickname used by sports writers), the faculty representatives passed a motion renaming the conference the Midwest Conference. The renaming turned out to be futile. A few days later it was discovered that there was already a Midwest Conference, and the action was rescinded by telephone vote. Inevitably, it came to be called the Big Seven Conference.

The minutes of the March 1 meeting of the faculty representatives show that attention was given to a plan for aid to athletes that had been developed by fans at the University of Nebraska. Funds raised were turned over to the university foundation, to be used as an "athletic achievement scholarship fund." The Nebraska representative reported that the foundation had received approximately five thousand dollars, four thousand of which had been disbursed to athletes in the form of two-hundred-dollar "grants in aid." The faculty representatives took a dim view of this kind of athletic aid. They ruled the fund illegal and ordered it discontinued.

All these developments were extraneous to OU's immediate problem: how to gain control of its athletic program. Cate and I realized that there was no way to do so as long as intercollegiate athletics were managed by a corporation that collected its own receipts and wrote its own checks without supervision of any kind by the university administration. An obvious solution was to dissolve the corporation and make intercollegiate athletics an auxiliary enterprise of the university, with personnel appointments, purchasing, contracts, travel applications, and policy approval handled in the same way that other auxiliary enterprises of the institution were handled, including internal audits by university auditors. Such a change would leave the Athletic Council to serve as an advisory board rather than as a corporate body.

It appeared, however, that the time was not right to try to dissolve the corporation. It seemed better to continue the Athletic Council as it was for the moment but attempt meanwhile to reach joint agreement between the Board of Regents and the council on the following procedures:

1. Require that all athletic income of any kind be deposited with the university controller instead of in a bank.

2. Require that expenditures from athletic funds be paid only upon presentation to the controller of disbursement orders approved by per-

61

sons specifically authorized to issue them.

3. Require that members of the intercollegiate athletic staff submit applications for all out-of-state travel before making trips, in the same manner that university employees applied for travel authorization, and that reimbursement for travel by members of the intercollegiate athletic staff be made on the same basis as for state employees.

4. Instruct the controller of the university to make no disbursements from athletic funds in excess of the budget approved by the Athletic Council at the beginning of the year or in subsequent budget revisions.

5. Assign to the auditing section of the controller's office the same responsibility concerning the monthly operating reports of the Athletic Council that it had concerning the operating reports of the various auxiliary enterprises of the university.

During preliminary discussions Wilkinson did not object to the suggested changes in the handling of athletic finances, but neither did he express any enthusiasm for them. Some members of the Athletic Council were doubtful that a successful athletic program could be maintained if athletic personnel were not free to spend in ways "not always known to the president of the university," but they did not actively oppose the changes. With this tacit approval the new procedures were recommended to the regents of the university, who agreed orally, and the plan was put into effect for the school year 1947–48.

The new policy gave the president's office some control over the employment practices of the Athletic Department, but the problems were by no means solved. It was difficult to police athletics to the extent that one could be sure each athlete was earning the money he received as athletic aid. The situation was complicated by the fact that an athlete obviously could not participate in a sport that required daily rigorous training, study enough to make the grades necessary to remain eligible for competition, and still work enough hours to earn a living. There were not enough hours available to accomplish all this. It was decided that the University of Oklahoma should face the problem squarely and try to persuade the other members of the Big Seven Conference and the officials of the NCAA to approve an athletic scholarship plan that would take care of the minimum educational expenses of a student athlete and require no service other than participation in the sport. This objective was finally achieved, but only after several years of effort.

CHAPTER 6

Wilkinson's First Season

1947

WILKINSON lost no time getting underway with the dual responsibilities he had been asked to assume. He organized a recruiting program that was to become one of the most effective in the country, and he conducted a successful spring practice. But he also displayed an active interest in sports other than football, an interest that extended to intramural sports and physical-fitness programs for all male students at the university. He seemed especially interested in the intramural program, and on several occasions we discussed the possibility of combining intramural and intercollegiate athletics under one management, so that the sports equipment and facilities of the institution could be used for the maximum benefit of the student body.

The 1946–47 season had marked the departure of two outstanding athletes from the OU football team. Both players had remaining eligibility at OU but decided to sign pro contracts. Joe Golding, one of OU's finest running backs of all time, signed with the Boston Yanks, and Plato Andros, a 220-pound All-America guard with two years' eligibility remaining, signed with the Chicago Cardinals.

While the loss of Golding and Andros to the pros must have been a discouraging blow to OU's young head football coach, things could have been much worse. Concerned OU fans spent much of the summer wondering to what extent the pro teams would be able to raid the squad Tatum and his staff had recruited. That only Golding and Andros were lured away must be considered a tribute to the leadership and persuasiveness of Wilkinson, who was able to convince the rest of the players that they would be wise to complete their formal education before beginning careers as professional athletes.

During the summer Wilkinson completed his coaching staff. He added Major Lou Hermerda, acting commandant of the university ROTC, and Cliff Matthews, a graduate student in geology, as part-time assistant football coaches. With Gomer Jones, Bill

Jennings, Dutch Fehring, and Walter Hargesheimer he had a staff of six assistant coaches on hand to begin the 1947 season. He had also a well-rounded squad, which included several who later would gain All-America honors and four who would become head coaches at major universities.

Wilkinson's first football season at OU was not a sparkling success, not indicative in any way that in later years his teams would break most of the records of modern football and establish a new record for consecutive victories—a record likely to stand for some time. His team defeated three of its nonconference opponents (Detroit University, Texas A&M, and Oklahoma A&M), but lost by decisive scores to the University of Texas and Texas Christian University. In conference competition there were four victories and a 13–13 tie with the University of Kansas. Thus for the second consecutive year OU and KU shared the conference championship.

I saw only the games played at home during the 1947 season. Mrs. Cross and I had planned to see the Texas game in Dallas on October 11, but a death in her family made it necessary for us to go to South Dakota. When we returned the following week, we found Oklahoma citizens astir over events that had occurred at the game. From newspaper and verbal accounts we gathered that the OU fans had bitterly resented the activities of one of the officials who worked the game—Jack Sisco, formerly football coach at North Texas State College then living in Dallas. Sisco's officiating thoroughly antagonized the Oklahomans.

The game started out in the torrid fashion that had characterized previous encounters. During the first quarter Bobby Layne, the Texas quarterback, piloted his team to a 7–0 advantage. During the second period, however, the Sooners developed a full head of steam and, with their forward wall ripping huge gaps in the heavier Texas line, staged a 61-yard drive that took them from their own 30 to their opponent's 9-yard line. At this point Oklahoma was penalized for unnecessary roughness and failed to score. But on their next possession they carried the ball across the goal line, tying the game at 7–7.

The tie was maintained until a few seconds before the end of the first half. As intermission approached, Texas had driven

64

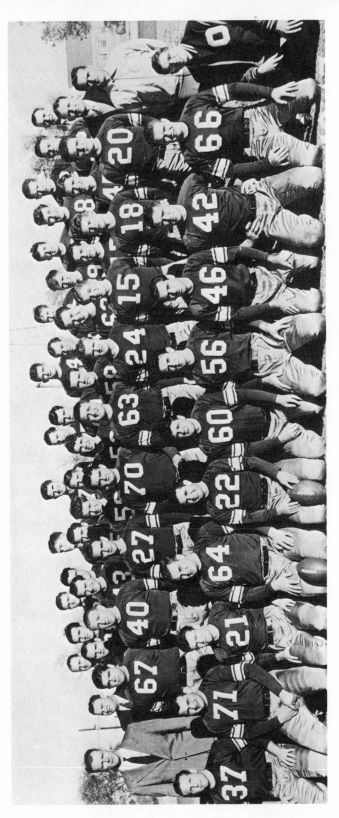

The 1947 team. FIRST ROW (FRONT ROW), LEFT TO RIGHT: Bob Cutsinger, John Husack, Darrell Royal, Stan West, Johnny Allsup, Wade Walker, Jim Tyree, Dave Wallace, Bill Morris, Eddy Davis (student manager). SECOND ROW: Bud Wilkinson (coach), Buddy Burris, Pete Tillman, Buddy Jones, Dee Andros, Ed Kreick, Bud Hoofnagle, Kenneth Parker, Dan Anderegg, Charles Sarratt, Joe Glander (trainer). THIRD ROW: Gomer Jones (assistant coach), Laddie Harp, Max Fischer, Frankie Anderson, Boyd McGugan, Truman Wright, Nute Trotter, Bill Remy, Bobby Goad, Dutch Fehring (assistant coach). FOURTH AND FIFTH ROWS: Walter Hargesheimer (assistant coach), Gene Heape, George Thomas, Ken Tipps, Charley Dowell, Homer Paine, John Rapacz, Myrle Greathouse, Jim Martin, Earl Hale, Bob Bodenhamer, Ray Pearcy, Ed Mays, Willie Manley, Jack Mitchell, Jim Owens, Merle Dinkins, George Brewer, Lou Hemerda (assistant coach). Courtesy Sports Information Department.

57 yards to the Oklahoma 3. With twenty seconds to go a Texas back gained 1 yard and the team hurriedly lined up, without a huddle, for a last minute attempt to score. But Texas back Randall Clay was gang-tackled and failed to gain as the clock ticked off the final seconds.

It was at this point that Sisco became conspicuous in the day's events. Oklahomans reported that he rushed to the pileup near the goal line, first signaling a touchdown but then quickly changing his signal to a time out. He later reported that Texas had called for a time out with three seconds left and thus had a bonus play after the half apparently had ended.

Jim Kennedy was selected to carry the ball on the final attempt. Kennedy fumbled, and the ball bounced off a Sooner's arm to the ground. One of the Texans retrieved it and lateraled to Clay, who scored from 6 yards out. Texas went into the second half with a 14–7 advantage. Oklahomans who saw the game were convinced that one if not both of Clay's knees had been on the ground at the time he received the lateral and that the ball should have been ruled dead at that point. In later conversations Sisco appeared sure that Clay had been on his feet after he received the ball. Impartial sports writers in the press box reported they had been mystified by the series of events.

The second half was a series of frustrations. Sooner end Jim Tyree threw a powerful block on OU's 14-yard line that enabled Darrell Royal to return a punt to the OU 25, but a red flag was thrown, and the Sooners were penalized to their 1-yard line for clipping. The Oklahoma fans, convinced that the block had been legitimate, expressed their displeasure loudly. The Sooners, kicking from deep in the end zone against the wind gave Texas the ball on the OU 33-yard line, and the Steers were able to carry it in for their third score of the day.

In the fourth quarter Sooner backs Thomas and Mitchell teamed up on an 80-yard lateral scoring run, which reduced the Texas lead to 21–14. After the ensuing kickoff the Texans drove from their 16-yard line deep into OU territory. Then Darrell Royal intercepted a Layne pass, and it appeared that the Sooners might be set up to tie the score; but Sisco declared a holding penalty, which gave the ball back to Texas on the Sooner 23-yard line. From this point the Steers were able to score a fourth touch-down just before the game ended.

The Sooner fans were angry throughout the second half and, on one occasion, vented their anger by throwing pop bottles and other objects onto the field. At the close of the game they rushed from the stands in pursuit of Sisco. But the Dallas police, sensing that something of that kind might happen, had assembled a hundred or more strong at the south end of the stadium. As the game ended, a police car wheeled onto midfield, and the game officials were surrounded by a barricade of officers. Sisco and his associates hurriedly climbed into the car and were driven from the stadium as the police patiently but firmly parted the angry crowd so that the vehicle could make its way off the field.

More than a quarter of a century later, one still hears the word "sisco" used occasionally in relation to an unsavory situation— "He pulled a 'sisco' on me," or "We were 'siscoed' in that deal."

The disturbances during and after the game prompted discussion during the following weeks about the advisability of discontinuing the Texas-Oklahoma series in Dallas. Dissatisfaction with the annual weekend south of the Red River had been expressed previously on many occasions. Many Oklahomans felt that the Dallas business circle had been using the game to exploit Oklahomans who made the annual pilgrimage. It was charged that room and food rates were raised during that weekend, and it was known that hotels and motels would not accept reservations for fewer than three nights. Moreover, in recent years, the weekend had developed into a sort of drinking orgy, with unruly crowds of students from the two universities and the local high schools taking over the streets of downtown Dallas the night before the game. Influential groups seemed about to unite in an effort to put the game with Texas on a home-and-home basis.

But several factors had to be taken into consideration. Each of the participating schools had received $41,406.06 as its share of the gate receipts for the 1947 contest. It was estimated that withdrawal from the series would cost the University of Oklahoma approximately $21,000 a year. Moreover, contracts with the University of Texas and the Cotton Bowl Association still had three years to run; Oklahoma's withdrawal would be a violation of the contracts. On November 29, at a special meeting of representatives of the university, the University of Oklahoma Association, the University Athletic Council, and the officers of the OU Dad's Association, the decision was made to complete the present contracts and then attempt to switch to a home-and-home arrangement.

A computation of the attendance figures for the 1947 season showed that a new record had been set for home games—a total of 148,938 and a game average of 29,787. The largest previous attendance had been in 1946, when 109,618 fans saw the four home games at OU. The average attendance was 27,404. The largest and second-largest home-game crowds assembled in 1947, when 34,547 saw Oklahoma and Kansas play, and 33,945 saw OU win over the Oklahoma Aggies by a score of 21–13 in the season's finale.

The first Wilkinson-coached team was rated sixteenth in the nation by the Associated Press national sports poll (the top team that year was Notre Dame). The team's record of seven victories, two losses, and one tie was actually better than that of the preceding year—as a matter of fact, it was the best for several years. In five of the seven victories, however, the team had had to come from behind to win and had not been impressive in winning. Although the team received (and turned down) bids to the Gator, Sun, Harbor, and Alamo bowls, many football fans were skeptical about Wilkinson's ability to make it as head coach at OU.

This skepticism was well illustrated by an incident that occurred at a party on the top floor of the Skirvin Hotel in Oklahoma City during the Christmas holiday season. At the party three enthusiastic supporters of OU football, Harrison Smith, Gene Jordan, and Robert Bowers, asked what I was going to do about the football situation at the university. They spent several minutes explaining that Wilkinson was too nice a person to get the job done; he had been reasonably successful during the past season only because of the momentum that had been generated by Jim Tatum. They assured me that this momentum would expend itself by the end of the next season or two and that I had better be looking for a coach more like Tatum. I reminded them that the season had been Wilkinson's first as head coach of any team and that he might have learned some things that would be helpful to him in subsequent years. My friends ended the conversation with the repeated admonition that I "had better be looking."

As I went about the state during the following weeks, I found that the opinion expressed at the party was the prevailing one. I remember talking with only one individual who had confidence that Wilkinson would make the grade at OU. He was H. V. Dowell, of Sand Springs, the father of Charles Dowell, a reserve center on the OU squad.

But this pessimistic attitude concerning Wilkinson's future as a football coach apparently was not prevalent beyond the state's borders. Early in January, 1948, Tom Hamilton resigned as football coach at the Naval Academy. The Navy football team had not enjoyed success comparable to that of the Army team, and the decision was made to hire a civilian coach who might be able to put football affairs in better order at the academy. Wilkinson was invited to visit Annapolis and discuss the situation with officials there, and he left Norman a few days later.

After he left, there was speculation in the local newspapers that he would accept a Navy offer. Hal Middlesworth, sports columnist for the *Daily Oklahoman,* wrote on January 27, "One of the things which causes coaches like Wilkinson to take a second look at offers like that of Navy is a distressing habit of fans and camp followers in this state who insist that a coach ought to win every game." He mentioned the "muttering" of Oklahoma fans during the past season, especially when OU lost to Texas Christian University. Other writers offered the opinion that Wilkinson would find it very difficult to resist an offer from Navy.

When Wilkinson returned from the East, he reported to me that Navy had made him an offer but that he had turned it down after careful consideration, partly because he was satisfied at OU and partly because several requirements were made of athletes at the Naval Academy that were not in vogue at West Point. He thought it would be very difficult, under the circumstances, for Navy to produce a team that could hope to beat the cadets.

He had scarcely left the house when the telephone rang. The

operator reported that Jim Tatum was calling from the University of Maryland. Tatum told me that he was under consideration for the coaching job at the Naval Academy and asked me to send a strong letter of recommendation. He said that I need not cover anything concerning his ability to coach or recruit, because the Navy officials were well acquainted with his record. But, he said, he did need a sort of "character reference," because Navy had been asking some questions about the part he had played in the dismissal of Jap Haskell, the subsidizing of football players at OU, and rumors that he had misused athletic funds. I told Jim frankly that I was in a position to write only about his ability as a recruiter of athletes and football staff and the quality of his coaching, that I was not able to write concerning his character. He then told me that I would probably change my mind when I learned that if he did not get the job Bud Wilkinson would be chosen—that he and Bud were the two top contenders for the position. He stressed that, in the interest of developing a good football program at the University of Oklahoma, I should make every effort to help him get the Navy job. I did not mention that Wilkinson had turned down a Navy offer but told him only that I would think about the matter carefully, as he had suggested, and make up my mind. As it turned out, it was not necessary for me to make a decision; shortly afterward it was announced from Annapolis that George Sauer, coach at the University of Kansas, had accepted the head coaching position at the Naval Academy.

The Annapolis incident was to be only the first of a series during the following years that involved keeping Wilkinson at the University of Oklahoma. Realizing that this probably would be the case, I recommended to the regents of the university, at their monthly meeting in April, 1948, that he be given the title director of athletics (he had served one year as acting director) effective May 1. The regents approved the recommendation.

CHAPTER 7

Eligibility Problems—The Touchdown Club 1948

DURING the spring and summer of 1948, a controversy over eligibility rules arose in the conference. As a background for understanding what happened, it will be helpful to point out that during the war eligibility standards had been relaxed throughout the country. With so many college men in service there had been a serious shortage of athletes in collegiate sports. The manpower shortage finally became so serious that one conference in the Middle West suspended all its eligibility rules. In 1944, OU's basketball team played a school from a neighboring conference that had one player with a bachelor's degree on its squad and another who not only had graduated from college but had played professional baseball as well.

When the war ended and the servicemen came back to resume their schooling, the faculty representatives of the Big Six Conference passed a number of very liberal rules covering postwar eligibility. Like most other conferences the Big Six awarded all former servicemen four years of varsity competition. It ruled also that no competition would be counted that an athlete might have incurred during the war while a member of a campus military unit. In some instances this rule made it possible for an athlete to participate for as many as six years. For example, Derold Lebow, Oklahoma's all–Big Six tailback of 1942 and 1943, was a member of a university ROTC unit during both of those seasons. Under the policy of the Big Six, when Tatum started spring practice in 1946, Lebow was eligible to compete four additional years, making a total of six years of competition.

But as time went on, a reaction set in. On March 2, 1946, the faculty representatives of the conference adopted a rule stating that all eligible veterans would have "a total not to exceed four years of competition." Later, at a meeting held on December 13, 1946, they changed the phrasing to read "a total of four years of participation." During the ensuing months several questions were raised about the meaning of those two almost identical phrases and about how the ruling would affect the eligibility of prominent athletes at several of the conference schools, especially Kansas State University, the University of Kansas, and the University of Oklahoma. It was thought advisable to clear up all these questions before the University of Colorado, which was being admitted to membership in the conference, began competition.

Therefore, during the winter, 1947–48, conference meeting, the faculty representatives took a careful look at the eligibility regulations. Earl S. Fullbrook, the newly appointed representative from Nebraska, reported that "It seemed clear that in passing the rules of March 2 and December 13, 1946, a majority of the faculty representatives had never intended to do more than permit four years of competition, whether it be varsity, freshman, or junior college." He then moved that "competition" be interpreted according to Article II, Section B, b, of the constitution of the conference, which states that "playing on a team or against a team in a contest in which either one of the institutions represented ranks above high school shall count as participation," with the exception that the first year of participation in a junior college did not count. Faculty representatives apparently favored the motion but decided to table it because the representative from the University of Kansas had left the meeting early.

The tabled motion was discussed thoroughly at the May, 1948, meeting of the group and passed by a vote of 5–2, over the vigorous opposition of the representatives from Kansas State and the University of Kansas.

As a result of the ruling Kansas State lost three players from the starting lineup of its championship basketball team. The University of Oklahoma lost a couple of third-string football players and one year of eligibility for Jack Mitchell, the leading ground gainer in the Big Six during 1947. The University of Kansas lost four football players, two from the first string and two reserves, and one member of the basketball team.

Wilkinson opened spring football practice late in February, and some of his drills were conducted in cold weather. He had some promising sophomores on his roster, including Claude Arnold, of Okmulgee; Harry Moore, of Blackwell; Frankie Anderson, of Oklahoma City; and Lindell Pearson, also of Oklahoma City.

In the minds of many Lindell Pearson was the most promising sophomore of the lot. He had been an outstanding athlete in high school and had been extensively recruited by coaches throughout the country. But his family dentist, Dr. C. B. McDonald, an enthusiastic OU fan, had been lining him up for OU since he first showed signs of athletic ability early in childhood. At the time of Lindell's graduation everything seemed settled; he announced that he would enroll at the University of Oklahoma in the fall of 1947.

But Lindell did not appear for enrollment in September, and a very concerned Wilkinson called Dr. McDonald to find out what had happened. Dr. McDonald expressed surprise at the boy's apparent defection and promised an immediate investigation.[1] He went to Lindell's home and talked with his parents. They professed ignorance of their son's whereabouts, but finally, following persistent inquiry by McDonald, Mrs. Pearson suggested that the boy's girl friend, who lived a block or so down the street, might know where he was and be willing to tell him.

McDonald went to the girl friend's home, and, after making maximum use of his considerable persuasive ability, he managed to learn from the girl that Lindell had gone to the University of Arkansas. A few hours later the good doctor was in Fayetteville trying to unravel the mystery, but he ran into a sizable roadblock: the university athletic officials would not let him see Lindell.

McDonald returned to Oklahoma City and sought out Eugene Jordan and Bob Bowers, OU fans who had been active in helping develop the football program at the university. Jordan and Bowers hired a detective to find Lindell, and a few days later, the detective reported success in his search—Lindell and one of the assistant coaches at Arkansas had been found in a hotel in Little Rock.

McDonald, Jordan, Bowers, and the detective went to Little Rock and registered at the hotel. That evening the detective

[1]The remainder of this chapter is based on information told to me by Paul Brown, an Oklahoma City attorney.

telephoned the assistant coach. Representing himself as an assistant coach from a southeastern institution, he said that he had stopped off at Little Rock on his way home and suggested that the two of them might spend the evening discussing football at their respective institutions. It was arranged that they should meet in the hotel coffee shop.

While the detective and the assistant coach were having coffee, McDonald and his two helpers went to Lindell's room and persuaded the boy to return with them to the University of Oklahoma. They helped pack his clothes and had him out of the room by the time his "bodyguard" returned.

Lindell enrolled at the University of Oklahoma the next day, but the problem of keeping him at OU was not yet solved. It had been anticipated (I was told years later) that some extraordinary inducements had been involved in Lindell's switch from the University of Oklahoma to the University of Arkansas and that some rather expensive gifts would need to be returned or paid for. To cope with this problem others were brought into the picture, including Paul Brown and Harrison Smith, both of Oklahoma City. Within a matter of hours a plan was devised whereby several OU fans would be invited to contribute money to "ransom" Lindell from Arkansas and provide the basis for a fund that might be used to meet such competition in the future.

The OU fans in Oklahoma City, and perhaps elsewhere, responded generously to the appeal for help, and several thousand dollars were contributed, much more money than was needed to ransom Lindell. The question then arose, How should the remainder of the money be used? The Oklahoma Cityans involved in the project, in cooperation with E. G. ("Big Boy") Johnson, of Norman, came up with the idea of developing a corporation for the purpose of receiving, holding, and disbursing money for the support of athletics, especially football, at the University of Oklahoma.

Paul Brown, an Oklahoma City attorney, prepared an application for a charter for the new corporation, which was to be known as the Touchdown Club. The application was approved, the charter was issued, and the Touchdown Club was organized on October 8, 1947.

The first president of the club was Harrison Smith. Smith,

Lindell Pearson. His unexpected switch to the University of Arkansas touched off a series of events that led to the establishment of the Touchdown Club. Courtesy Sports Information Department.

with the aid of Jordan, Bowers, McDonald, Brown, Johnson, and others, launched a fund drive that brought in $30,000 in a very few days. At the end of three months $75,000 had been collected.

Paul Brown realized from the beginning that contributions from the club to OU athletics must be made through the university and not directly to the Athletic Department or to the athletes. Accordingly, arrangements were made whereby the funds would be transferred periodically to the University of Oklahoma Foundation and made available to the Department of Intercollegiate Athletics as needed.

Actually the Touchdown Club did not at any time provide extremely large amounts of money for recruitment purposes but instead concentrated its efforts on developing a substantial fund from which only the income, plus the annual individual membership dues of fifty dollars, would be made available to the university.

75

CHAPTER 8

The 1948 Season—Sugar Bowl I
1948–49

ALL in all, prospects looked pretty good for the 1948 season. Of course, the peacetime draft that had been proposed by Congress was a threat to the nonveterans on the squad—twenty-one in all—but most of the experienced players were draft-exempt veterans. One loss from the squad caused special concern. John Rapacz, the outstanding center of the 1947 squad, became ineligible because he had signed a contract with a professional team. There were, however, several promising young centers to fill the vacancy, including Pete Tillman, of Mangum; Charles Paine, of Enid; Harry Moore, of Blackwell; Charley Dowell, of Tulsa; and Bob Bodenhamer, of Waurika. While I was watching spring practice that year, it occurred to me that the squad was pretty well equipped with talent at every position. The coaching staff for the coming season was in good shape also. Dutch Fehring had resigned, and Frank ("Pop") Ivy, All-America end at OU in 1939, was named to fill the vacancy.

The Sooners opened their second season under Wilkinson against Santa Clara, at Kezar Stadium in San Francisco. The team flew to San Francisco on Friday, September 24 in a chartered plane, and I went along.

The game the next day provided a good example of the principle that a groggy opponent can be dangerous—that pressure must be maintained throughout an athletic contest. Things seemed to go very well for OU during most of the first half. The line played brilliantly, blunting Santa Clara's rushing attack and blocking the Sooner backs to a net of 231 yards, more than double that gained by Santa Clara. Darrell Royal was effective at quarterback, and with twelve minutes left in the half the Sooners led 10–0.

Then, after an exchange of punts, Royal fumbled to Santa Clara on the Sooner 18-yard line, a misadventure that was followed by a scoring pass to an uncovered Santa Clara receiver in Oklahoma's end zone.

76

Oklahoma halfback George Thomas picks up ten yards on this play in the game with Santa Clara. Courtesy Sports Information Department.

Jack Mitchell then replaced Royal at quarterback. On his first play he handed off to George Thomas, who, with excellent blocking, was able to go 82 yards for a touchdown. Leslie Ming kicked the extra point, and OU led 17–7 at half time.

OU was unable to score during the second half, but Santa Clara completed two long passes, each of which led to a touchdown. The Sooners were behind 17–20 when the game ended.

The disappointed OU squad discussed the game freely as they flew back to Oklahoma that evening. The linemen, who had played so well—Jimmy Owens, Homer Paine, Buddy Burris, Stanley West, Dee Andros, Wade Walker, and Bobby Goad—and the linebackers—Myrle Greathouse, Pete Tillman and Charley Dowell—were inclined to be a little critical of the defensive secondary personnel. But Wilkinson put the game in proper perspective in his newsletter the following week: he said that the Santa Clara team had shown superior hustle during the second half, and it was obvious that the OU team would need to learn to "carry the fight to the opponent 60 minutes instead of 15."

During the next few days Wilkinson had practically no support from Oklahoma fans. Monday-morning quarterbacks were loud in their opinion that he did not have what it took to develop a successful football program at the university and that it would be only a matter of time until OU would be looking for another head football coach. Certainly no one would have been willing to predict that Wilkinson-coached teams would not lose again until they had compiled a record of thirty-one consecutive victories.

After the disappointing loss to Santa Clara, the coaching staff and squad settled down to serious business. The results were apparent the following weekend, when, playing before a home crowd on Owen Field, the Sooners rolled convincingly over the Texas Aggies by a score of 42–14. Wilkinson used forty-three players during the game, and all of them played with the effort and aggressiveness that was to characterize OU teams for the next several years. Darrell Royal was again at quarterback but shared his duties with an unheralded sophomore, Claude Arnold, from Okmulgee, who tossed a touchdown pass to Leon Heath. Lindell Pearson, the much-publicized ransomed sophomore from Oklahoma City, who had missed the Santa Clara game because of illness, made his first appearance for OU and gave promise of future greatness when he carried the ball from the Aggie 33-yard line to the 3, setting up the final touchdown of the game,

65 seconds before it ended. Also noteworthy was the Sooners' improved pass defense, which yielded only 78 yards on twenty attempts and intercepted twice.

With this satisfying victory under their belts, the Sooners began preparation for their annual tilt with the University of Texas the following week. The Texans were enjoying a string of eight consecutive wins, and, although the Sooners had played well against the Texas Aggies, there seemed little reason to hope that they would be able to interrupt the Longhorn winning streak. But, as Wilkinson put it in his newsletter, "Our boys always battle Texas hard, and while I'm not optimistic about the game, I feel sure that our team will play to the full limit of their ability at Dallas."

An all-time record crowd assembled in the Cotton Bowl the following Saturday, October 9, to see the two schools renew a rivalry that had been initiated in 1900—one that, through the years, had been largely dominated by the University of Texas. The oddsmakers had named the Texas team as two-touchdown favorites.

The squad and coaches arrived at the Cotton Bowl about 11:00 A.M. Saturday morning. The trainers immediately went to work in the Sooner dressing room, taping ankles and wrists. The players suited up and held a light workout for an hour or so before the start of the game. When I saw them return from the field, I went to the dressing room to see how Wilkinson handled them during the final few minutes before kickoff. I found the entire squad resting in various positions on the floor. Wilkinson was sitting in a corner, saying nothing but methodically shuffling large cards on which were diagrams of plays. I could feel the tension developing as game time approached. On that and several later occasions, I noted that Wilkinson, by sitting quietly in a certain position and going through certain motions with his hands and cards, could bring his team to the proper mental and emotional attitude immediately before the start of a game. He seldom if ever used emotional oratory to bring his team to a peak before kickoff or between halves. He always spoke briefly, quietly, and logically, with restrained emotion.

The largest crowd in the history of southwestern sports gathered that day. The Cotton Bowl, which the preceding year had seated 45,195, had been enlarged into a saucer-shaped bowl that, according to the newspapers, could accommodate 67,435 fans. Construction workers had been busy that morning installing and numbering the last of the new seats, and the final work was completed only about an hour before the game started. Many Oklahomans were dissatisfied with their seating locations in the stands; an option to purchase many (perhaps most) of the choice seats had been given to the Dallas businessmen who had advanced the money to enlarge the stadium.

However, the total viewing audience for the game was not confined to those seated in the stadium; an additional three thousand or so spectators in the Dallas–Fort Worth area were to see the action on television. Station WBAP-TV of Fort Worth, said to be the only television station operating between St. Louis and Los Angeles, was scheduled to broadcast the game as part of the introduction of television to the Southwest.

Shortly after the kickoff it became apparent that the 1948 edition was not to be a repetition of past contests dominated by the Longhorns. The Sooner line, operating with poise and precision, seemed clearly superior to its Texas counterpart. Sooner fans, sensing early that their team might be fulfilling a date with destiny, created an uproar that compared favorably with the din produced by at least double the number of Texans.

The first two drives put underway by the Sooner offense were interrupted by a pass interception and a fumble, but about midway in the second quarter, with Jack Mitchell at quarterback, a drive was launched that went 73 yards for a touchdown. Crisp, rhythmic blocking by the line that gave the backs (Darrell Royal, Junior Thomas, and Leon Heath) opportunities for ground-gaining thrusts and sweeps and a surprise pass from Mitchell to Frankie Anderson put Royal in a position to cross the goal line with the ball at 6 minutes, 39 seconds before the end of the first half. Ming converted, giving the Oklahomans a 7–0 lead, which they carried into the second half.

A second touchdown in the third period seemed to give OU reasonable control of the situation as the final quarter of the game got underway with the score 14–0. The Texas team had

The Texas offense operated from a T, here with a flanker to the left. Courtesy Sports Information Department.

been unable to develop a serious scoring threat; it had been held in check by great defensive play, sparked by the superb linebacking of Myrle Greathouse. But early in the fourth period the Longhorns threatened to change the trend of the game. After being checked on their first drive deep into Oklahoma territory, they forced the Sooners to punt and received the ball on the OU 49-yard line. Then three passes by their clever quarterback, Paul Campbell, to a pair of talented receivers resulted in a touchdown, and the score stood 14–7.

The stung Sooners retaliated immediately; their powerful front wall blocked Heath loose for a 68-yard run before the Texas secondary was able to bring him down on their 12-yard line. On the next play Thomas scrambled through the center of both teams for a touchdown. Ming missed the extra point, making the score 20–7. It was apparent that the game was not over, because two touchdowns had been scored within a minute and a half, and there were still 5 minutes, 20 seconds of play remaining.

Any complacency the Oklahomans had felt was quickly dispelled when the Sooner kickoff was received by Perry Samuels (a sprinter on the Texas track team), who traveled 65 yards to the OU 20 before he was brought down by Royal. Three plays later Tom Landry, Texas fullback, lugged the ball across OU's goal line, and following a successful conversion attempt, the score was 20–14, with 3 minutes, 51 seconds remaining. (Landry,

Oklahoma Sooners enter the Cotton Bowl for the first victory over Texas in nine years, 1948. Courtesy Sports Information Department.

Myrle Greathouse provides superb linebacking in OU's 1948 victory over Texas. Courtesy Sports Information Department.

a fine athlete, later played pro football with the New York Giants and then became head coach of the Dallas Cowboys.)

After receiving the Texas kickoff, OU was unable to advance the ball, but Royal got off a good punt, and the Longhorn receiver was brought down on his own 37-yard line. In the final minutes of the game Texas made a frantic passing effort, and the Texas fans were frenzied in their calls for action. On the first play the quarterback's pass went wild; on the second the quarterback was buried beneath three Oklahoma tacklers, led by Buddy Burris, before he could get rid of the ball; on the third attempt the quarterback got rid of the ball, but the pass was deflected by an Oklahoman and intercepted by Thomas. With time left for only one play Mitchell wisely took no chances. After receiving the snap from the center, he dropped to the ground and snuggled the ball securely to his midsection. As the final seconds ticked off, Oklahomans chanted in unison "7-6-5-4-3-2-1-0" and then let out a mighty roar as they rushed from the stands to the Oklahoma goal post.

The wooden goal post, bedecked with red-and-white ribbons, came down easily, and was first carried the length of the field and leaned against the Texas post. It was later broken into pieces

Bud Wilkinson receives congratulations from President and Mrs. Cross following OU's defeat of the Texas Longhorns in 1948.

that were taken home as souvenirs by the enthusiastic students and others who had invaded the field. The OU band played for a while, and the crowd gradually left the bowl for downtown Dallas, where they celebrated far into the night.

Mrs. Cross and I flew home with the team. I had in my possession the game ball and the Bronze Hat. The latter was a rotating trophy that had been donated by a Texas fan in 1941 and, because of the eight consecutive Longhorn victories, had never been north of the Red River until that evening. The happy squad landed in

Jubilant Sooners admire the game trophy, the bronze cowboy hat, in the dressing room after the 1948 victory over Texas. Darrell Royal, the future Texas coach, is under the hat. Courtesy Sports Information Department.

Oklahoma City about 8:00 P.M., to be greeted by a large, enthusiastic crowd at Will Rogers Airport.

Oklahoma opened its conference competition the following weekend with a home game, rolling over Kansas State College by a score of 42–0. The outstanding play of the game was a punt return executed by Darrell Royal with only one minute left in the first quarter. Jack Mitchell received the punt on the OU 4-yard line but handed off to Royal on a crisscross maneuver; Royal first retreated to the goal line and then broke up the east sideline for a touchdown—the longest return made by an Oklahoma player in modern times. The play was perfectly executed: every Kansas State player was knocked off his feet, and Royal crossed the goal line untouched. Trotting by his side was huge guard

85

Stan West, looking hopefully for a chance to make a final block.

The fifth game of the season, against Texas Christian University, at Fort Worth, was quite a different story. Shortly after kickoff Darrell Royal, back to punt, was unable to handle a bad pass from center. In the scramble that followed, an OU player recovered the ball but was downed in the end zone for the first score of the game. Things improved after that, and, although the Sooners fumbled seven times during the contest and lost the ball on five of those mishaps, they led in the fourth quarter, 21–16, with a minute and half left in the game. They had possession of the ball on their own 11-yard line, fourth down, and 2 yards to go. To the audible amazement of the fans they did not go into punt formation. Instead, Mitchell received the snap and quickly retreated to the end zone, dodging and evading tacklers in an apparent effort to find a running opportunity. He was finally downed in the end zone, and it dawned on the OU fans that their team had elected to give an intentional safety, which cost two points, in return for a free kick from the 20-yard line rather than a punt from behind the goal line. After receiving Royal's free kick from the twenty, Texas Christian threw a scare into the Oklahoma fans by completing a 42-yard pass to OU's 20-yard line, but the Sooners held at that point. Thus the first and last scores of the game were safeties scored against OU.

Several players were injured during the contest, including Myrle Greathouse, Pete Tillman, Nute Trotter, Wade Walker, and Bobby Goad. Goad injured a shoulder on the opening kickoff but stayed in the game. I saw him on the campus the following week, with his shoulder in a cast and his arm in a sling. I asked him when he had received his injury, and he told me it had happened during the first play after kickoff. I asked him if it had not been painful to play with his shoulder in that condition. He replied, "Not really. My opponent wasn't very good; I was able to block him pretty well with my other shoulder." He admitted, however, that he probably would not be playing any football for the next couple of weeks at least.

Fortunately, the sixth opponent of the season, Iowa State College, though plucky, persistent, and keyed up for the game (played at Ames), was undermanned, and the Sooners, despite the injuries sustained the preceding week, won by a score of 33-6. Alternate quarterback Claude Arnold completed five of seven forward passes, one for a touchdown, and Frankie Anderson, recently converted from guard to end, turned in a remarkable performance on defense and as a pass receiver.

During the following week there were several suggestions in the newspapers that the University of Oklahoma might be invited to participate in one of the major postseason bowl games. Wilkinson reacted to these speculations with caution, pointing out that the opponent of the week, the University of Missouri, had been having a splendid season. Their team was undefeated in five contests and was nationally ranked. A comparison of their record with Oklahoma's appeared to make them a definite favorite in the upcoming contest. One comparison made freely that week was that OU had defeated Texas only 20-14, whereas Southern Methodist had won from Texas by the somewhat more impressive score of 21-6 in a game played at Austin before a Longhorn home crowd. But Missouri had whipped Southern Methodist 20-14, administering the only defeat the Mustangs, quarterbacked by Doak Walker, had had during the past two years.

A record crowd of 38,500 assembled at the OU stadium to see the action. Many additional thousands listened to Bill Stern's NBC broadcast, Curt Gowdy's account over KOMA, and eight additional local broadcasts originating at the stadium in an improvised addition to the press box that extended over the fans in the top rows and was supported by steel pipes.

The so-called experts had picked Missouri to win, and early in the game their predictions seemed justified. During the first quarter the Tigers carried the game to OU aggressively and scored early, following an OU fumble that was recovered by Missouri on the OU 6-yard line. OU managed to tie the score in the second period, and the half ended 7-7. But the Sooners really came to life during the second half with a four-touchdown scoring spree in the third quarter, including a 70-yard touchdown jaunt by Jack Mitchell. A sixth touchdown in the fourth period made the final score an amazing 40-7.

To most spectators it was obvious that the play of the OU line, coached by Gomer Jones, had made the one-sided win possible.

In the dressing room after the game Wilkinson commented that "our line made the difference," and in the Missouri dressing room losing coach Don Faurot acknowledged that "Oklahoma's two lines beat the heck out of us." Analyzing the game in his column the following Monday, John Cronley, sports editor of the *Oklahoma City Times,* wrote, "By now it must be conceded that the University of Oklahoma possesses one of the top lines—if not the best—in the entire nation."

OU fans were now confident that the Sooners would play once again in a major bowl. The only question was which bowl it would be. Polls were conducted and opinions aired. Most of the OU fans seemed to think that the team was headed for the Orange Bowl, but Wilkinson stoutly maintained that his coaching staff and squad would not give any thought to bowl contests until after the remaining three games on the schedule—Nebraska, Kansas and Oklahoma A&M.

The Sooners had no trouble defeating two of their remaining opponents, winning from Nebraska at Owen Field, 41–14, and from Kansas at Lawrence by an overwhelming 60–7. But it was a different story against Oklahoma A&M at Stillwater. Mitchell had been injured in the Kansas game, and, while he was able to play, he was not much of an offensive threat, a fact that the Aggies fortunately did not discover until the second half. The field was wet at the beginning of the game, and the soft turf soon was chewed into mud. The OU backs found it difficult to maneuver, and the linemen, outweighed by their Aggie counterparts, could not find footing to take advantage of their quickness. Royal replaced Mitchell for part of the second half, but with three minutes to go when the score was 19–13 in favor of the Sooners, who had the ball on their 3-yard line, it was decided to send Mitchell back in to use up time before giving an intentional safety. Mitchell downed the ball twice and then deliberately used up the twenty-five seconds allotted for a huddle, bringing a penalty which moved the line of scrimmage to the 1-yard line. Royal then went in to punt but instead ran with the ball, weaving and dodging in the end zone before he was finally pulled down with ten seconds remaining. But one of the Aggies had been offside, and so it was necessary for Royal to repeat his maneuver, while the final seconds ticked away. The 19–15 win cleared the way for OU to participate in a major bowl game.

That evening OU accepted an invitation to play in the Sugar Bowl at New Orleans on New Year's Day against the University of North Carolina. The same evening Oklahoma A&M accepted a bid to meet William and Mary in the Delta Bowl at Memphis. Representatives from both bowls had been in the stands during the afternoon and it was generally conceded that the Aggies' remarkable performance against OU before thirty thousand fans —the largest number to assemble for an athletic contest in the history of the Stillwater school—was a determining factor in their selection by the Delta Bowl officials.

With a 9–1 season completed, Oklahomans finally were convinced that Wilkinson had been a fortunate choice for the head coaching job. His 1948 squad had won a Big Seven championship. It was ranked fifth in the national poll, behind Michigan, Notre Dame, North Carolina and California. Two members of the squad, Buddy Burris and Jack Mitchell, received All-America recognition. However, only one national record was set, and that one unsought: a national record for fumbles lost during the season— 35.

The squad was given the week off following the battle in the mud at Stillwater but resumed practice in time to put in a couple of weeks of work before Christmas. Coaches and players moved to Biloxi, Mississippi, the day after Christmas to make final preparations in warmer weather than we were having in Oklahoma. Wilkinson had arranged for the squad to work out daily at Biloxi through the afternoon of December 31. The players and coaches would then move to the Algiers Naval Base to rest for the night, well insulated from the noisy celebrations of New Year's Eve in New Orleans.

The approaching contest was the fifteenth Sugar Bowl game, and most regional sports writers predicted that the game would be the best of the series. Early in December, the oddsmakers had established North Carolina as a nine-point favorite, possibly because Carl Snavely, coach of the Tar Heels, had a considerable edge over Wilkinson in experience and because the once-beaten Sooners had played a somewhat less rigorous schedule than their

OU meets North Carolina in the Sugar Bowl, January 1, 1949. Courtesy Sports Information Department.

opponent had. But in late December, the odds dropped and the consensus appeared to be that neither team would be more than a one-point favorite at game time.

The University of Oklahoma official party left Will Rogers Airport on the morning of December 30 and arrived at Moisant International Airport a few minutes before noon. Mrs. Cross and I were in the plane with our twelve-year-old son, Bill. We were invited to the Sugar Bowl Press and Radio dinner, sponsored by the New Orleans Mid-Winter Sports Association at Antoine's Restaurant on New Year's Eve. When Mrs. Cross and I arrived at Antoine's, we were shown to the head table and seated with Frank V. Schaub, president of the New Orleans Mid-Winter Sports Association; de Lesseps S. Morrison, mayor of New Orleans; Governor and Mrs. Roy Turner of Oklahoma, and dignitaries from the University of North Carolina.

I had very little opportunity to savor the famed food of Antoine's. I was served turtle soup at the beginning of the meal, and just as I was about to sample it, I was interrupted by someone who asked if I would mind participating in a short radio interview. I left the table to do so, and when I returned, my soup had been replaced with a second course—some kind of fish, I believe. Those at the head table were about halfway through the second course, and I realized that I would need to hurry to catch up, but I had scarcely picked up my fork when a representative of another radio station asked if I could give him a few minutes. Returning a second time to the table, I found that the main course had been served, but my serving had been omitted, probably because the waiters thought the seat was not occupied. It did not make much difference, because I was immediately interrupted again by an employee who asked if I would accept a phone call from a sports writer who had been unable to attend the dinner and wanted to ask a few questions about my impressions of the game the next day.

By the time I was able to settle down for the evening, waiters were serving the dessert, and the famous *café brûlot diabolique* was being prepared in the corner of the dining room. *Café brûlot diabolique* is made by adding an alcoholic beverage of some kind, brandy or bourbon, to the regular strongly brewed New Orleans coffee. On that evening the hot mixture, with its rapidly evaporating alcohol, was poured back and forth between pitchers held by the head coaches of the opposing teams. On the first pour a torch was applied to the drink, and the lights were turned out. The coffee was enveloped in a sheath of fire as it was poured to the pitcher below. The flame continued to burn as the coffee was passed several times from one pitcher to the other, creating a weird impression of pouring fire in the darkened room. After this brief ceremony, *café brûlot diabolique* was served to the guests, most of whom professed to enjoy it greatly, although I remember thinking that one would need to acquire a taste for it.

A program followed dinner with speeches of welcome by Mayor Morrison and various Sugar Bowl officials. Governor Roy Turner gave a short response for the guests from Oklahoma, and the party ended a few minutes after eleven, a rather hectic but none-

Among interested fans at the 1949 Sugar Bowl game were, left to right: Mrs. Bud Wilkinson, Mrs. Roy Turner, Governor Turner, Mrs. Cross, and President Cross. Courtesy Sports Information Department.

theless memorable occasion. After dinner we took Bill to Canal Street for the New Year's Eve revels. As the last few seconds of 1948 ticked away, the noise on Canal Street reached a crescendo that I had never experienced before except at athletic contests, but a few minutes after midnight things began to quiet down, and we made our way back to the picturesque St. Charles Hotel for a good night's sleep.

At about 12:30 the next afternoon Mrs. Cross, Bill, and I were driven to the stadium in a limousine provided by the Sugar Bowl officials. The weather was perfect—a bright sun and just a hint of chill in the air; the field appeared to be in excellent condition.

We made our way to Box 8, where we were soon joined by Erl Deacon, president of the OU regents, and Mrs. Deacon; Governor and Mrs. Roy Turner; Mr. and Mrs. Walter Billingsly; Senator and Mrs. Bill Logan; and Mrs. Bud Wilkinson. The OU band put on a good pregame show with formations of oil wells and a "surrey with the fringe on top," setting the stage well for the main event that would follow.

North Carolina had been a slight favorite in the last forecasts preceding the game, probably because Carl Snavely had used the single-wing formation so impressively in defeating nine opponents and tying the tenth during the regular season. His chief offensive threat was Charlie ("Choo Choo") Justice, an All-America halfback, who could run, pass, or kick the football superbly well. But also in his backfield was Hosea Rodgers who many coaches in the Southeastern Conference throught was an even more valuable back than Justice. Art Weiner, an all-conference end, was Justice's favorite pass receiver. Len Szafaryn, a huge tackle, was a candidate for all-conference and All-America honors.

During his two years as head coach at OU, Wilkinson had been experimenting with a variation of Don Faurot's split-T formation, which Jim Tatum had installed at OU in 1946. In the split-T, the offensive linemen take their places on the line of scrimmage with intervening spaces of a yard or more, in contrast to the single-wing, where the interior linemen get set in tight formation, elbow to elbow. The halfbacks are placed six or seven yards apart. The splitting forces the defensive linemen to split in similar fashion and thus give a wider target for straight-ahead thrusts by the halfbacks and fullback.

In the single-wing formation the ball is snapped from center to either the fullback or tailback, both approximately four yards back of the line of scrimmage, thus making it necessary for the ball carrier to move four yards forward before gaining yardage. In the split-T formation, as Wilkinson used it, the quarterback receives the ball from the center on the line of scrimmage and then considers several options. He may hand off to one of the halfbacks or the fullback, or he may glide laterally along the line of scrimmage, waiting for the defensive linemen to commit themselves before deciding whether to run with the ball or pitch it to one of the backs for a wide sweep. The single-wing is based more on power thrusts, running, and passing; the split-T, on quickness, deception, and timing.

Wilkinson used the forward pass only sparingly, but it was always a threat in his attack. He used a single cycle of plays in his offense, which involved a handoff to one of the three running backs, a jump pass, a quarterback option, a running pass, a fullback counter and a quarterback sneak, a fullback counter pass, and a reverse. All these plays started out in exactly the same way—as if a quick-running thrust was developing. Because the plays all looked alike at the start, defending against them had been a baffling problem for nine of the OU regular season opponents during the 1948 season. Many were eager to see the two very different offensive systems in action against each other and make their own comparisons.

The game started out as though it might be a bad day for OU. The Tar Heels returned the opening kickoff to their 36-yard line and then staged a drive to the OU 15, a drive that included two completed passes by Justice, one for 13 yards and another for 23. Then, with a first down on OU's 15-yard line, Justice tried another pass, far to the right. But Myrle Greathouse, OU's great linebacker, had diagnosed the play perfectly and had reacted so quickly that he was in position for an interception; he tucked the ball under his arm and traveled with it 70 yards downfield before he was upended on the North Carolina 15-yard line.

Quarterback Jack Mitchell carried the ball for the next five downs and ended the series on the North Carolina 2-yard line. But at that point the Sooners received a backfield-in-motion penalty, which left them on the 7-yard line with three downs to go. Junior Thomas managed to get to the 1-foot line in two carries, and Mitchell sneaked the ball into the end zone on the last down; Ming's conversion made the score 7–0.

The Tar Heels were able to score in the second period, but the try for the extra point went wide, and the half ended 7–6.

In the third period OU scored once again, largely as a result of a remarkable pass play. The Sooners threw the ball only three times during the entire game, but one of these was a 44-yard heave from Darrell Royal to Frankie Anderson, who made the reception on the Tar Heel 10-yard line. Thomas then gained 3 yards, and Lindell Pearson carried for the touchdown; Ming once again kicked the extra point.

The fourth quarter was largely a punting duel between Royal and Justice. The Tar Heels threw a slight scare into the Sooners when they took over on the 50-yard line. But after advancing to OU's 36, they lost possession when Bobby Goad intercepted a Justice pass.

When the game ended, the exuberant Sooners poured out onto

OU kicks off after taking a 7–0 lead in the 1949 Sugar Bowl game. Courtesy Sports Information Department.

the field, and I worked my way to the sidelines to congratulate the coaches and squad. I suddenly found myself being tossed into the air, and I somehow landed on the shoulders of Pete Tillman and Myrle Greathouse. Other members of the squad picked up Wilkinson, and the two of us were transported bumpily to the door of the Sooner dressing room.

After spending a few minutes shaking hands with the coaches and players, I went to the North Carolina dressing room to compliment the Tar Heels' personnel on the fine game they had played. I found a disconsolate group. Charlie Justice was sitting on a bench in the dressing room, bent over facing the floor with a blanket over his back and pulled down to cover his face. He was sobbing with grief; it was his second and last appearance in the Sugar Bowl—two years before he had played as a sopho-

President Cross makes remarks to the radio audience between halves of the OU-North Carolina game. Courtesy Sports Information Department.

Excited fans pour onto the field after OU's 14–6 defeat of North Carolina, 1949. Courtesy Sports Information Department.

President Cross is carried to the Sooner dressing room following the first Sugar Bowl victory, 1949. Courtesy Sports Information Department.

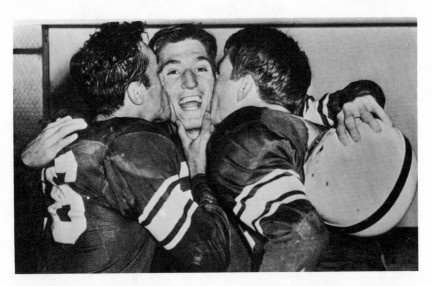

LEFT TO RIGHT: Jack Mitchell, Bobby Goad, and Myrle Greathouse celebrate in the dressing room after OU's first Sugar Bowl victory, 1949. Courtesy Sports Information Department.

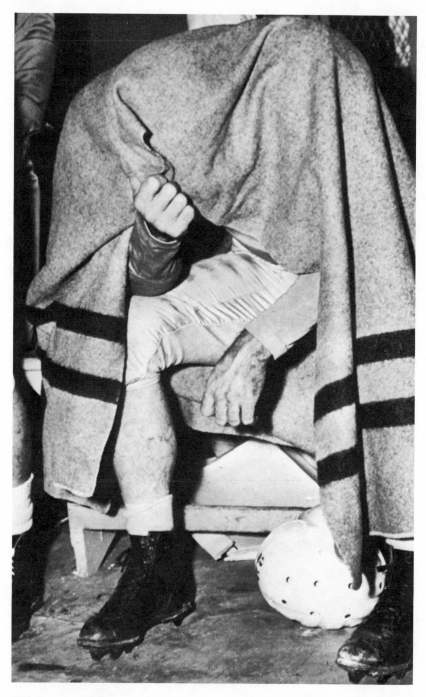

Things were different in the North Carolina dressing room. All-American Charlie ("Choo Choo") Justice sobs beneath a blanket. Courtesy Sports Information Department.

more, and North Carolina had been upset by Georgia. I did not bother him—merely patted him on the shoulder and went on.

There was a victory dinner that evening in the Roosevelt Hotel. As the festivities were getting under way, we learned that Oklahoma A&M had lost to William and Mary that afternoon in the Delta Bowl, 20–0.

It was announced at the dinner that Jack Mitchell had won the Warren V. Miller Memorial Trophy as the outstanding player in the Fifteenth Annual Sugar Bowl Football Game. This trophy, a memorial to the first Sugar Bowl president, was awarded on the results of a poll of sports writers who had seen the game. Many of the same sports writers spent much of their time at the Sugar Bowl party discussing the future of Bud Wilkinson. It was the consensus of most that the University of Minnesota, Wilkinson's alma mater, and the University of Wisconsin would be bidding for his services on a basis hard for the University of Oklahoma to match. Speculation continued in the newspapers the following week, as Oklahoma writers devoted many columns to praise of the Sooner coach, and to suggestions about what to do to keep him.

The team and coaches remained in New Orleans for a couple of days of relaxation before returning to Norman on January 4. I knew that Wilkinson would leave that same day to attend a meeting of coaches at the NCAA convention in San Francisco, to begin on January 5. I saw him briefly between planes and told him that the regents had verbally agreed to give him a five-year contract totaling fifteen thousand dollars a year and separate his job as athletic director from that of head football coach to give him greater security at OU. He told me that he was very well satisfied at the University of Oklahoma and had no intention of leaving. He did not mention that he had spent a couple of hours the preceding Sunday with William Sarles, chairman of the athletic board at the University of Wisconsin, and that he had agreed to visit the Wisconsin campus after the San Francisco meeting.

After returning to Norman, Wilkinson took off for Wisconsin without telling anyone. He admitted later that he thought he could pay a secret visit to the Badger State by flying to Milwaukee and going by automobile to Madison. But he was met by reporters when he got off the plane at Milwaukee, and there were headlines

99

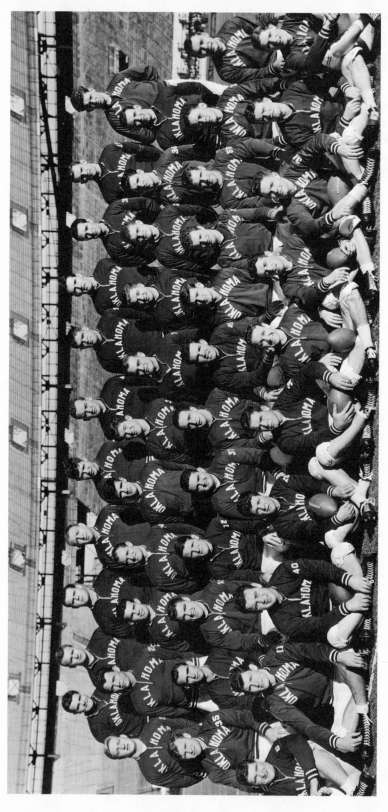

The 1948 team. FIRST ROW (FRONT ROW), LEFT TO RIGHT: Joe Horkey, Jim Owens, Nute Trotter, Wade Walker, Homer Paine, Tommy Gray, Jack Mitchell, George Brewer, Darrell Royal, Bobby Goad. SECOND ROW: Norman McNabb, Buddy Jones, Lindell Pearson, Myrle Greathouse, Dee Andros, Clair Mayes, Al Needs, Ed Lisak, Leon Heath, Harry Moore, Charles Paine. THIRD ROW: Bob Wheat, Ken Tipps, Bill Remy, Calvin Steinberger, Bob Bodenhamer, Charley Dowell, Dean Smith, Ken Parker, George Thomas, Joe Cunningham, Joe Leguenec. FOURTH ROW: Bob Ewbank, Harold Hoofnagle, Les Ming, Pete Tillman. Willie Manley, Stan West, Buddy Burris, Gene Heape, Claude Arnold, Art Jones, Frankie Anderson. Courtesy Sports Information Department.

in most of the Oklahoma and Wisconsin papers the next day announcing his arrival and reporting that he had been offered twelve thousand dollars a year to coach at the University of Wisconsin.

After his return Wilkinson told me that he had not been offered a job, that he had only taken part in a general discussion of Wisconsin coaching problems, and that he had gone only because "at the time of the Sugar Bowl game in New Orleans, I promised to make a courtesy visit to Professor William D. Sarles." He seemed honestly surprised that the visit had caused so much publicity. On Saturday, January 15, he said he was eager to dispose of the matter and agreed to sign a contract that provided a total annual salary of fifteen thousand dollars a year for five years, a separate appointment with salary stipulated as athletic director, and a professorship in physical education in addition to appointment as head coach of football.

At the next meeting of the regents a member of the board reminded his colleagues that the salary of the university president was only fourteen thousand dollars a year, whereupon the group hurriedly went into executive session and raised my salary to sixteen thousand. According to newspaper reports a month later, the governing board of Oklahoma A&M College, hearing what had happened at OU, raised President Henry Bennett's salary from fifteen thousand to sixteen thousand. Thus the two presidents also received tangible benefits from Wilkinson's success.

CHAPTER 9

The Stadium Enlarged—The 1949 Season—Sugar Bowl II

1949-50

WITH the problem of keeping Wilkinson at OU solved, at least for a time, it was possible to give attention to some other matters relating to athletics—especially a proposal to enlarge the stadium. The existing facility consisted of two wings that had been built in 1925 on the east and west sides of Owen Field. A clock tower and scoreboard stood at the north end of the field, and beyond that was the "mirror pool." A cinder track encircled the field, with a spur extending several yards out of the stadium to the south on the east side, providing a straightaway for the beginning of a race.

The two wings had a seating capacity of approximately 31,500, and it had been apparent since the 1946 season that they were not nearly large enough to accommodate the crowds. The pressure for tickets reached a crisis at the Missouri game in 1948, when Bill Cross estimated that between fifteen and twenty thousand people had tried and failed to buy tickets. The Athletic Council was asked to study the problem and make a recommendation to me about enlarging the stadium, perhaps financing the project through self-liquidating bonds.

The first two wings, which had cost $288,000, had been financed in part through gifts, but largely through self-liquidating bonds issued by the Stadium-Union Corporation. The corporation was organized because until 1945 an institution of higher learning in Oklahoma could not issue self-liquidating bonds except by special act of the legislature. The Stadium-Union Corporation also raised money for the construction of the Student Union Building. The two completed structures were named Oklahoma Memorial Stadium and Oklahoma Memorial Union respectively, commemorating OU students who lost their lives in World War I.

But in 1945 and 1947 the Oklahoma legislature passed a law making it possible for state institutions to issue their own bonds, and OU planned to take advantage of this legislation to enlarge the stadium. The bonds involved would not be an indebtedness of the state of Oklahoma, the University of Oklahoma, or the Board of Regents of the University of Oklahoma; they would be a special-obligation series, payable entirely and solely from net revenues of the stadium. Because the bonds that had been issued to finance the original two wings had long been retired, it was not anticipated that there would be any difficulty in selling bonds to increase the seating capacity. But the problem of how to enlarge the stadium most efficiently proved to be a vexing one. There were three possibilities: either one or both ends of the stadium could be closed, adding 17,500 or 35,000 seats; a second deck could be constructed above the existing stadium on one or both wings, providing 8,000 or 16,000 additional seats; or the playing field could be excavated to a depth of six to twelve feet, the cinder track eliminated, and the seating extended down to or near the edge of the playing field.

The idea of building a second deck above either of the existing wings was carefully considered but soon discarded because the estimated cost seemed excessive—approximately $70 a seat. Additional seats produced by closing either end of the stadium or by excavating the field would cost something less than $30 each. The Athletic Council finally recommended that the north end of the stadium be closed and the field excavated to a depth of approximately six feet, thus providing approximately 24,000 new seats. The council decided against recommending that the south end of the stadium be closed, because that would encroach too much on the practice field. But the recommendation did include provisions for the construction of a new press box above the west wing.

The need for a new press box had been obvious since the season of 1947, when it had been necessary to construct a special facility for Bill Stern to use in broadcasting the Missouri game. Under the supervision of Harold Keith plans for a new press box had been developed in 1947 and submitted for bids early in 1948. But the bids, ranging from $89,950 to $99,800, seemed excessive to the regents, and the project was postponed until a time when postwar inflation subsided.

The tentative plans for the stadium enlargement and the new press box were presented to and approved by the regents at their meeting in December, 1948. The board approved final plans and authorized the taking of bids in January, 1949. Roscoe Cate, who had been working on a bond issue to cover the cost of construction, was instructed to make the issue sufficiently large to include a press box.

The new press box, Keith assured us, would be among the finest in the Southwest. The working drawings, prepared by architects Wright and Selby, provided for three levels with adequate accommodations for sixty-four sports writers, eight broadcasting booths, and space for television equipment, photographers, and scouts.

One feature of the project that was almost unique in stadiums was an elevator for transporting personnel and equipment from the ground level to each of the three areas of the press box. The idea of installing an elevator had been difficult to sell to certain members of the Athletic Council, and even to some of the regents. It was argued that sports writers and other personnel should be healthy enough to climb to their posts and should not need to be hoisted in an elevator. An alumni member of the Athletic Council argued that it was folly to invest so much money in equipment that would be used only five times a year (he did not seem to realize that what he said was true of the entire stadium). But Keith insisted that there should be an elevator, and I, in turn, insisted when the matter came to the regents; it was finally approved.

In January the university advertised for bids for the sale of bonds and for construction. The sealed bids were received and were opened on February 9, 1949; the successful bidder for the bonds was the B. J. Van Ingen Company of Chicago, while the Harmon Construction Company of Oklahoma City submitted the low bid for construction.

It would be some time before the proceeds from the sale of the bonds would be available, but temporary financing was arranged through an Oklahoma City bank, and Harmon got underway immediately. They plowed up the turf, brought in dirt-moving equipment, and removed the fence and clock tower and scoreboard at the north end. With good luck the project could be completed and the sod reestablished in time for the opening game that fall.

In the meantime other plans had been in the making for improving the management of the business operations of intercollegiate sports at OU. Two years before, Bill Cross, perhaps worried about his struggle with the ticket-buying public, had asked to be relieved of the responsibility for ticket sales. It did not seem feasible or possible at the time to grant his request but, with the enlargement of the program, it did appear that it would no longer be possible for one man to do both jobs. Early in 1949 a plan was approved whereby Cross would be moved to the Administration Building, where he would handle the funds of the Athletic Department under the terms of the stadium-bond contract. His removal to the Administration Building was scheduled for the summer of 1949.

To take over responsibility of ticket sales and other matters having to do with certain promotional activities associated with the athletic program Wilkinson recommended Clee Fitzgerald, a senior law student scheduled to receive a degree that spring. The regents set the price of tickets for 1949 football at $17.50 for the season, $3.50 for individual reserved seats, $3.00 for general admission for adults and $.50 for children.

As Wilkinson planned his program for spring practice that year, he often stressed the problem of replacing certain of his 1948 squad who would be lost through graduation or completed eligibility. Gone would be such standouts as Buddy Burris, All-America guard; Homer Paine, three times all–Big Seven tackle; and Pete Tillman. Gone also would be Myrle Greathouse, the linebacker who had played such a decisive role in several close victories during the past season. The team also lost Jack Mitchell, All-America quarterback, who became ineligible for further competition under the recent reinterpretation of conference rules.

There were some promising linemen from whom to pick replacements, and, to succeed Mitchell, Wilkinson could choose from Claude Arnold and Bob Ewbank, both of whom had lettered the preceding year, and Darrell Royal, who had played some at quarterback, but had spent most of his time at halfback. Avail-

Oklahoma Memorial Stadium as it appeared during World War II and the early postwar years. U.S. Navy official photo.

able also was a promising freshman from Crooked Oak, Oklahoma, Frank Silva. Wilkinson gave each of the boys a try at quarterback during the spring sessions, but at the end of the practice period he said that no decision had been reached.

Walter Hargesheimer was lost from the coaching staff that spring when he accepted a job at the University of Southern California. Houston Elder was named to replace him. The Sooner squad had a good spring practice, which ended with a game played in Oklahoma City against a very strong alumni team. The game had been arranged as a benefit for the OU Club Lounge,

Oklahoma Memorial Stadium after it was enlarged in 1949. Courtesy Sports Information Department.

a facility included in the enlarged stadium plans. The alumni practiced three or four times before the game but did not scrimmage. During the first half things looked rather bleak for the 1949 edition of Sooner football; at the end of the half, the alumni, despite their lack of practice and no scrimmage, were leading 13–0. But during the second half the collegians pulled themselves together and managed to win 14–13, giving some promise of another good season in the fall.

Wilkinson and his staff worked hard in early season practice to ensure that they found promising replacements for the outstanding athletes lost from the 1948 squad.

The season's opener with Boston College had been scheduled for Friday evening, September 23, on Braves Field, owned by the Boston Red Sox. Mrs. Cross and I left by air with the team on September 22. When we arrived at our hotel, we found the

New York Yankees there waiting to play the Boston Red Sox the next afternoon. A heavy rain Friday morning made it necessary to postpone the baseball game for twenty-four hours, and we spent most of the day in the hotel lobby, where we met some of the Yankees, including Casey Stengel and Yogi Berra. It was announced in the afternoon that the football game would be postponed until Saturday night, after the baseball game, to avoid tearing up the muddy field.

Saturday afternoon Mrs. Cross and I went to the baseball game. I've forgotten how the game came out, but I remember that Ted Williams hit a home run far into the left-field bleachers.

As we were leaving for the stadium Saturday evening, I was alerted by Gomer Jones to watch the opening kickoff carefully if OU was receiving, because the coaching staff had planned something that "might be interesting." Seated in the press box with the president of Boston College, who was rather cool to us, and the genial mayor of Boston and looking out over a poorly lighted field, we saw the official signal that OU would receive, and I mentioned Gomer's admonition to watch carefully.

Boston kicked off to the Oklahoma 5-yard line, where George Thomas took the ball and, with the aid of exceptionally fine blocking, managed to wriggle down the right side of the field for a touchdown. I was never able to figure out just how this sort of thing could have been "planned" by the coaching staff, and I forgot to talk with Gomer about it afterward. The team went on to drub Boston College thoroughly, 46–0.

The following week the Texas Aggies came to Norman for the first game to be played in the newly enlarged stadium. Unfortunately, but perhaps not unexpectedly, the stadium had not been completed in time for the contest; on the day of the game three or four sections of concrete were still to be poured in the north-end enclosure, though the forms for the concrete were in place. The contractors promised that everything would be ready for the Oklahoma-Kansas game on October 15.

The approximately forty thousand completed seats were well filled that day, because the Texas Aggies were highly regarded. They came with a rather impressive victory over Texas Technological College (26–7) the preceding week.

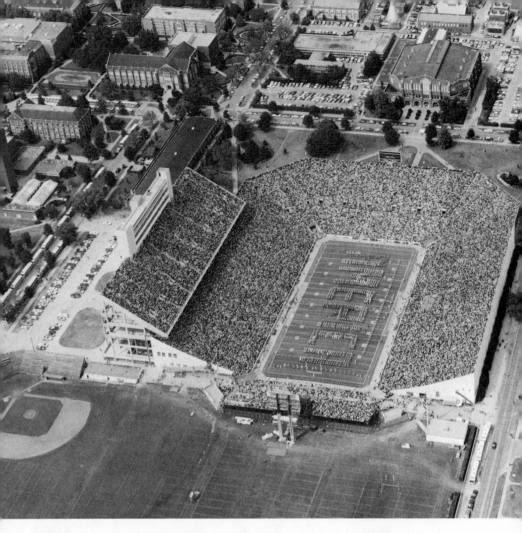

University Memorial Stadium after further enlargement in 1975. Courtesy University of Oklahoma Publications.

At kickoff time a wind that must have gusted up to fifty miles an hour, blew from the south. The Sooners won the toss and chose the wind. The Aggies, held for downs early in the first quarter, were forced to punt against the turbulent breeze. The ball rolled off the kicker's toe nicely and started a graceful spiral into the air. But after traveling for perhaps 25 yards, it was caught in the wind and returned to the ground 5 yards behind the line of scrimmage. OU guard Stan West recovered it on the Aggie 19-yard line. The Sooner offense, with Darrell Royal at quarterback, took quick advantage of this early break and escorted the ball across the goal line in six plays. The Sooners went on to win, 33–13—an auspicious dedication of the enlarged stadium.

With two victories tucked away early in the season, the coaches and squad started preparation for the annual foray with the University of Texas in the Cotton Bowl on October 8. The Sooners prepared for that forty-fourth annual battle with Texas mindful that OU had won only twelve of the forty-three games and only one of the last nine encounters. Scouts reported that the current Texas squad might well have the greatest potential in the history of Texas football. On the other hand, Texas scout Jack Gray reported to Coach Blair Cherry that "this is the greatest Oklahoma team, by far, that I've watched while scouting them for the past eleven seasons." Obviously an interesting Saturday afternoon was in prospect.

The game, and its aftermath, gave me the first hint of the impact that Wilkinson and his winning squads were to have on Oklahomans in the years ahead. The pregame antics on the streets of Dallas that Friday night reached a frenzy that exceeded anything in the memory of those who had been making the annual trip for years. The game was a sellout—75,347 tickets—a record for the Southwest.

There was a high wind at kickoff, and soon it began to rain heavily. The first quarter was scoreless, but the action was mostly in Sooner territory. The Texas offense was stopped once on the 6-yard line, and again on the 20; but with only 47 seconds gone in the second period, the Longhorns scored a touchdown, kicked the goal, and led by seven points. The Sooners retaliated quickly after receiving the kickoff and scored a touchdown in six plays; the try for point was successful. The rest of the game, played for the most part in a blinding rain, demonstrated the superiority of the Sooner squad. The final score (Oklahoma 20, Texas 14) was the same as the preceding year, but the Sooner ground game was definitely superior—216 yards rushing to 118 for Texas.

Despite the weather Sooner fans demonstrated for several minutes on the field after the final gun had sounded. The OU Roughnecks made repeated efforts to "collect" at least one of the goal posts, but were frustrated in their efforts by several dozen unsympathetic Dallas policemen.

The demonstration was continued on the campus of the University of Oklahoma the following day. The streets near the campus that Sunday were filled with caravans of automobiles—horns honking and occupants shouting, "Holiday tomorrow!" About 2,500 to 3,000 students assembled in front of my house that evening and demonstrated for about an hour. Their demands for a holiday were denied, with the reminder that they had the option of attending classes or staying away—the university rule at the time was that a student must attend 70 per cent of the class periods during a semester to earn credit.

The crowd finally left the house, but the celebration continued through the night and into the following Monday, when groups of students made repeated efforts to interrupt class sessions, sometimes successfully. About 10:00 A.M. a group decided to invade Oklahoma City, where they managed to tie up traffic in the downtown district for several minutes. They then visited the state capitol to call on Governor Turner. The governor cautiously appeared on the fifth-floor balcony of the Capitol Building and greeted the students on the fourth-floor rotunda. He made a short speech, commenting that he appreciated their spirit and, except for his need to preserve his dignity, would gladly join the celebration himself. The students showed their appreciation by presenting him with a Texas flag; he responded by saying, "Thanks for this flag from a great neighboring state," and then quickly disappeared. Finally, exhausted from their prolonged emotional spree, the students returned to the campus, and things settled down.

But I have the impression that the 1949 OU-Texas football game marked the turning point in the development of what might be described as "overinterest" in OU football. From that time, wherever I appeared in the state, the first question I was asked related to prospects for the Big Red team. The following spring, when I bought gasoline at a small town in southeastern Oklahoma, the station operator noticed my Cleveland County license number and asked what I thought the next season would be like.

The Sooners had little trouble with the rest of their schedule.

Darrell Royal, Wade Walker, and Jim Owens were selected for All-America recognition in 1949. Others selected that year were Stan West and Junior Thomas. Courtesy Sports Information Department.

Their well-balanced squad, sparked by the extraordinary play of such standouts as Wade Walker, Stan West, Jim Owens, George Thomas, and Darrell Royal, swept through the remaining games, winning by lopsided scores. Only their return game with Santa Clara University was close — 28–21.

At the end of the season the Associated Press rated OU second in the nation behind Notre Dame. They were second in the nation also in rushing yardage, having averaged 320.3 yards a game; they led the nation in rushing defense, allowing an average of only 55.6 yards a game; they were sixth in the nation in total defense — allowing only 202.7 yards a game. Royal, Walker, West, Owens, and Thomas received All-America recognition. Thomas led the nation in scoring with a total of 117 points. Wilkinson was named coach of the year by the National Football Coaches Association.

A bid to play in the Sugar Bowl for a second time was approved by squad vote in the Owen Field dressing room following OU's 41–0 defeat of Oklahoma A&M in the final game of the 1949 season. The opponent had not been selected. Tulane University, a likely prospect, had been upset by Louisiana State University the same day, thus making LSU a possible choice. But Louisiana

112

needed the approval of the Southeastern Conference before it could accept a bid, and there was some doubt that permission could be obtained because the conference had a rule that prohibited a member team from playing in a bowl game if it had been defeated twice within the conference during the regular season, and LSU had lost two conference games. But approval finally was forthcoming, arrangements were completed, and OU fans began making plans for the second invasion of New Orleans —a game on Monday, January 2, 1950.

Once again Wilkinson made arrangements for the football team to practice first at Norman and after Christmas at Biloxi. The pregame activities at Biloxi proceeded quietly and apparently smoothly, during the final week before the game. At least things were quiet until Friday evening, December 30. The squad and coaches returned to their hotel late in the afternoon following the final day of heavy work. There Coach Wilkinson found in his hotel box a message to call a number in Biloxi. The message was labeled "urgent." Wilkinson called the number and talked to a man who identified himself as Clarence Johnson, of 801 Lee Street. Johnson told him that the squad's Thursday and Friday practice sessions had been watched by three men from the roof of a garage in his neighborhood. The trio, according to the informant, worked with a camera, binoculars, and a large scout's chart.

Johnson said that the three men had crawled on top of the garage, just beyond the north end of the playing field, and had pulled a tarpaulin over themselves before scouting the drills. He believed that the men had been successful in their scouting because a neighbor of his reported that, as they walked past his house, he heard one of them talking about devising a certain kind of defense that would stop at least one of OU's offensive maneuvers.

It would be an understatement to say that Wilkinson was upset by the report. He was positively furious. He spent the evening arranging for a counterattack against the unwelcome spectators. Dr. C. B. McDonald (the OU fan from Oklahoma City who had won a reputation as a detective in the recovery of Lindell Pearson); Ned Hockman, an employee of the University of Oklahoma and a motion-picture photographer; John Askin, Jr., a Biloxi policeman; Bill Dennis, a Biloxi photographer; and John Scafidi, a former Tulane football player who had gone into professional football, were assigned to surveillance of the garage roof during the next practice session.

When they arrived at their station, the five immediately spotted a man between two garages, standing on a ladder and looking over a canvas fence that had been erected to ensure secret practices. He was screened from the field with a blanket suspended between the two garages.

When the suspect saw the five people approaching with photographic equipment, he hurriedly got down from the ladder, hid behind the door of one of the garages, indulged briefly in profanity, and threatened to smash the camera if anyone tried to photograph him. Scafidi interrupted his discourse by reaching behind the door, pulling him out into view, and holding him firmly by the collar. The victim quickly covered his face with a handkerchief, but Dr. McDonald snatched it away so that Dennis could get into action with his camera. Moments later the man broke from Scafidi's grasp and ran into a house on Lee Street. The owner of the house granted him sanctuary and threatened to prosecute anyone else who entered his house.

Dennis had his film developed immediately, and a print was put on display at the OU alumni registration booth in the Roosevelt Hotel lobby, where OU fans could see it all day Sunday. None of the Oklahomans could identify the interloper, but several New Orleans residents were sure that it was Piggy Barnes, a former LSU football player currently associated with the Philadelphia Eagles, a pro team. Investigation revealed that the house into which he had fled was occupied by Elbert Manuel, an LSU football player of the 1930's.

Wilkinson made no statement to the press about the event, but of course news of what had happened circulated widely and received much attention in the press. LSU officials vehemently denied that the personnel of the school had been involved in any way. They suggested that someone had perpetrated a hoax with the object of stimulating the OU team to greater effort come January 2.

Dr. C. B. McDonald, an OU fan, confronts Piggy Barnes, former Louisiana State player, who was accused of spying on OU practice sessions in Biloxi, Mississippi, before the Sugar Bowl game. Holding Barnes by the collar is John Scafidi, former Tulane football player. Joining the proceedings is John Askin, Jr., a Biloxi policeman. The photographer was Bill Dennis. Courtesy Sports Information Department.

The incident was discussed at the annual Sugar Bowl press and radio party held at Antoine's restaurant on Saturday evening. There T. P. Heard, the LSU athletic director; Gaynell ("Gus") Tinsley, football coach at LSU; and Wilkinson became involved in an exchange about what had happened. Heard told Wilkinson that he (Wilkinson) had been the victim of a ballyhoo plot designed to excite his football players. Wilkinson, fortified by the snapshot and other information, countered with the accusation that someone connected with LSU had sent a former LSU player to spy on OU's secret practice sessions. The discussion became somewhat heated, and Heard indulged in some impressive oratory having to do with the ethical standards of the members of the LSU squad and coaching staff and his regret that the Coach of

115

the Year should question their integrity. Coach Tinsley listened for a few moments and then shrugged his shoulders and walked off. Later one of the scheduled speakers suggested that Wilkinson and Tinsley put on boxing gloves and "fight it out with everybody watching—ten-round championship, no decision."

After dinner Coaches Wilkinson and Tinsley shook hands and, according to Sugar Bowl tradition, performed the *café brûlot diabolique* ceremony, managing not to burn each other.

The next morning the papers carried the gist of the remarks Heard had made at the dinner and treated the whole matter as something of a joke. Wilkinson, who up to that time had made no statement to the press and had not released the names of those who had been involved in the incident, was further nettled because what he considered a serious incident was treated so lightly in the newspapers. On Monday morning, the day of the game, he issued a statement describing in detail what had taken place on Lee Street, and he invited Piggy Barnes and Elbert Manuel to present themselves for identification by the three neutral witnesses who had accompanied McDonald and Hockman in the effort to trap the alleged spy.

Neither Barnes nor Manuel presented himself for identification. Their failure to appear was duly noted in the papers, and the football fans were free to draw their own conclusions. Whatever credence the fans gave to the spy story, they certainly were in unanimous agreement that the incident, and the newspaper publicity that accompanied it, gave added emphasis to the already intense interest that had been generated in the contest.

The day of the game came with a gray dawn and heavy clouds. There was an alumni breakfast at the Roosevelt Hotel. George Cummings, assistant executive secretary of the University of Oklahoma Association, had made the arrangements for the affair, which was attended by six hundred OU fans. It was reported at the breakfast that Oklahoma was an eight-point favorite the morning of the game despite Louisiana's impressive record, having defeated three teams—Rice, North Carolina, and Tulane—that had won championships that year in their respective conferences.

The two teams had similar offensive styles; each depended primarily on a strong rushing attack with sparing use of the pass.

116

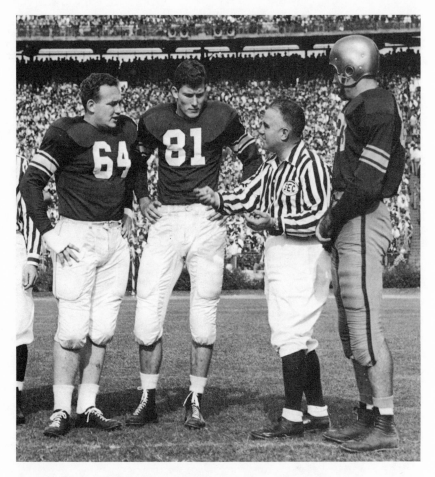

Co-captains Stan West (64) and Jimmy Owens watch the flip of the coin preceding the Oklahoma-Louisiana Sugar Bowl game, 1950. Courtesy Sports Information Department.

However, during the season LSU had used the two-platoon system
— complete offensive and defensive units. Oklahoma had used
its best athletes on both offense and defense, though with liberal
substitutions.

During the first quarter it appeared that the contest might be
very close because neither team was able to score, and the Sooners
did not move the ball into LSU territory.

But it was a different story the remaining three quarters, during
which the Sooners accumulated thirty-five points while holding

After Oklahoma's 35–0 rout of Louisiana State, Leon Heath, (left) receives the Most Valuable Player Award, and Bud Wilkinson holds the Sugar Bowl trophy. Courtesy Sports Information Department.

their opponents scoreless. The Tigers were completely outclassed, utterly bewildered by tricky reverses, laterals, and forwards thrown from laterals, and frustrated by savage defensive play when they were on the offense.

OU scored twice in the second period, once in the third, and twice again in the fourth. Ken Tipps kicked all five extra points to set a new Sugar Bowl record. Other records were set also: the 35–0 score was the worst defeat of a team in Sugar Bowl history. Leon Heath set an individual record for yardage on a touchdown run in the third quarter, when he took a handoff from Royal and journeyed 86 yards for the third score of the game. Heath gained a total of 170 yards, enough to win the Warren B. Miller Memorial Trophy, which he received at the

118

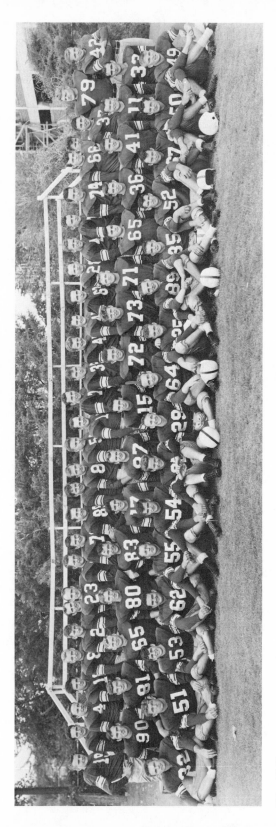

The 1949 team. FIRST ROW (FRONT ROW), LEFT TO RIGHT: George Brewer, Charlie Dowell, Boyd McGugan, Dee Andros, Harry Moore, Bob Bodenhamer, Frankie Anderson, Tommy Gray, Stanley West (co-captain), George Thomas, Cliff Bradley, Jack Lockett, Sam Carnahan, Fred Smith, Floyd Murphy, Bill Ricks. SECOND ROW: Gene Heape, Jimmy Owens (co-captain), Norman McNabb, Bobby Goad, Ken Tipps, Frank Silva, Harold Hoofnagle, Claude Arnold, J. W. Cole, Leon Manley, Jim Weatherall, Bert Clark, Dick Heatly, Blythe Carney, Darrell Royal, Buddy Jones. THIRD ROW: Bob Ewbank, Bob Siebert, Phil Kidd, Joe Cunningham, Bill Price, Al Needs, Art Janes, Bill Lambeth, Delton Marcum, Joe Horkey, Ed Mays, Bob Clark, Bill Beckman, Bill Covin, Bob Greenburg, Joe Leguenec, Lindell Pearson, Ed Lisak, Curtis French, Clair Mayes, Nolan Lang, Leon Heath, Geronimo Davis, Ed Rowland, Harry Pace, Wade Walker, Larry Cotton, Gordon Hoopes, Ken Parker. Courtesy Sports Information Department.

banquet that evening as the outstanding player of the 1950 Sugar Bowl game.

With two Sugar Bowl championships stashed away, the Sooner squad and the coaches, with their wives, took off on Tuesday, January 3, for a two-day holiday in Cuba. Among their activities in Havana was a reception in their honor at the American embassy.

The champions arrived back in Norman on Thursday, January 5. They probably spent Friday and the weekend catching up on what enthusiastic sports writers in Oklahoma had reported about their great victory in New Orleans. Accolades reached a crescendo in local papers after the game, and the Oklahoma sports world seemed unanimous in the belief that OU's 1949 edition was the best team in the nation.

For the first couple of weeks in January, 1950, enthusiasm about the victory remained so intense that it was practically impossible to talk for even a few moments with members of the university family—alumni, students, or faculty—without mentioning it. It seemed to me that all of this was having a disrupting influence on university affairs and I began to question the desirability of postseason football competition. Anticipation of OU's second Sugar Bowl contest had hindered the students' classroom work throughout December, and the same effect was continuing into the new year as the game was replayed endlessly. But things finally quieted down, and the campus gradually returned to normal. The coaching staff, of course, immediately got underway with its recruiting program. One disadvantage of playing in a postseason contest is the loss of recruiting time in December, but this disadvantage was perhaps countered by the publicity associated with a bowl game.

On the morning of February 14, I was shocked and grieved by news from Ardmore that Lloyd Noble had just died in Houston. Noble was one of the finest men I have known, and his passing meant a great personal loss as well as a loss to the university he had served for so many years with loyalty and effectiveness. Many people had misunderstood his interest in the university, thinking only of the active part he played in the development of the athletic program. But athletics were not his primary interest; his

Bud Wilkinson (left) receives the Coach of the Year Trophy and the congratulations of Joe Williams (center) sports editor of the *New York World Telegram and Sun,* and Dutch Meyer, past-president of the American Football Coaches Association, January, 1950. Courtesy *Oklahoman and Times.*

first concern, which he expressed frequently, was a good counseling program for undergraduate students, especially entering freshmen. He believed that counseling and instruction should come first in university planning, but he realized that strength in research and public service were necessary for the institution to make a maximum contribution to the citizens of Oklahoma. In his conversations with me he had always evaluated athletics correctly—as interesting and exciting extracurricular activities.

121

Wilkinson received important national recognition early in the year. In January he was awarded the Coach of the Year Trophy by the American Football Coaches Association. The United States Junior Chamber of Commerce selected him as one of the ten outstanding young men of the nation. He received the award on February 21 at an appreciation banquet given by the Norman Chamber of Commerce for the "1949 Football Kingpins of the Midwest." The banquet was held at the Normandie Club, a huge, barnlike eating establishment (later destroyed by fire) west of Norman on what was then known as the "Football Highway." Lawrence Campbell, of Miami, Oklahoma, state president of the Junior Chamber of Commerce, presented the award to Wilkinson with appropriate remarks. Each player and coach received a set of cocktail glasses upon which were stamped in red the scores of the 1949 games. The regents of the university rose to the occasion and awarded a certificate of excellence to each player and coach. The graduating seniors of the squad drew numbers to determine who would get the game footballs of the perfect season. It was a gala occasion; the athletes, coaches, sports writers, state dignitaries, and other guests looked to the future with enthusiasm and confidence.

But Oklahoma's prospects for the 1950 season were to be jolted within the next couple of weeks. Faculty representatives of the Big Seven, at a meeting held in Kansas City on March 3 voted six to one that Lindell Pearson, OU's fine left halfback, would not be eligible for further competition, though he was a junior and had had only two years of intercollegiate competition.

It will be recalled that Pearson, after making initial plans to attend OU, had enrolled at the University of Arkansas. The Southwest Conference, of which Arkansas was a member, had a regulation that permitted its member schools to combine their varsity "B" teams with the freshmen and play a schedule of games. Pearson played in some of those games. This, the faculty representatives decided, constituted a year of competition.

Loss of Pearson was a serious blow, but there seemed adequate time to find his successor in the OU backfield. Dick Heatly had been his understudy during the 1949 season, but Frank Silva, a sophomore quarterback in 1949, whose jaw had been fractured

122

in the Boston College game, was also a likely prospect, providing the quarterback situation could be worked out satisfactorily following the graduation of Darrell Royal. Then there were some promising freshman backs who might make the grade. Among them was a lad from Cleveland, Oklahoma, named Billy Vessels. Leon Heath was the only member of the starting lineup from the preceding year who would be eligible for the 1950 season. Graduation and loss of eligibility took ten of the eleven starters of 1949, as well as a number of capable reserves.

The varsity-alumni game, played at Taft Stadium in Oklahoma City following spring practice, did not provide a reassuring experience for the fans. The alumni won, 20–14, although they had practiced only four days. But the impressive thing about the game was the way in which the alumni won. They outrushed the varsity 350–176 net yards, and their offense was so good that they never had to punt.

At the close of spring practice, Norman McNabb and Harry Moore were elected co-captains for the 1950 season. Wilkinson was cautious in his comments about the prospects for 1950, giving no hint that he had a national championship in mind. He was quoted in the *Sooner Magazine* of May, 1950, as saying: "Frankly I don't know who will win the Big Seven in 1950. It could be anybody."

CHAPTER 10

Aid to Athletes—Problems with Politics 1950

AT this point, I should back up a bit and give consideration to signs of problems in the offing. During the fiscal year 1948–49, $68,100 had been budgeted and spent in our program of aid to athletes—aid in return for which the athletes were, under the regulations of the conference and the NCAA, expected to perform some minimum services for the university. I had serious doubts during the year that many of the athletes were performing the required services. When I expressed these doubts to the coaches of the various sports, I was assured that the athletes did do some work, though perhaps not very much, in return for the money they received. I was assured repeatedly that in this respect we were doing as well as if not better than most of the schools with which we competed.

But my skepticism increased during the summer of 1949, when I received a letter from Wilkinson, dated July 8, in which he reported that four budgetary accounts had been overspent during the preceding year. One of these accounts was the basketball-ticket and game-expense budget. Wilkinson explained that it had been necessary to spend $265.59 to hire ushers for the basketball games because of a new plan for reserved seating that had been put into effect that year. Investigation revealed that athletes had not served as ushers, and in a letter of July 9, 1949, I replied as follows:

It is difficult for me to see why it should be necessary to hire ushers for basketball games when we have so many athletes on our payroll. Surely this is a service which athletes might be expected to perform, and to perform creditably.

I hope to have an opportunity to discuss with you the general problem of service from athletes, with the idea of bringing our situation a little more in line with the rules of the NCAA and our own conference.

There is nothing in my memory or files to indicate that Wilkinson responded to this suggestion, but early in September I received a request from him that the student-labor budget for intercollegiate athletics be increased to $82,084, with the suggestion that $50,000 of this amount be made available through the intramural department for the football team and $32,000 be channeled through the Department of Physical Plant (landscape and grounds and janitor services), for the benefit of basketball, baseball, track, swimming, and wrestling.

These amounts were finally approved and represent the extent of the university's expenditures for aid to athletes during the 1949–50 season. As near as I could determine, similar aid was being provided in two or three other schools of the conference and lesser amounts at the remaining schools. From what I could learn also, the athletes receiving the aid performed little, if any, service in return at any of the schools. This disturbed me a great deal, because it meant that the institutions of the conference were in violation of their own regulations and, of course, in violation of the regulations of the NCAA.

Still another problem had come into prominence with the Lindell Pearson recruiting incident—that of overenthusiastic supporters providing unusual and unreasonable inducements in their efforts to recruit promising high-school athletes. These practices, it was rumored, were widespread throughout the conference, sometimes with the knowledge of the coaching staffs involved but more frequently on an under-the-table basis.

It seemed obvious that steps needed to be taken to develop better controls. At a meeting of the Big Seven presidents in 1950 I suggested that the member schools of the conference recognize that an athlete could not possibly meet the demands placed on him by the practice periods involved with his sport, maintain an academic average that would ensure his eligibility for participation in his sport, and still have the time and energy to perform work in return for the financial aid he was receiving. I suggested that the Big Seven regulations be changed to allow an athlete board, room, tuition, books, and a small amount (fifteen dollars a month) in return for devoting his time to a university activity. I suggested that to do otherwise really meant institutional exploitation of the talents of some of its students in the quest for publicity and gate receipts. However, I was not able to sell

125

my ideas to the Big Seven presidents. All but one of them thought we should continue with the current policies and insist on compliance with the regulations. It was to be two or three years before the institutions of the country were to face their problems squarely and develop policies of aid to athletes that were workable and could be enforced.

Still another problem emerged during the spring of 1950, one that led to the reorganization of the Business Office of the Athletic Association and a change in the relationship of the Department of Intercollegiate Athletics to the University of Oklahoma.

Early in January, 1950, I received from Bill Cross a financial report concerning the Sugar Bowl as follows:

Estimated Sugar Bowl Income	$110,000
Estimated Sugar Bowl Expenses	90,000
Net	$ 20,000

The report reminded me of past difficulties in getting complete information concerning athletic receipts and expenditures. It seemed clear that the time had arrived to make a new effort to reorganize the administration of the Department of Intercollegiate Athletics, and I recommended to the regents of the university at their meeting on March 8, 1950, that intercollegiate athletic activities at OU be designated an auxiliary enterprise under the title "Athletic Department," that the department be subject to the same management and control as any other department or auxiliary enterprise of the institution, and that the position of treasurer of the Athletic Council be abolished.

The regents unanimously approved the recommendation, and on April 8, Wilkinson, Fitzgerald, and I met to discuss the mechanics of administering the new policy. During the conference Fitzgerald made the surprise announcement that he had been seriously considering the practice of law and offered his resignation effective May 1. The regents named Kenneth E. Farris business manager of athletics at their regular monthly meeting on April 19, 1950. Farris was an alumnus of the university, a three-time broad-jump champion of the Big Seven Conference, and had worked in Harold Keith's office during his student days. Since his discharge from the Marine Corps he had been employed

Kenneth E. Farris, an alumnus of OU, was appointed business manager of athletics by the Board of Regents in April, 1950. Courtesy Sports Information Department.

by the institution as superintendent of the physical plant, North Campus, and supervisor of inventory and receiving. In these posts he had demonstrated unusual ability to organize and handle details.

A bit of good news came during the spring of 1950. Estimates made in the business office of the Department of Athletics indicated that, by the middle of April, approximately $150,000 would be collected through advance sale of football tickets for the 1950 season. It appeared that none of this cash would be needed for operating expense for six months or more, and Roscoe Cate recommended that the money be invested in short-term government obligations, such as Treasury bills. The rate on Treasury bills at that time was 1.148 per cent. The regents approved investing the surplus funds in this manner, and in later years it was found possible to develop a rather substantial surplus.

A bit of confusion developed during the summer of 1950 concerning the radio broadcasts of the OU games. During the summer tentative arrangements had been worked out with Radio Station KOMA in Oklahoma City to broadcast the contests, but the signing of the formal contract had been delayed pending the selection of a sponsor or sponsors for the broadcasts. In the preliminary agreement the university had reserved the right to approve or disapprove sponsorship, being concerned that cigarette or beer advertisers might become involved, with damage to the institution's reputation.

Sometime during August, while my family and I were on vacation, several members of the Democratic party, including H. W. McNeil, a personal adviser to Governor Turner, called on T. R. Benedum, a member of the university Board of Regents to discuss the possibility that the Democratic party might sponsor the broadcasts until the general election on November 7. Benedum told me later that he had expressed some doubt about the advisability of such sponsorship but that it would be up to the regents of the university, acting as a whole, to make the decision. He explained to his visitors that the university had a lot of good friends among Republicans as well as the Democrats and that the Republicans, naturally, would feel some resentment if the institution permitted its football team to be exploited for political purposes. Benedum said that he had the impression that the Democratic party subsequently decided to abandon the proposal.

But just to be sure that there could be no misunderstanding, I called Joe Bernard, general manager of KOMA, and told him that under no circumstances would I recommend to the OU governing board approval of a contract calling for political sponsorship of the broadcasts. I told him I was certain that the regents would not take such action without my recommendation and that he should look for other sponsorship if he wanted his station to broadcast the games.

Shortly thereafter, to the apparent surprise of everyone except those directly involved, officials of the Democratic party announced that they had signed a contract with KOMA to sponsor the broadcasts. The announcement was accompanied by the appearance of twelve billboards distributed throughout Oklahoma, each of which displayed a donkey wearing a football helmet and a jersey and running with a football. Conspicuous on the sign above the donkey was "OU Football" and below, "presented by the Democratic party."

Within hours I was besieged, at both my home and the office, with phone calls from indignant Republicans protesting what they said was discrimination against their party. I immediately released a statement that the university had not been involved in any contract that would permit its football games to be broadcast under sponsorship of any political party and that I would not recommend to the regents that any such arrangement be approved.

But, despite my statement, when he was queried by reporters, James Arrington, chairman of the state Democratic party, was quoted as saying:

As far as we know, we have a contract for sponsorship of the games. KOMA of Oklahoma City is handling it.

We are trying to get the games for Oklahoma A&M as well as OU. These are the two greatest institutions in Oklahoma and they were both built under Democratic administrations.

The billboards had appeared on Saturday, September 2. After reflecting on the situation for a few hours and listening to protests from the Republicans, I decided that I needed to get support from the OU regents. On Sunday, September 3, I arranged a telephone conference with members of the board and received authorization to issue the following statement: "The Regents of the University of Oklahoma by telephone conversation have ruled unanimously that a political party is not an acceptable sponsor for broadcasts of university activities."

Despite this statement Joe Bernard of KOMA took the position that there was a binding contract between his station and the Democratic party and that he thought he had a binding agreement with the university. He was reported as saying that he would fight to keep the Democratic party as sponsor of the university football games, and he asked for a meeting with university officials on Tuesday, September 5. A meeting was arranged for 3:00 P.M. that day. There Bernard argued, rather ingeniously, that "sponsorship of the game broadcasts did not constitute a university endorsement of any product or group—but that an

129

arbitrary decision not to allow any certain sponsor did put the school in the position of being opposed to that certain sponsor's product, application or philosophy," thus suggesting indirectly that the university's refusal to allow Democratic sponsorship of its football games put it in the position of being opposed to the Democratic party. Bernard left the meeting apparently still thinking that he was right but finally convinced that the university would not approve political sponsorship of any of its activities.

Later someone came up with a proposal that the broadcasting of the games should be sponsored jointly by the Democratic and Republican parties—an idea rejected almost immediately by both university officials and the Republican party. When the regents met on Wednesday, September 13, Bernard was on hand to represent KOMA with a proposal that the Anderson-Prichard Oil Company would sponsor the away-from-home games and that another nonpolitical sponsor would be secured later for the home games. The regents approved a contract on that basis. Thus ended OU football's first involvement with Oklahoma politics—but not its last.

CHAPTER 11

The First National Championship and Consecutive-Win Record

1950

THE Sooners looked a little undermanned as they took to the field in their opening game, at home against Boston College—especially in the backfield. Leon Heath seemed adequate at full-back, but the two halfbacks, Tommy Gray, of Seminole, and Buddy Jones, of Holdenville, although splendid athletes, weighed only 157 and 155 pounds, respectively. Claude Arnold, senior quarterback from Okmulgee, had never been fully tested, having played for the past three years behind Jack Mitchell and Darrell Royal. But the Sooners scored on their first possession and again just before the half ended, after experimenting with calling two plays in a huddle instead of one—looking to the future when it might be important to save time.

Several sophomores saw action, including Buck McPhail, Billy Vessels, and Eddie Crowder. Although the play as a whole was not particularly impressive, Oklahoma did manage to win by a score of 28–0.

The Texas Aggies were scheduled for the following week, on October 7, at Norman. It was decided to open the activities of that afternoon with an invocation by Stewart Harral, director of university public relations. It was the consensus in the president's office that a brief interlude of prayer before each of our home contests might serve to remind the increasing numbers of fans of their spiritual heritage.

In that first prayer Harral referred to "Christ our Lord." This brought protests from several on the grounds that many OU students, and perhaps others in the crowd or listening on radio, were not of the Christian faith. It was stressed that we should have an interreligious prayer or no prayer at all. After pondering for a day or so, I asked Harral to omit references to Christ in future prayers, and at the next home game he came up with what I thought a splendid interreligious effort. But to my dismay the following week, I received letters protesting his failure to mention

Christ, and pointing out that Western civilization, of which we are a part, was based on Christianity. To each of these correspondents I explained, as best I could, that the pregame prayer was intended to be useful to people of all faiths and that each one who heard the prayer was free to interpret the message as he considered appropriate.

The game with the Texas Aggies was a thrilling seesaw battle, with perhaps the wildest, most exciting finish of any in OU football history. The score was tied, 21–21 at the beginning of the fourth quarter, but 27 seconds later the Aggie fullback, Bob Smith, swept around left end for a 50-yard jaunt that ended with a touchdown, followed by a conversion, putting OU in the hole, 21–28.

OU's drive for a tie, following the ensuing kickoff, was terminated by Leon Heath's fumble on the Aggie 39-yard line, but the Sooners forced the Aggies to punt after four plays and once again started their march down the field. This time they were successful: Claude Arnold passed to Billy Vessels for a touchdown, 3 minutes, 33 seconds from the end of the game—score 27–28. Gloom pervaded in the ranks of Sooner fans when Jim Weatherall missed his attempt for the extra point, his first miss in eight tries. But the crowd gave the big tackle a strong ovation as he walked to the sideline, went down on one knee, and appeared to sob.

The Sooners then kicked off to the Cadets, and a seemingly inspired OU defense forced a punt on the next series. The ball was returned to OU's 31-yard line with 1 minute, 46 seconds left.

A bit of confusion in our box followed, because M. T. Harrington, president of Texas A&M College, and D. W. Williams, vice-chancellor, had to leave the game to catch a plane back to Texas. After their departure I seemed to sense a curious air of expectancy sweep through the crowd, a sort of tense awareness that something dramatic was about to happen. This feeling was shared by our son Bill, who leaned over and said to me, "Dad, we're going to win this game."

The crowd's hopes soared when Arnold completed a 30-yard pass to Vessels. They sagged on the next play, when Heath failed to see a perfectly thrown pass because he lost the ball in the

132

sun that was beginning to set toward the southwest corner of the stadium. There were three mighty roars when Arnold completed a pitch to Gray for 11 yards, one to Heath for 14 yards, and, finally, one to Gray who traveled 10 yards to the Aggie 4.

Then, with 44 seconds left to play, Arnold brought the attack back to the ground. He took the snap from center, faked a play through the line, and tossed a long pitchout to Heath, who went around left end to score what was to be the winning touchdown. This time Weatherall was successful in kicking the extra point, and Oklahoma took the lead, 34–28.

During the final few seconds of the game the Aggies tried three desperation passes but completed none of them. The game ended with the crowd in a frenzy. The air was full of red cushions thrown skyward as the crowd broke out of the stands onto the field. Wilkinson, Heath, and other players were carried in triumph to the dressing room.

Walking home from the stadium that afternoon, I became a little tired of Bill's repeated insistent demand, "Didn't I tell you we were going to win, Dad?"

The next week a story made the rounds that Gomer Jones, OU's great line coach, whom everybody, including players, called Gomer, had been in telephone contact with an OU coach stationed in the press box. During the final seconds of the game, when the Aggies were making their last desperate effort, the coach in the press box had an idea about something that would be useful in OU's defensive strategy. He got on the phone and asked to speak to "Jones." Gomer, on the other end of the line, was so excited he failed to realize that the name was his own. He looked along the sideline and called frantically to the other coaches and players, "Where's Jones? The press box wants Jones!"

The third game of the 1950 season was the annual brawl with the University of Texas. When the record-breaking crowd, numbering in excess of 76,000, assembled in the Cotton Bowl that afternoon, the thermometer stood at about 90 degrees. Correspondingly high humidity made it sticky and uncomfortable in the stands. I remember wondering what it would be like down on the playing field and which of the two teams would have the greater reserve strength.

If OU could win that day, it would be only the second time in history that the Sooners had three consecutive wins over the Longhorns. The trick had been turned back in 1910, 1911, and 1912, when Coach Bennie Owen's Sooners won by scores of 3–0, 6–3, and 21–6. Before the 1950 game records of the series showed twenty-nine victories for Texas, thirteen for OU, and two ties.

Starting at halfback for the Sooners was the promising sophomore Billy Vessels. Vessels had played some in OU's opening game against Boston College and had looked good, and in the Texas Aggie game he had carried the ball fifteen times for a gain of 56 yards, caught two passes for a gain of 60 yards, and completed a pass on a pass-option play for a gain of 8 yards. His performance as a reserve in the first two games earned him a starting role against Texas.

The game got under way in typical slam-bang fashion, with OU scoring early in the first quarter on a 52-yard drive, which featured ball-carrying heroics by Claude Arnold, Billy Vessels, and Leon Heath. Vessels scored the touchdown, Jim Weatherall kicked the goal, and OU led 7–0, 4 minutes, 12 seconds after the opening kickoff.

Texas dominated the play during most of the rest of the first half, tying the score 7–7 early in the second quarter. The Texans continued to dominate the play in the third quarter, and took the lead early in the fourth period, when one of their backs intercepted an OU pass and ran it back 45 yards for a touchdown. Fortunately, from OU's point of view, the try for conversion was missed, and the score stood 13–7 in favor of Texas.

This was the situation, with 6:17 left in the game, when Texas attempted to mount another scoring drive after receiving a punt on their 23-yard line. The OU defense stiffened to meet the challenge. Two power plays into the line were stopped cold, and on a third, similar attempt the ball carrier was tackled for a 9-yard loss, creating a punting situation. Moving with the snap, the OU forward wall surged onto the kicker, buried him before he could get the kick away, and took possession of the ball on the Texas 11-yard line, with 4:45 in which to score.

Only two plays were necessary to accomplish this. Arnold gave the ball to Vessels on the first down, but the sophomore, who

All-American Jim Weatherall and President Cross share a happy moment after OU's victory over the Texas Longhorns in 1950. Courtesy Sports Information Department.

had had such a great day, failed to gain. The second down featured a fake to Heath, who plowed into the Texas line in a determined effort to attract attention, then a pitchout to Vessels, who was running to the right from his left-halfback position. Two Texas tacklers were on hand to interrupt Vessels' trip to the end zone, but fortunately the two were not close together, and Vessels simply lowered his head and plowed between them as he traveled goalward.

With the score 13–13, the huge crowd, wet from perspiration and limp with suspense, awaited the try for point. Weatherall, seemingly untroubled by the fact that he had missed a crucial kick the preceding week, boomed the ball squarely over the goal posts into the crowd beyond the end zone.

The OU defense, given moral support by the frenzied roar of OU partisans in the stadium, kept the Longhorns well in check during the waning moments. Oklahoma was winning another squeaker. At the game's end, the OU fans swarmed onto the field and in a matter of moments were breaking both goal posts into souvenirs. The Cotton Bowl officials, convinced that there was no way to protect the posts following any OU-Texas contest, had erected special posts that could be dismantled easily. The Texas fans filed dejectedly from the stadium, governors and university presidents shook hands and exchanged pleasantries, and it was all over for another year. OU had won its third consecutive game with Texas and its twenty-fourth consecutive contest over opponents.

After Texas, homecoming on October 21 seemed something of an anticlimax, because Kansas State College was not considered a strong opponent. But the student body worked enthusiastically that week preparing floats for the parade and decorating houses. The organizations got a little behind in their preparations, and the administration obligingly gave them a half-day holiday on Friday afternoon to get things in final shape for the weekend.

The theme for homecoming decorations and floats was titles of songs, and many interesting ideas evolved. The float of greatest interest to the Cross family was being prepared in the back yard of the Pi Kappa Alpha fraternity, next door to us. A good view of what was going on there could be obtained from Braden's bedroom, which overlooked the property. The boys had backed a flat trailer into the yard, built a platform on it about six feet square, and then appeared with two-by-fours, chicken wire, and several bags of plaster of Paris.

They built a cross on the little platform and then began to mold the chicken wire around it into the form of a human bust, shoulders and head. Then they put cloth over the wire and applied plaster of Paris.

Each evening that week Braden watched the proceedings with fascination as the figure became more realistic. One evening while watching, he yelled excitedly, "Mother, they're making Daddy!" Mrs. Cross went to the window in time to see the boys finish inserting a pipe into the mouth of the plaster figure. The pipe no doubt gave Braden the real clue, but when the float was finished, it turned out to be a remarkable likeness. It appeared in the parade on homecoming morning, labeled "The Old Rugged Cross." The float got a lot of attention in the parade, but I believe it did not win a prize.

The football game in the afternoon, as many had predicted, was not much of a contest. The Sooners defeated Kansas State 58–0 in a game that featured the punt returns of Merrill Green, a sophomore from Chickasha, Oklahoma. He returned four Kansas State spiral offerings for a total of 68 yards.

The Sooners had little difficulty with any of the remaining games of their 1950 regular season. Iowa State, quarterbacked by Bill Weeks, the nation's leading passer, was defeated at Ames 20–7 on October 28. Claude Arnold had a good day; he brought his total pass attempts without interception to fifty-nine. Billy Vessels continued to look impressive also; he carried the ball sixteen times for 72 yards.

The University of Colorado gave the Sooners their closest game of the remainder of the season at Boulder on November 4. Although Oklahoma was in front with respect to statistics, the final score was 27–18. Injuries were a prominent feature of the game. Tommy Gray, a defensive halfback, injured a knee; Buddy Jones, safety, left the game with an injured hip; and Frankie Anderson, right end, was knocked out on the first play of the game and saw no further action. With both Jones and Gray out of the OU defensive secondary, Colorado was able to profit with its passing attack. But Leon Heath played well despite an injured leg and ailing shoulder, and Billy Vessels had a great day, rushing for a net of 120 yards on twelve carries.

The bruised and battered team that flew home from Colorado that evening still faced what many thought the most difficult three games of their conference schedule, with always dangerous Oklahoma A&M College for the finale. But coaches and players appeared to be in a good mood at the airport, very much aware that they had that day established a modern American record for number of consecutive wins—twenty-seven.

Actually, Wilkinson and his high-flying squad had very little difficulty with the remaining games. They easily defeated Kansas (at Lawrence) and Missouri (at Norman) by scores of 33–13 and

41–7, respectively. Following the decisive defeat of Missouri, Oklahoma was ranked number one in the AP poll—for the first time in history.

Nebraska, with a great running back, Bobby Reynolds, and a fine quarterback, Fran Nagle, managed to hold the Sooners to a 21–21 tie during the first half. But the dam broke in the second half, and the final score was 49–35 in favor of Oklahoma. The Sooners retained their number-one spot in the AP poll that week, with the strongest showing in the poll's history, 337 points of a possible 350.

During the week preceding the Nebraska game, rumors were rife that an invitation from the Sugar Bowl would be presented to the Sooners after the game and that an announcement would be forthcoming that evening. But the crowd waiting at the dressing-room doors to hear the news was disappointed. There was no announcement that evening; it came on Monday. Presumably the invitation was extended on Saturday and presented to the squad at a meeting held the next afternoon. On Monday, November 27, newspapers throughout the South and Southwest carried headlines that the Oklahoma squad had voted unanimously to accept an invitation to meet the University of Kentucky in the Sugar Bowl on New Year's Day, 1951. The announcement pleased most Oklahomans.

The season's final game with the Oklahoma Aggies was won by Oklahoma, 41–14, in a game played at Stillwater. Coach Paul ("Bear") Bryant, who had led his Kentucky squad to the championship of the Southeastern Conference and a seventh place ranking in the AP poll, was present to scout the Sooners and visit with friends in Oklahoma.

Bryant returned the following Friday, December 8, to be featured with Wilkinson at a "postseason" quarterback luncheon held in the Civic Room of the Biltmore Hotel in Oklahoma City. Wilkinson and Bryant were to hold interviews about the forthcoming Sugar Bowl game, and a movie of one of Kentucky's games would be shown—perhaps Kentucky's 48–21 victory over Mississippi State, or maybe its 7–0 loss to Tennessee.

An overflow crowd turned out for the luncheon. The two coaches exchanged encomiums, and Wilkinson complimented his team, the OU alumni, the fans, and even the president of the university. Bryant displayed his skill as a public speaker, telling several anecdotes that kept the large crowd in excellent humor. It fell to his lot also to explain why no film of a Kentucky game would be shown that day. It had failed to arrive. But he said that the two schools had agreed to exchange films of four games played during the past season. A film of the OU-Kansas contest was shown, and everyone seemed content. Bryant spoke somewhat plaintively of the overemphasis on basketball in Kentucky. He said: "We had a big banquet last week and Adolph Rupp, the basketball coach, was given a big beautiful four-door Cadillac. I got this cigarette lighter."

The climax of the luncheon came when Bill Bryan, of KTOW, presented Wilkinson with the Sportsman of the Year award, the tangible portion of which was a beautiful pen set. The crowd gave Wilkinson a standing ovation, his second of the day.

Throughout 1950, and especially during the football season, the ever-recurring rumors had spread that Wilkinson would leave the University of Oklahoma to accept a coaching job elsewhere at the end of the season. Speculation centered on the coaching job at the University of Minnesota. Bernie Bierman, under whom Wilkinson had played there in the mid-thirties, had been having difficulty with his won-loss percentages, and the alumni of the institution were demanding a replacement. Wilkinson assured me that he would not follow Bierman at Minnesota—presumably out of regard for his old coach. "If Bierman couldn't make it there, I don't think I could either," he said one day.

Nevertheless, late in the year, Ike Armstrong, athletic director at Minnesota, came to Norman to try to persuade their distinguished alumnus to take the job. After he returned to Minneapolis, Armstrong had President J. L. Morrill call me to ask permission to make Wilkinson an offer. It seemed a little late to be asking my permission, but I gave it. Morrill did make an offer, but I never learned the terms. On December 8, according to an article in the *Daily Oklahoman* Armstrong issued a statement that Wilkinson had been offered the job and had turned it down. I wondered momentarily why the refusal was publicized in this manner, but I soon realized that Armstrong probably had released the statement to get rid of the pressure from the Minnesota alumni who were demanding that Wilkinson return home. When Wilkinson was asked for a statement concerning the negotiations, he was reported (Laymond Crump, the *Daily Oklahoma*) to have said: "I appreciate being contacted relative to the Minnesota job but in view of the fact my contract at Oklahoma still has three years to run it is impossible for me to consider any other coaching situation. I am very happy at Oklahoma." Following Wilkinson's statement there were suggestions that Bear Bryant, who was thought to be mildly unhappy at Kentucky, working in the shadow of Adolph Rupp, would become the new Minnesota coach, but they did not materialize.

Official recognition of Oklahoma's first national football championship came at a lavish banquet held on Tuesday night, December 19, in the Persian Room of the Skirvin Tower Hotel. The main feature of the event was the presentation of the Reverend J. Hugh O'Donnell Memorial Trophy, a plaque emblematic of the national championship, sponsored and presented by the Monogram Club of Notre Dame University. Oklahoma was to retain possession of the trophy until another team won the national championship. There was a provision, however, that any team winning three national championships would take permanent possession of the prized award.

Frank Leahy, head football coach at the University of Notre Dame, came to present the award on behalf of the Monogram Club. The choice of Leahy for the presentation was appropriate: his team had won the plaque the preceding year, and OU was scheduled to meet Notre Dame at South Bend in 1952. Leahy, a talented public speaker and a master of the quip, warned of "another day" when, after presenting the trophy, he said, "Last year they carried me off the field at the end of a perfect season; this year we lost four games, and they ran me off."

Co-captain Harry Moore introduced each of the football coaches and players, with special mention of All-Americans Leon Heath, Jim Weatherall, Buddy Jones, and Frankie Anderson. He pointed out that quarterback Claude Arnold had led the nation in another statistic—only one interception in 114 passes.

Following the festivities that December came serious prepara-

140

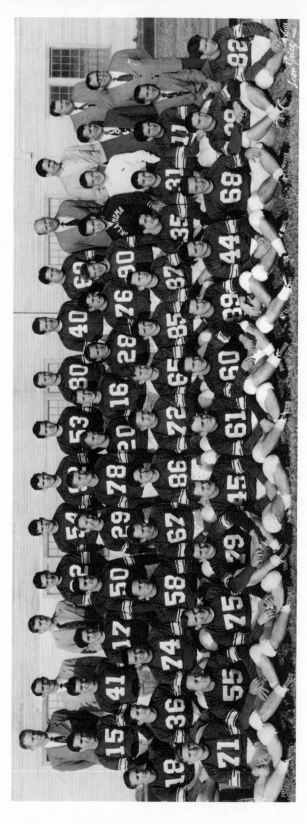

The 1950 team. FIRST ROW (FRONT ROW), LEFT TO RIGHT: Jim Weatherall, Harry Moore (co-captain), Art Janes, Joe Horkey, Ed Lisak, Dean Smith, Clair Mayes, Ed Sampson, Sam Allen, Bobby Gaut, Jack Santee, Frankie Anderson. SECOND ROW: Bill Blair, Dick Heatly, Ed Rowland, Bill Covin, Fred Smith, John Reddell, J. W. Cole, Norman McNabb (co-captain), Jack Lockett, Kay Keller, Billy Vessels, Larry Cotton, Joe Cunningham, Joe Glander (trainer). THIRD ROW: Claude Arnold, Buck McPhail, Frank Silva, Bert Clark, Tommy Gray, George Cornelius, Merrill Green, Eddie Crowder, Dale Crawford, Melvin Brown, Jerry Ingram, Eugene Ball, Omer Kirschner (manager), George Lynn (coach), Orville Tuttle (coach), FOURTH ROW: Bud Wilkinson (coach), Buddy Jones, Al Needs, Jim Davis, Tom Catlin, Sam Carnahan, Harry Pace, Bill Beckman, Leon Heath, Raymond Powell, "Pop" Ivy (coach), Bill Jennings (coach), Gomer Jones (coach). Courtesy Sports Information Department.

tion for the third Sugar Bowl contest, to be held on January 1, 1951. The Sooners worked at Owen Field until Christmas and then flew in two chartered planes to their now-favorite training spot, at Biloxi, Mississippi, for the training.

Mrs. Cross and I decided that we would not represent the university this time and arranged for Vice-President and Mrs. Roscoe Cate to go in our places. Later Mrs. Cross and I were invited to fly to New Orleans the day of the game with other guests in a Phillips Petroleum Corporation plane and return on January 2. Mrs. Cross decided not to go, but I was unwilling to pass up an opportunity to see the game, free of appearances or speeches.

We flew to New Orleans on January 1 and went immediately to the Sugar Bowl. The weather was a trifle chilly, with a gusty wind and threatening clouds—a dreary prospect that was not brightened by the events that followed, especially the final score, Oklahoma 7, Kentucky 13. Losing the ball five times on fumbles and mishandling a punt provided substantial handicaps for the OU team, but Kentucky's aggressive play probably caused most of the errors. Kentucky's quarterback, Vito ("Babe") Parilli, had a good afternoon, completing nine of twelve passes. Claude Arnold tried only five passes, completing two for 21 yards. On other occasions when he tried to pass or run with the ball, he frequently was tackled behind the line of scrimmage. He ended the game with a net loss of 21 yards.

Kentucky's right tackle, Walt Yowarsky, played brilliantly on defense. That evening at the party for the two teams he was awarded the Warren V. Miller Memorial Trophy as the outstanding player of the game, the first time the award had gone to a lineman since it was first presented in 1948. Another Kentucky tackle who played well was Jim MacKenzie, a young man destined to be named head football coach at OU in 1965.

The loss ended the longest winning streak in modern football history—thirty-one consecutive victories—a somber thought for Oklahomans but a happy one for the Kentuckians. At the game's end Bear Bryant was hoisted to the shoulders of a couple of husky players and carried from the field, leaning down frequently to shake hands with well-wishers. Wilkinson followed slowly to the Wildcat dressing room to congratulate the winning coach and his squad. He then returned to the Sooner dressing room, where several of the younger athletes were sobbing as they removed their sweat-drenched jerseys and pads. To the sports writers he said simply, "I'm proud of the kids. They never quit. Those bad breaks kept hitting them in the face, but they never stopped scrapping. An average team would have quit after all those breaks."

Wilkinson, who had been named coach of the year by the National Football Coaches' Association in 1949, received similar recognition for his coaching performance in 1950, when he was named coach of the year by a poll of the Associated Press. But the young man's increasing prominence in the football world brought increasing problems to the president of his university, because of the persistent rumors that he would leave OU and accept a more attractive position elsewhere. Every move that he made seemed to give rise to another rumor. He was scheduled to speak to a group of fans at Clinton, Oklahoma, on February 5, 1951. That turned out to be the date of a farewell dinner for Bernie Bierman, who was leaving his coaching post at the University of Minnesota. Wilkinson asked the Clinton fans to change the date of his appearance, so that he could attend the dinner, and a later date was set. But fans jumped to the conclusion that Wilkinson was making another trip north to discuss the job at Minnesota, and his vigorous denial did little to dissipate the rumors.

Fortunately, the matter was settled temporarily when Wes Fesler was appointed head football coach at the University of Minnesota late in January. I say temporarily, because rumors began circulating shortly after Fesler's appointment when it was learned that he had received a three-year contract—a contract that would expire at the same time Wilkinson's contract expired at the University of Oklahoma. Charlie Johnson, sports editor for one of the Minneapolis papers, came up with the suggestion that the Fesler appointment was an interim one, a stopgap measure until Wilkinson became available.

Johnson had been a great admirer of Wilkinson for some time. In his articles he insisted that Wilkinson was eager to return to

143

his alma mater but could not do so because of his contract with OU. This did not accord with statements Wilkinson had made to the Oklahoma press—that he was satisfied at Oklahoma and wanted to remain there "as long as the fans want me." Some Oklahomans were unkind enough to suggest that Wilkinson was telling the Oklahomans one thing and the Minnesotans another. Others took the position that he was satisfied at the University of Oklahoma but did not want to offend his Minnesota friends by saying that he was not interested in their offer, and so used his contract at OU as a shield while professing interest in the Minnesota job. Only Wilkinson knew the answer.

Oklahoma writers seized on the interim-coach suggestion and came up with several interesting interpretations. Fesler, they pointed out, had voluntarily resigned as coach at Ohio State University on December 9. He had given poor health as the reason for his resignation. Now, only a little over a month later, he had accepted a position as head coach at the University of Minnesota (to coach a downtrodden team that his Ohio State squad had defeated 48–0 the past season). Why had he done this in the light of his supposed ill-health? Surely, it was argued, some arrangement must have been made with him for temporary duty at Minnesota, pending the time when enthusiastic alumni could arrange for Wilkinson's return.

After the holiday season there was much discussion of the low morale of some male students at OU. During a week's time one hundred men dropped out of school without completing the semester's work. It appeared that there would be a sharp decline in enrollment of men for the second semester, perhaps as much as 20 per cent—about double the usual drop. Reporters scurried about interviewing teachers about the cause for the drop in morale. Of course, the outbreak of the Korean War was a factor: in response to inquiries, several students expressed the belief that a degree would not do anyone "much good in Korea."

A few members of the faculty expressed the view that the war was not all of the problem. The attitude of the faculty was summed up neatly by one member, who said: "The football craze throughout the entire first semester occupied too much of the students' time and resulted in low grades and class cuts." I was inclined

144

to agree that football had been a factor. It seemed to me that a winning team had done a great deal for the state of Oklahoma, but not nearly as much for the university. I resolved to do everything that I could to prevent the university from taking part in a postseason game after the 1951 season.

In between composing denials that Wilkinson planned to leave the university, I found time to work on some other problems confronting the university. Enrollment for the second semester dropped alarmingly to below the 8,000 mark. It had been 10,500 the year before and 11,800 at the beginning of the first semester of the 1949–50 session. The decrease threatened to cause serious budgetary difficulties for the institution, because each veteran lost from the student body meant a loss of $120 which was paid to the institution by the Veterans Administration.

I appeared before the joint House-Senate Appropriations committee of the state legislature early in February in an attempt to explain OU's needs for increased appropriations. Governor Murray had recommended that the university receive $6,950,539 from state appropriations for the biennium. I was asking for $10,600,000, a difference of $3,659,461. I carefully described the university's situation to the committees, explaining in detail why the increased appropriations were needed and how the money would be used. As I closed my thirty-minute presentation, I thought with satisfaction that I had done a good job, that I had been persuasive and convincing.

After I backed away from the lectern, the chairman of the combined committees thanked me for appearing and then asked if anyone had a question. A sleepy-looking senator, just to my right on the front row, raised his hand and said: "Yes, I'd like to ask the good doctor why he thinks he needs so much money to run the University of Oklahoma." For a moment I was completely nonplused. Then came the depressing realization that I had failed to get my message across. After groping for an answer, I concluded that nothing by way of logic would impress my questioner, and so I replied that "I would like to build a university of which the football team could be proud." My remark brought a laugh and scattered applause but when Governor Murray's budget was finally approved, I didn't get the funds I had requested.

However, I was surprised by the attention my remark received in the newspapers and other news media. The quote appeared in most of the state's papers, and there were several semihumorous analyses of athletics versus academics at the university. Then papers across the country started picking up the story. Some readers missed the gentle irony, and one day I received a letter from the editor of a newspaper in Indiana who scolded me vigorously for overemphasizing athletics at the university. He concluded with the statement that he could see little hope for higher education in the country as long as university presidents placed football ahead of academic programs.

Another communication came a few months later from *Reader's Digest*. There was a check for ten dollars in the envelope and a slip of paper with my quote at the top. Below the quote was a message: "The attached item, attributed to you, is scheduled to appear on page 6 of our August issue. We take pleasure in enclosing our check for $10 in payment." Later the quote appeared in *Time* and *Life* magazines. It appeared also, astonishingly, in at least three foreign newspapers; clippings were sent to me by friends traveling abroad.

Wilkinson had a rugged schedule of speaking engagements and appearances during the spring of 1951. He got back from Bernie Bierman's farewell dinner in Minneapolis just in time to go to Muskogee with me to attend the annual banquet of the Muskogee Quarterback Club, given in honor of Muskogee's high-school team, which had won the state championship in 1950. We left for Muskogee in the university's Beechcraft Bonanza (I was the pilot) about 4 o'clock on the afternoon of February 17 and soon were flying above the oak-hickory forests of eastern Oklahoma. Wilkinson seemed somewhat troubled and ill at ease during the trip, and I wondered at first whether he might be a little worried about my skill in handling the little plane. Then I realized that he was trying to prepare me for an unpleasant possibility. He said that, despite his statements to the reporters, he was not entirely satisfied with the situation at OU. He mentioned several problems of coaching, including the difficulty of recruiting in competition with two other state schools and the Southwest Conference. He mentioned also that not all the prom-

Muskogee fans express their well-merited appreciation of OU in February, 1951: a Cadillac to Coach Wilkinson and a cigarette lighter to President Cross. Courtesy *Oklahoman and Times.*

ises made to him had been kept by the university. For example, one thousand dollars in expense money that he had been promised had not been forthcoming. I could not recall any unfulfilled commitments, but I assured him that if there were any I certainly would see that they were met.

The banquet honoring the Muskogee football players was held at the Severs Hotel. Camp Bond was the toastmaster. Wilkinson was the guest of honor, but to be impartial, the Muskogeans had also invited J. B. Whitworth, coach at Oklahoma A&M, and

Buddy Brothers, coach at Tulsa. Paul Young, coach of the Muskogee High School football team, made a talk, praising the squad and emphasizing that twenty-one of the players were seniors.

Wilkinson offered congratulations to the team but did not make a recruiting pitch. He spoke briefly of the program at OU, mainly to express the hope that "we can continue to play the kind of football at Oklahoma that the people of this state will be proud of."

Whitworth also spoke briefly, concluding by saying that "any of you boys who want to learn how to plow, come up and see me."

Brothers had a somewhat more direct approach. He spoke of his Hurricane squad and mentioned that "our scholarships are practically filled at TU, but we have twenty-one left."

Pete Smith, president of the Muskogee Quarterback Club, then presented his annual Pete Smith Trophy to the outstanding player of the squad, Max Boydston. Bill Nichols followed by presenting the award for the most valuable player of the year to Curt Burris (both Boydston and Burris later were to attend OU and play outstanding football; Curt Burris was a brother of Buddy Burris, All-America guard at OU in 1948).

Near the end of the program gifts of appreciation were presented to Whitworth and Brothers. Then Wilkinson was called to the speaker's stand and given the keys to a 1951 Cadillac sedan, with the compliments of the OU Alumni Association.

The final presentation of the evening was a cigarette lighter, given to me as a testimonial that "higher education was appreciated in Muskogee."

Wilkinson and I spent the night in the Severs Hotel and flew home the following morning. I don't recall how he got his Cadillac home. Later we were photographed together, he sitting in the Cadillac, and I holding the cigarette lighter.

CHAPTER 12

More Politics—Scandals in Athletics— Wilkinson Resigns

1951

INTERESTING developments took place at the state capitol during the next month. It had become apparent after enrollment for the second semester was completed that the state system of higher education would not have enough income to operate for the rest of the school year, and the regents for higher education had presented a request to the legislature for a supplemental appropriation of $1,950,000, the amount needed to bolster the budgets of the various schools so that the second semester's work could be completed. Of this amount the Norman Campus of the University of Oklahoma was to receive $507,893.

The request for a supplemental appropriation created a furor in both houses of the legislature, but it was in the senate that the situation came to a head as far as the University of Oklahoma was concerned. This may have been due in part to a little trouble I had had with a member of the senate at the beginning of the football season just ended. Dr. Louis B. Ritzhaupt, state senator from Guthrie had visited my office just before the start of the 1950 season and asked to be exempt from the university requirement that recipients of complimentary tickets to the football games must pick up their tickets in person the day of the game. He told me that, because of his responsibilities as a physician, he could not arrive in Norman in time to pick up his tickets and asked to have them mailed to him. I explained that I could not make an exception to the policy, because it had been established by the university regents. I also pointed out that, if an exception was made for one member of the legislature, exceptions must be made for all. He appeared unconvinced and described in some detail the much better treatment he was receiving from other schools. He finally left my office, clearly unhappy with the results of his visit.

When Ritzhaupt learned that a supplemental appropriation for higher education had been requested, he decided to investigate the spending by the University of Oklahoma. He found several items of which he disapproved, including a portrait of me as president of the university, a frame for the portrait, and a window air conditioner for the guest room in the president's home. But the most damning items, in his opinion, were records of the purchases of a set of Egyptian earrings and a brazier from an Egyptian tomb.

In an address to the senate the afternoon of March 7, Ritzhaupt listed wasteful expenditures that the university had made, totaling $14,349.96. He ended his oratory with the accusation that the university had "bought earrings and brassieres out of state funds."

Ritzhaupt's revelations naturally caused a stir in the senate, and a committee was immediately formed to investigate the university's expenditures. Chairman of the committee was Senator Frank Mahan of Fairfax; other members were Senators Oliver C. Walker of Dale, Ray Fine of Gore, A. E. Anderson of Elk City, and Leroy McClendon of Idabel.

Roscoe Cate and I were "invited" to meet with the committee, preliminary to the weighty investigations that supposedly would follow. We went to the state capitol at the appointed time and waited in the reception area of Senator Mahan's office. While we were sitting there, a delegation from the press came into the room, headed by Bill Henthorne of the *Tulsa World.* Henthorne looked at Cate and me and asked: "What are you fellows going to tell this committee? Are you going to break down and confess to wasting state money, or are you going to give the committee a lot of reasons why the items you bought were necessary for the development of a championship football team?"

Cate gave a little thought to the question and then replied in his usual bland manner, "With the exception of the brassieres, we're going to make a clean breast of the whole business."

Henthorne pointed his finger at me and asked, "Can I print that?" To this I replied, "No! Don't you dare print it! We are not approaching this investigation in any spirit of levity; we are taking the whole matter very seriously."

Although for several moments the group continued to chuckle at Cate's quick wit, none made any mention in the stories that

150

followed of his mild correction of Senator Ritzhaupt's mistake.

The meeting with the committee was friendly enough. The misunderstanding concerning the earrings and brazier was straightened out to everyone's satisfaction, and the members accepted our explanation of the other expenditures.

A major furor over what turned out to be a relatively minor matter developed that spring when a story appeared in the *Oklahoma Daily,* OU's student newspaper, on betting on athletic contests by OU athletes. The article claimed that circulation of parlay cards and betting on athletic contests had been a common practice among the residents of Jefferson House, the home of many OU athletes. It was alleged that bets ranging from five to one hundred dollars had been placed. The writer said that a Sooner football player had distributed the cards during the 1950 season; however, he reported that betting had been commonplace as far back as 1948, when members of the football squad made an impressive amount of money betting on the Missouri game at Norman and the North Carolina game in the Sugar Bowl. On both occasions OU had been the underdog.

The story might not have attracted a great deal of attention except that a betting scandal had developed in the East during the past winter, when athletes at Long Island University and City College of New York had been accused of accepting bribes to influence the outcome of basketball games. The newspapers alleged that a jeweler named Salvatore Sollazzo, of New York City, had been involved. Before the scandal broke, OU's basketball team had made a trip east to play City College of New York. OU had won, something of an upset in view of the fact that City College was a past NCAA champion and a National Invitational Tournament champion.

Word got back to Norman that some of the OU players had accepted an invitation to visit Sollazzo in his apartment. This led to a rumor that Jim Terrell, a member of the Sooner squad, but not a starter, had been offered a bribe by Sollazzo. All of this was included in the betting story.

The situation on the campus was a little tense for the next few days while investigations were conducted. It was determined that parlay cards had indeed been seen on occasion in Jefferson

151

House but apparently had not been distributed regularly by any-one. There had been some side bets among the players on the outcome of certain games—especially point margins.

When we checked with Terrell about his visit with Sollazzo, he denied that he had been offered a bribe at any time; Sollazzo had merely said to him: "It's too bad you don't bet on games, because you could pick up some easy Christmas money." This might have been interpreted as an invitation to explore the matter further, but certainly it was not an offer of a bribe. Three other players who had gone with Terrell (Tom Churchill, Marcus Frie-burger and Doug Lynn) insisted that there had been no mention of bribes during the evening. There was no reason to believe that any OU player had received a bribe in connection with the game, which OU had won with an innovative offense that came to be known as the "Drake Shuffle" (named for Coach Bruce Drake). However, in the minds of some, there was the unhappy possibility that one or more of the City College athletes might have accepted a bribe to influence the outcome of the game, thus casting a cloud over the victory.

After receiving assurances from the Athletic Department that OU's athletes had been admonished not to bet on athletic con-tests and that reasonable precautions would be taken to prevent the distribution of parlay cards in Jefferson House, we decided to forget about the matter.

I had seen Wilkinson several times in February after our return from Muskogee. He had behaved oddly, appearing tense and re-served. Early in March he came to my office and announced rather tersely that he had decided to resign from OU and accept a position in public relations with a Texas company headed by Eddie Chiles, an alumnus of the university. He pointed out that resignation under these circumstances was not a violation of his contract, because it provided that, while he could not resign to accept another coaching position, he could resign to enter private business. Shortly afterward I received a letter from him in which he announced his resignation, effective at the conveni-ence of the university, but not later than "the close of the next football season."

Wilkinson's resignation posed a considerable problem. When

should it be effective? Because of his undoubted genius as a football coach, I was tempted to try to keep him through the 1951 season and possibly win another national championship. But I knew that the matter could not be kept secret and that, after it became known, his effectiveness at OU would be greatly reduced. Accordingly, it seemed best to make his resignation effective immediately and start the search for his successor.

It occurred to me that Wilkinson himself was probably the best source of advice on finding his successor. With this in mind, Mrs. Cross and I invited the Wilkinsons to pay us a farewell visit. After spending a few minutes together in the living room, Wilkinson and I went to the small library on the north side of the first floor, where a cheerful fire was burning in the fireplace. We talked for a while about the future of football at OU and his own future in the business world. He made several good suggestions about possible successors. But as he spoke, I sensed that he was not satisfied with what was happening—that he had at least mild misgivings about the prospect of leaving the university. When this dawned on me, I began trying to talk him out of resigning. I stressed the importance of what he was accomplishing at the university in ways other than winning football games. I mentioned the impact he had had on the personal development of the members of his football squad and the great respect of the faculty for the integrity of his program. I asked him whether, after his years of working with young athletes in such significant ways, he could find fulfillment as an employee of a business, where his sole responsibility would be improving profits for the corporation.

After a couple of hours Wilkinson announced that he had changed his mind: he would not resign. He suggested that we break the news to Mrs. Wilkinson.

Mrs. Wilkinson stared unbelievingly when her husband stood in the door and announced, "Mary, we're not leaving." She had just spent an evening explaining to Mrs. Cross why her husband had decided to leave OU. But she quickly recovered from her surprise and expressed her pleasure in the news.

As our guests left that evening, Wilkinson said, "Be sure to tear up my letter of resignation." I replied that I might keep it among other memorabilia but that I would not tell anyone about it. The next day I placed the letter in my scrapbook, where it still remains. The story is now shared with those interested in OU sports history.

In retrospect, the spring of 1951 was a time of an unusual number of minor crises. Scarcely had the uproar over betting died down when a new storm center developed over the televising of football games. In the few years since the first football game had been televised in Texas, the television industry had expanded greatly in the Southwest. E. K. Gaylord had put WKY-TV into operation on June 6, 1949. The success of the university's football team, along with the statewide interest this success aroused, made the telecasting of its games a highly popular program for Saturday-afternoon viewers. The first game was aired at Owen Field on October 1, 1949. During the 1950 season WKY-TV televised the university's five home games and paid the institution the impressive sum of three thousand dollars for the privilege.

But as television made its impact on the sports scene, those responsible for intercollegiate athletics became uneasy about the effect it might have on attendance at football games—gate receipts might decline. This uneasiness found tangible expression in the Southwest Conference after the 1949 season, when the members of the conference voted that there would be no live television of any game unless it was a sellout or a likely sellout a week ahead of time. The conference agreed that television movies could be filmed, but for showing only after 6:00 P.M. the day after the game. This action stimulated a vigorous reaction from newspapers in Texas; strongly worded protests appeared, including an unusually lengthy analysis on the editorial page of the *Fort Worth Star-Telegram* of May 23, 1950. OU officials and regents were concerned about what might be done in the Big Seven Conference and, more specifically, at the University of Oklahoma. But the NCAA relieved the conference and the university of responsibility for at least part of the decision when the members met at Dallas, Texas, early in 1951. The NCAA declared what amounted to a year's moratorium on the televising of football games, with the provision that a member institution could televise one home game and one game away from home, from September 22 to November 24, inclusive. There were no restrictions before or after those dates.

When the news got out early in March, 1951, that the OU football games would not be televised that fall because of the NCAA regulation, there was a flurry of protest throughout the state, especially in the area served by WKY-TV.

In the second week in March a bill to lift the ban on television and make the televising of football games mandatory at the University of Oklahoma and Oklahoma A&M College was introduced into the senate. Senator George Miskovsky of Oklahoma City was principal author of the bill. Fortunately, Senator Joe Smalley of Norman was on hand to request a committee hearing, so that officials of the university would have a chance to express their views. Miskovsky vigorously protested what he termed an effort to delay or kill the bill, with the following rather ingenious reasoning:

The state is composed of stockholders who are the citizens, and the senate and house are the board of directors with the governor as chairman. You ask the stockholders and 999 out of 1,000 will say "yes, let's televise the football games." Are we going to let one or two people at the university tell us what to do?"

Smalley countered with the suggestion that a simple resolution urging the institutions to televise might be a more effective weapon in getting the NCAA to lift its ban than a law that would compel them to do so.

The education committee of the senate met on March 14 to hear from university officials and from representatives of WKY-TV. Wilkinson and I represented the university, and P. A. Sugg, manager of WKY-TV, was there to represent his station. Wilkinson and I explained that the University of Oklahoma could not hope to retain membership in the NCAA unless it was willing to abide by association regulations. We described the possible consequences of expulsion from the association, stressing that such action would ruin the sports program at OU.

Miskovsky pooh-poohed this idea. He said, "I lay $1,000 on the table that the NCAA or Big Seven Conference won't throw the Big Red out of the conference." Wilkinson immediately replied, "I'll take that bet." At this somewhat tense moment I managed to get a laugh by reminding them of the betting scandal that had erupted earlier in the month. I suggested that there should be no betting between a member of the state senate and OU's football coach on any issue having to do with athletics.

Wilkinson and Sugg then exchanged comments. Wilkinson tried to explain that the NCAA moratorium on television had been an effort to protect small colleges that lie within the radius of major TV football screenings. "The NCAA is concerned with keeping the big institutions from becoming too big and building up the little ones," he said. But Sugg was unimpressed by this line of reasoning. He said that he had been watching Wilkinson's lips as he spoke of the smaller schools, and he could observe no expression of sympathy. He went on to inquire whether anyone had ever heard of coaches of big schools giving little ones a break. If Wilkinson wanted an athlete from Edmond High School, would he go after him, or would he try to steer him to Central State College? He then went on to suggest that Wilkinson had been shedding "crocodile tears" when he spoke of the problems of the smaller colleges.

Miskovsky then made a somewhat impassioned speech to the members of the committee about the responsibilities of the president of the university and the football coach to the people of Oklahoma. With glances in our direction he said that the president and the coach were "servants" of the people. He asked what our position would be if the senate should pass the pending legislation. Thinking that the time had come to be somewhat conciliatory, I said, "Whatever this legislature asks, I shall do—for obvious reasons." Wilkinson promptly followed with, "We're certainly going to do the will of the legislature at the University of Oklahoma."

The committee of the senate then voted to approve the resolution, rather than the bill, to be sent to the senate that afternoon.

After a stormy session in the afternoon—a session embellished with a lot of oratory, including a somewhat startling statement by Senator Paul Ballinger of Holdenville that if Oklahoma should be the first state to pass a law defying the NCAA "other states would get up on their hind legs and assert themselves"—the senate

156

voted 21–17 to reject the resolution but postponed action on the bill until Monday.

Driving back to Norman that afternoon, Wilkinson and I agreed that it would be a catastrophe if the senate bill was passed on Monday. We decided that it was time to get some help from the Big Seven Conference and possibly also from the NCAA. The next day (Friday, March 16) I called Reeves Peters, secretary of the conference, at his office in Kansas City and asked him to poll faculty representatives of the conference on what action would be taken if the University of Oklahoma should be compelled by state law to televise its home football games. Peters said that he would take the poll and have the results ready for me before the legislature went into session the following Monday. I then got in touch with George D. Small, of the University of Tulsa, a member of the NCAA executive council, and asked him for a statement concerning probable action of the NCAA if the proposed legislation was passed. Small gave me the following statement: "If any member institution is forced to violate the NCAA television policy because of action by their state legislature, such institution shall be required to resign from the NCAA and its resignation should be accepted without prejudice."

Reeves Peters completed his poll on Saturday and reported to me that the faculty representatives of the six other schools in the Big Seven Conference had voted unanimously by telephone to cancel athletic contests with the University of Oklahoma "if the university decides or is compelled to live televise its football games this fall." I gave Peters' report and Dr. Small's statement to Senator Smalley. He suggested that I should go to the capitol on Monday and give the information to the senate myself — a most unattractive prospect.

I arrived at the capitol building early on the morning of March 19, found a seat in the senate chamber, and waited for the membership to drift in.

I awaited my appearance before the membership with some apprehension, because I was almost sure that I would be accused of "rigging" matters with the conference and the NCAA — which, in effect, I had done. My report to the senate was indeed followed by a blast of indignation from several of the strong proponents

157

of the bill, but to my surprise none of the indignation was directed toward me; it was all against the NCAA and the Big Seven Conference. Senator Miskovsky and Senator Oliver Walker of Dale urged strongly that the legislature defy the NCAA and the conference, but cooler heads prevailed. Senator Boyd Cowden of Chandler, president pro tempore of the senate, made a strong statement that had a quieting effect on the turbulent group. He said:

> I'd say that it's a dictatorial attitude the members of the conference are assuming.
>
> The legislature is mindful of the fact that the university is a tax supported institute, and we feel like the people are entitled to have television if that is what they want.
>
> However, the legislature also is mindful of the plight we would put athletes and the university in, and we have no desire to do anything that would cripple the athletic or educational program. The final decision of the legislature will be made upon these premises.

After speeches by a dozen or more members of the senate, a motion was made to return the bill to the education committee for further study, and the motion passed by a vote of 25 to 13. Senator Smalley then introduced a resolution directing the regents and officials of the university to do everything possible to get the National Collegiate Athletic Association and the Big Seven Conference to lift the ban on television, and the resolution was approved.

But Senator Miskovsky, never one to acknowledge defeat, went down fighting with the announcement that he was sending all the information concerning the issue to H. G. Morrison, assistant United States attorney general in charge of investigation of violations under the Sherman Antitrust Law. When questioned later by the press, Morrison acknowledged receiving a communication from Miskovsky, and was quoted as saying that he had been "hearing about this" from other sources as well. But I have no evidence that his office did anything about the matter.

The basketball betting scandals in the 1950–51 season, and perhaps to a lesser extent the NCAA's moratorium on the televising of football games, focused the attention of the news media of the country on intercollegiate athletics, especially the "subsidizing" of athletes and the commercialization of sports. Perhaps the greatest effort to explore and report to the public was made by the *New York Times,* which published a series of six articles, beginning in the March 18, 1951, issue, on the impact of athletics in education. The author of the articles, Charles Grutzner, took the position that the situation in intercollegiate sports had deteriorated in many respects in the twenty-two years since the Carnegie Foundation for the Advancement of Teaching had published an exposé and condemnation of commercialism in college athletics.

The articles described conditions claimed to have been found in forty institutions of higher learning that had become prominent in intercollegiate athletics, especially in basketball and football. The University of Oklahoma was included among the forty. Its aid to athletes was described as follows:

Each scholarship provides free tuition and $55.00 a month for living expenses of which the student gives the university $40.00 for room and board. Married athletes get $75.00 a month.

Besides the largess from the Touchdown Club, which was distributed through official university channels, athletes pick up extra money by holding campus job sinecures. The job titles include janitorial services and grounds maintenance, but even the university president doesn't pretend they work at them during the playing season.

The report was accurate with respect to the amounts involved for a full athletic scholarship, but inaccurate in the statement that athletes picked up extra money by "holding campus job sinecures." I explored the situation carefully with Wilkinson and was convinced that, except for money a few athletes earned selling football programs, the players did not receive any money from the university over and above their scholarships. But I could find little or no evidence from questioning a somewhat reluctant Wilkinson that any of our athletes performed any work for the university in return for their scholarship stipends—a violation of the NCAA's regulations.

The *Times* articles marked the second time in less than a year that the news media had taken notice of what was going on in athletics at OU. In the October, 1950, issue of *True* magazine, Paul Gardner had written a lengthy—and highly exaggerated—

159

account of how OU's football program was financed. His article appeared under the title "Oklahoma and the Touchdown Club." The subtitle was: "How does a third-rate college football team suddenly become one of the best in the country? It isn't so tough —if there are 700 millionaires busy helping it along." Gardner reported that dues to the Touchdown Club were five hundred dollars a year for senior members and one hundred dollars a year for junior members, "plus added assessments whenever the need for them arises." He said that funds were available to persuade "hot shot school boys to enroll at Norman" and, after enrollment, for tuition, board, room, and incidental expenses— including "such needs as ice cream sodas, movies, dates and other physical and social requirements of a growing boy." Gardner also reported, accurately enough, that the same aid was available to all members of the squad, whether star halfback or unsung lineman. Wilkinson had indeed insisted that this must be the rule because he knew full well the damage that could develop from jealousies between ball carriers and blockers.

Completely erroneous, however, was the portion of Gardner's report alleging that Tatum had been forced to leave his coaching position at OU because of differences with members of the Touchdown Club. The club had not been organized until October, 1947, several months after Tatum's departure from the university.

Moreover, Gardner had grossly exaggerated the number of millionaires in Oklahoma. It is doubtful that seven hundred millionaires could have been found in the state of Texas, much less in Oklahoma.

CHAPTER 13

A National Championship—Football Losses— To Bowl or Not to Bowl?

1951–52

SOONER sports fans, highly enthusiastic about winning a national championship in football in the fall of 1950, probably gave little thought to the possibility of national championships in other sports that school year. But the wrestling and baseball teams, coached by Port Robertson and Jack Baer, were destined to come through and give OU its first, and to date only, three-sport win in NCAA competition.

While the winter and spring sports were in progress, Wilkinson and his staff were, as usual, making preparations for the 1951 football season. The spring practice sessions ended with the varsity-alumni game on April 21. The alumni won, 21–24, largely because of the appearance of such former stars as John Rapacz, Darrell Royal, Frankie Anderson, Leon Heath, and Lindell Pearson. But Wilkinson later expressed satisfaction with the performance of his squad. He told me he really didn't want his team to defeat the alumni. A victory might give them a false impression of their ability and make them less "coachable" in the fall. (It might also, incidentally, discourage the alumni, whom he hoped to attract back for future games.)

Early in the spring it occurred to me again that I should be considering the potential problem of a bowl game following the 1951 football season. I suggested to Wilkinson that we ask the regents to announce that the university would not participate in a bowl game at the end of the season, regardless of the team's record. Wilkinson did not share my concern. He commented by letter that "we should either state unequivocally that we will not play in bowl games or not alter our present policy." He went on: "It is my sincere belief that the record of our team in years ahead will not be sufficiently good to merit an invitation to play in a bowl game often enough to become a problem."

It seemed obvious that I would not receive much support from Wilkinson in my attempt to restrict OU's participation in post-

161

season games. And I had little confidence in his prediction that future teams would perform in such fashion as to eliminate the problem of too-frequent participation. I knew that he had and would maintain a superb coaching staff. In addition to Gomer Jones, Pop Ivy, and Bill Jennings from his staff of 1950, he had brought in Pete Elliott, winner of twelve sports letters at the University of Michigan, to replace George Lynn, who had resigned to go to Stanford University. Dee Andros, an outstanding guard from the 1949 Sooner squad, had been added as line coach.

Moreover, it seemed likely that Wilkinson would continue to recruit exceptional high-school athletes for his future squads. OU alumni living in the Southwest had been organized into a highly efficient recruiting operation. Many of these OU graduates had become successful in the oil industry and were in a position to exert marked influence on recruiting—influence that was to cause the university certain problems with the NCAA a little later.

It appeared to me that the whole matter of football could easily get out of hand. Fans were beginning to talk about OU leaving the Big Seven Conference for membership in the Southwest Conference which, except for the University of Arkansas, consisted of Texas institutions.

With these misgivings in mind, I proposed to the regents, at their meeting on March 14, that OU announce its decision not to take part in a postseason football game following the 1951 season. I did not ask for action at the meeting, only for informal discussion. The regents appeared generally sympathetic to the proposal, but I had the impression that a little pressure from OU fans at the proper time might change their minds.

Late in April the newspapers reported that Governor Murray had appointed Quintin Little, of Ardmore, to the OU Board of Regents to succeed Joe McBride, whose term had expired. Little, a native of Indian Territory who had attended Oklahoma Baptist University, had been an extremely successful independent oil operator in Ardmore since 1931. He was a most enthusiastic football fan, and I suspected that he would not have much patience with any idea of limiting the sport at the university.

The 1951 football season got under way at Norman on September 29 with William and Mary as the first opponent. A crowd of

162

approximately thirty-eight thousand, reported to be an all-time record for an opening game at Owen Field, was on hand to see how the reorganized Sooners would perform. The game was not much of a contest; Oklahoma won 49–7; Wilkinson used forty-four players, nineteen of whom had never played college football before—five freshmen and fourteen sophomores.

Perhaps the most impressive and encouraging aspect of the game was the blocking of the offensive line—center Tom Catlin, guards J. D. Roberts and Roger Nelson; tackles Jim Weatherall, Jim Davis, and Art Janes; and ends Hugh Ballard, Gene Ball, and John Reddell. But fullback Buck McPhail, Leon Heath's successor, ran well, gaining 65 yards on three attempts—one a 57-yard sprint for a touchdown. Frank Silva and Billy Vessels started at halfback, but Max Boydston, Larry Grigg, and Dick Heatly were also used at that position.

Quarterback Eddie Crowder's passing was effective—seven completions out of nine attempts for 141 yards. He was relieved later in the game by Jackie Ging, OU's 152-pound reserve quarterback. Jim Weatherall, in addition to playing very well at tackle, kicked a goal after each touchdown.

The coaching staff seemed pleased with the team's performance but were aware that errors by William and Mary early in the game had been a big factor; the Sooners ran up a 21–0 lead in less than eight minutes of play. The coaches knew that most of the opponents remaining on the schedule would not be as cooperative, especially the Texas teams on the itinerary the following two Saturdays. The first of these was Texas A&M College, in a game scheduled for October 6, at College Station.

The Texas Aggies were expected to be tough. They had had the finest rushing offensive in college football during the 1950 season, and essentially the same personnel were on hand in 1951. They had defeated the University of California at Los Angeles in their season's opener, and their fullback, Bob Smith, was an almost unanimous preseason favorite for All-America honors.

The game was played in the evening in extremely bad weather. A strong north wind, seasoned with intermittent showers, lashed the huddled crowd—everyone, that is, except the A&M students. That group, about seven thousand young men in cadet uniforms, stood throughout the game, cheering constantly; they maintained a high-pitched roar that, though it varied in intensity, never died out entirely until several minutes after the game in an Aggie victory—7–14. OU's one touchdown came as the first half ended, when Billy Vessels, after receiving a lateral from Eddie Crowder, ran 74 yards for the score. Time ran out as he was crossing the Texas 30-yard line.

The third opponent of the season, as usual, was the University of Texas. The sports writers generally favored Texas; the Steers were unbeaten in three outings, having defeated Kentucky, Purdue, and North Carolina. On the morning of the game, Texas was favored by six points. The margin turned out to be two points; the final score was Texas 9, OU 7. Two successive defeats so early in the season were discouraging; no Wilkinson-coached team had lost two games in a row, although the 1947 team had lost to Texas, tied Kansas, and lost to Texas Christian on successive weekends.

The coaching staff began making plans to salvage the season as the Big Seven competition approached. The problem in 1951 was obvious to those who had watched the first three games: that of getting the offense to play well consistently. The defense had been effective, except for an occasional lapse in punt coverage at critical times. But the offense had been erratic; it would look good for a few plays, and then a missed signal or a fumble would halt a drive, cause a turnover, or bring on a punting situation. Wilkinson analyzed the problem in his football letter of October 16, 1951: "A good football team is built on the work it does on Monday, Tuesday, Wednesday, and Thursday of each week of its fall season. Our team has been very ordinary on these days, and they haven't been able to make up for it on Saturday."

But the problem was solved pretty well before the opening conference game with Kansas on October 20, Dad's Day at Norman. In that game there was no sputtering on offense. Each time—five times in all—the Sooners pushed inside the Kansas 40-yard line, they went on to score. Especially significant was the team's poise—its ability to mount a scoring drive under pressure. There was pressure indeed early in the fourth quarter, when

164

Kansas took the lead 21–20. But OU received the kickoff on its own 46-yard line and launched its fourth touchdown march of the day. A few minutes later a fifth and final touchdown gave the Sooners a 33–20 victory. This come-from-behind effort may well have been the turning point of the season. It gave the team and the coaches the confidence to come from behind and win.

The game was memorable in that two of the OU backs rushed for a total of 336 yards. Buck McPhail carried the ball twenty times for a total of 215 yards, to set a new modern OU rushing record. In fifteen attempts Buddy Leake gained 121 yards. Billy Vessels did not play; he had strained a knee in the Texas game, and, as it turned out, he was to spend the rest of the season getting his knee back in shape for his final year of competition in 1952.

The OU offense remained effective for the rest of the season, and the Sooners had little difficulty with any of their remaining opponents—the closest score was their 34–20 win over the University of Missouri in a game played at Columbia—as they rolled to another conference championship.

The Big Seven champions finished tenth in the national poll. Jim Weatherall and Tom Catlin received All-America honors, and the Football Writers' Association of America awarded the Outland Trophy to Weatherall as the nation's outstanding tackle or guard.

As the 1951 season came to a close, there was the usual speculation that OU might participate in a postseason game, though the regents had on two or three occasions unofficially indicated that they did not favor a fourth successive bowl appearance. At their October meeting (from which Regents Shepler, Shartel, and Little were absent) they had voted against a bowl game that season, with instructions that Wilkinson was to be told of their decision after the Texas game. Officials of the Orange Bowl extended tentative feelers to Wilkinson for an appearance in Miami, with Georgia Tech as the opponent. It was a poorly kept secret that the coaching staff and the squad would welcome an opportunity to revisit Miami and try to wipe out the sting of the defeat suffered there against Tennessee more than ten years before. But, though the three absent members of the board might have favored participation in the Orange Bowl, the other members supported

The 1951 team. FIRST ROW (FRONT ROW), LEFT TO RIGHT: Larry Grigg, Harry Lee, Billy Bookout, Jack Ging, Eddie Crowder, Buck McPhail, Art Janes, Dick Bowman, Doc Hearon, Fred Smith, Billy Vessels. SECOND ROW: George Cornelius, Ed Sampson, Carl Allison, Jack Lockett, Hugh Ballard, John Reddell, Jerry Ingram, Dale Crawford, Roger Nelson, Dick Heatly, Jerry Wilkes, Jack Van Pool. THIRD ROW: Frank Silva, Sam Allen, Bob Gaut, Kurt Burris, Allie Robards, Jay Gaynor, Jennings Nelson, Bill Beckman, Jim Davis, Ross Ansburn, Dick Ellis, Bill Covin. FOURTH ROW: Gene Calame, Chet Bynum, Jack Santee, Max Boydston, Buddy Leake, J. D. Roberts, Ray Powell, Larry Cotton, Bert Clark, Ed Rowland, Jim Weatherall, Tom Catlin. Courtesy Sports Information Department.

my recommendation that OU should not compete, and the matter was finally dropped by the sports writers and fans, who turned their attention to the upcoming season.

The usual spring practice ended on April 5 with the annual varsity-alumni football game. Lost from the 1952 squad were such outstanding players as tackle Jim Weatherall and guard Bert Clark. But a number of promising players were on hand. Billy Vessels, fully recovered from his knee injury, ran well once again. For the third consecutive year the alumni came through with a win, 27–20, but the fans left the stadium with the feeling that the 1952 edition of Sooner football held promise.

CHAPTER 14

Some Administration Problems
1952

AFTER the 1951 season I had had several talks with Wilkinson about his future and the future of football at the university. Although he professed satisfaction with conditions at OU, I was never sure that he really intended to make his career at the university. He would occasionally express doubt about the value of what he was doing—whether a life spent coaching football could bring him fulfillment. He often mentioned the lack of security of those in his profession, the fickleness of fans, the pressure to win, and so forth. He addressed these themes in speeches he made across the state. He repeatedly warned that Oklahoma's bubble could burst; injuries to valuable players, such as Tom Catlin or Buck McPhail, could mean the loss of half or more of the games. He usually ended his commentary with the understatement that "undoubtedly this wouldn't please the alumni."

Wilkinson had two years left on his five-year contract. In obvious reference to that, he said in more than one public appearance that "sometimes it isn't too good business for a coach to move into the last season of his contract. It is mutually beneficial both to the school and coach to have a long-term agreement, thus assuring a stable situation." He would usually follow this comment with the suggestion that a short-term contract makes it too easy for disgruntled alumni to force the firing of a coach after one bad season. He would add that "a long term contract would spike the rumors of other offers" or of a coach's impending departure for another school.

It became clear to me that Wilkinson was worried about the prospect of a bad season in 1952 with only one more year to go on his contract. I had the same uneasy feeling about him that I had had earlier, just before he submitted his letter of resignation. Because I considered him an exceptional person quite apart from his expertise as a coach, I very much wanted to keep him at the university. Sometime in late January or early February I discussed with him the kind of arrangement that could be made to relieve his anxiety. He suggested a ten-year contract as athletic director and head football coach, with the right to retire as coach and continue as athletic director at a time of his choosing. He asked for a salary of fifteen thousand dollars a year—five thousand dollars as coach and ten thousand dollars as director of athletics.

At their meeting in February, I recommended to the regents that Wilkinson's five-year contract with the university be canceled by mutual consent and that a new contract be executed under the terms he had requested. The board, with Dr. Oscar White as chairman, unanimously approved the recommendation.

When informed of this action, Wilkinson asked us not to release the information about his changed status. He pointed out that the university does not announce changes in salaries of professors or administrative officials and said that he did not want to be singled out for special attention. Although he did not say so, I had the impression that he was concerned about possible faculty reaction to his salary increase. The regents rather reluctantly agreed to his request. They would have preferred to tell the public that they had done everything within reason to retain Wilkinson. I said that I too was somewhat opposed to withholding the information from the public, because I was certain that it could not be kept secret very long. I was wrong about that. The newspapers did not get the story until the middle of April, more than two months later. Reaction to the new contract was very favorable, but reaction to withholding the story was extremely critical. Casey Cohlmia commented in the May 1, 1952, edition of *Enid Events:*

The fact that a person as well known and highly regarded in his profession as Wilkinson has signed a ten year contract is NEWS whether Bud, Georgie, or Oscar think so or not. They owe it to the public, which pays through the nose in taxes and football tickets, to announce such information.

Several regents were disturbed by the swell of criticism, but they and their successors were to learn that football fans, and some sports writers, are inclined to regard the sport as belonging more to the public than to the university and to consider football more important than anything else that goes on in the institution. An increasing number of Oklahomans thought of the university primarily in terms of the "Big Red."

Early in 1952, Wilkinson talked with me about a problem involving new recruiting regulations passed during a meeting of the Big Seven Conference in December, 1951. The new rules, enacted perhaps partly in reaction to the recent basketball scandals, covered a number of points that had long needed attention, including a provision that athletes could receive athletic scholarships covering the cost of fees, tuition, and books, and would be permitted to earn an additional fifteen dollars a month.

Recruiting sessions with athletes off campus were prohibited, and, while athletes could be invited to visit the various institutions, their expenses for the trips could not be paid by the schools, the alumni, or fans. Furthermore, all postseason competition, including NCAA events, was eliminated.

On the whole, the new regulations were very positive steps forward by the conference, especially in their recognition that athletes could not earn all of their financial aid. I had been advocating such an awareness for more than three years. But the idea that an athlete would have time to earn fifteen dollars a month while participating in sports was, in my opinion, unrealistic.

Wilkinson was bothered most by the recruiting restrictions and the elimination of postseason games. The last would prevent Big Seven athletes from participating in Olympic competition.

Equally troublesome was the rule that prohibited coaches from talking with high-school athletes in their home towns. The Southwest Conference had no such regulation. That conference and other institutions in the area with which OU competed for athletes were operating under regulations of the American Council on Education, which permitted college coaches to talk to high-school athletes in their home towns but not to offer athletic scholarships. The ACE insisted that all scholarships, including those for athletes, must be administered by a committee of faculty members. Wilkinson was understandably upset by such handicaps. He suggested that he and his coaches should continue to make recruiting contacts despite the new regulations.

I did not tell Wilkinson that I had reported the problem to the OU regents at their meeting on December 13, 1951, immediately after the new rules were adopted. Regent Little had moved that "if the conference does not modify these regulations the University of Oklahoma will go independent," and his motion was passed unanimously by the five members present, Shepler, White, Benedum, Morgan, and Little (Regents Shartel and Foster were absent). But I did tell the worried coach that the matter would be on the agenda for the regents' meeting on January 9, 1952.

When the board met in January, all the members were present except Benedum. After discussion of the controversial rule, it was agreed that the chairman of the board should appoint a committee to confer with Wilkinson about whether the university could get satisfactory schedules in football and other sports if it withdrew from the conference. Regents White, Foster, and Little were named to the committee, and they agreed to report back to the board at the February meeting.

After conferring with Wilkinson, the committee came to the February meeting with contradictory reports about his attitude on withdrawing from the conference. Regent White, the committee chairman, thought Wilkinson had said, "If they insist on enforcing the rules, we should pull out." But Regent Foster reported a rather different interpretation: "I believe it was Bud's thought that we should not pull out from the Big Seven but that we should tell them we would abide by the rules of the Southwest Conference, inasmuch as our competition is there."

After the report I recommended that our faculty representative, Walter Kraft, be instructed to tell the faculty representatives of the conference that the new regulations on recruiting and participation in events authorized by the NCAA were not acceptable to the university and that OU would operate under the regulations of the Southwest Conference unless the rules were changed and leave it to the conference to decide the question of OU's continued membership in the Big Seven. My recommendation was approved unanimously.

There were two changes in the membership of the board that spring: Kent Shartel died on February 21, and Governor Murray appointed George Short, of Oklahoma City, to succeed him. Ned Shepler's term expired in March, 1952, and Joe McBride was appointed to fill the vacancy.

The next meeting of the faculty representatives of the conference was convened at the end of February in Kansas City, Missouri. At that session Kraft, following instructions from the regents, tried hard to get the restrictive regulations modified but without success. When he returned to Norman and reported to me, I called the presidents of the six member institutions and explained that OU could not accept the regulation that restricted coaches from making contacts with promising athletes and that we would follow the rules of the Southwest Conference. With one or two exceptions the presidents were sympathetic and indicated that no action would be taken to expel Oklahoma from the conference. However, both Chancellor Murphy, of the University of Kansas, and President McCain, of Kansas State University, suggested that possibly the presidents of the Big Seven institutions should meet with the faculty representatives to discuss the issue. McCain offered to make the arrangements for a meeting, and Murphy agreed to serve as "a sort of clearing house for possible items" to be included on the agenda.

In the meantime, reports of activity by the American Council on Education and the North Central Association of Colleges and Secondary Schools in the regulation of intercollegiate athletics caused concern in Big Seven circles. Clearly a joint meeting of the faculty representatives and presidents was needed. After the basketball scandals of the 1950–51 season the ACE had become interested in the problem, and after a thorough study had made several recommendations in a statement dated February 15, 1952. One suggestion, a sensible one, was that athletic as well as academic ability might be taken into consideration when scholarships were awarded. But the ACE suggested also that the six regional accrediting agencies accept the responsibility of policing intercollegiate athletics for the institutions within their jurisdictions. Only one of the regional accrediting agencies, the North Central Association of Colleges and Secondary Schools, accepted that responsibility.

Unfortunately, the North Central Association disagreed with

the ACE that athletic ability might be taken into consideration when scholarships were awarded. The association strongly opposed providing financial aid related in any way to athletic ability and announced, at a meeting held on April 7, 1952, that the prohibition would become effective September 1, 1952. The announcement was received with consternation by the athletic conferences (especially the Big Seven and Big Ten) within the association's jurisdiction. It was apparent that these institutions would be seriously handicapped in competing for athletic talent with institutions that were not members of the North Central Association.

With this added problem now to be considered efforts were made to expedite the joint meeting of the faculty representatives and the presidents of the Big Seven. The meeting was called for 5 P.M. on April 24 at the Muehlebach Hotel in Kansas City.

Somewhat to my surprise, all the presidents showed up for the meeting (Charles E. Friley, of Iowa State College; James A. McCain, of Kansas State College; R. L. Stearns, of the University of Colorado; Franklin Murphy, of the University of Kansas; F. A. Middlebush, of the University of Missouri; R. G. Gustavson, of the University of Nebraska; and I). All but one or two of the faculty representatives were there, and they had sent substitutes.

Early in the meeting I described in detail the problems of the University of Oklahoma in trying to compete for athletes handicapped as we were by Big Seven regulations that prohibited our coaching staff from talking with high-school athletes. I objected also to the regulation prohibiting OU athletes from participation in Olympic competition. I ended by reporting that the regents had instructed the Athletic Department to operate in what amounted to open violation of the Big Seven regulations. Curiously enough, those present did not seem greatly disturbed by OU's rebellious attitude and instead wanted to talk about the NCA's new regulation that after September 1, 1952, athletic ability could not be taken into consideration in awarding scholarships.

It was agreed that if the NCA enforced this edict, athletic programs in the north-central area would deteriorate, but it was recognized that the association was in a good position to enforce any regulation, because it controlled the accreditation of all the institutions within its jurisdiction. After lengthy discussion it appeared to be the consensus of the presidents and the faculty representatives that, since their institutions were members of the NCA and intended to remain in good standing with the association, each institution, through its organization responsible for intercollegiate athletics, would determine what actions it must take to comply with the new policy and be prepared to report at a later meeting. It was decided also that the conference should attempt to persuade the ACE to assume leadership in the development of a uniform code of principles to be used by the several accrediting agencies of the country.

Near the end of the meeting we decided that the Big Seven Conference should meet twice a year, once in the summer and once in the winter, and that the next such meeting would be held in June—a one-day meeting in Boulder, Colorado. The details of future meetings were to be worked out by Reeves Peters, executive secretary of the conference.

Information about the Kansas City meeting leaked to the press the following week, and early in May several articles appeared suggesting that OU's defiance of a portion of the conference regulations was the first step in a withdrawal from the Big Seven, the next step being to seek admission to the Southwest Conference. While most of this was wishful thinking by some alumni and football fans, official thought had indeed been given to seeking admission to the Southwest Conference. Wilkinson told me privately on several occasions that he thought there would be many advantages in making the change. Regent Little made a strong effort to promote the move at several board meetings. At the February 13, 1952, meeting he reported that he had talked with several OU alumni in Texas, all of whom had urged that OU try to make the change. Declaring, "That is what Bud wants," Little moved that a committee be appointed to study the matter of transferring to the Southwest Conference. The motion passed unanimously.

As I reflected on the events of the past few weeks, I decided that the University of Oklahoma had got off track in defying the regulations of its conference. With the much more strict regulations of the NCA that were to become effective on September 1, it seemed to me that OU should not jeopardize its position in the academic world by refusing to abide by conference regulations, however distasteful they might be. Accordingly, at a meeting of the regents on May 14, 1952, I recommended that "the University of Oklahoma immediately comply with the regulations of the Big Seven Conference and announce publicly that it will do so." Evidently the regents had also had second thoughts. My recommendation was approved unanimously.

The board took up another matter related to athletics—one that later became a problem complicated by political overtones— the matter of the concessions at the OU football games. McClure's Concessions, Inc., had operated the stadium concessions for a number of years. The facilities had deteriorated, and the fans were critical of the service and of the appearance and lack of cleanliness of those who sold food and drinks at the games. Improvements were needed.

After several conferences with Wilkinson, Kenneth Farris, and Roscoe Cate, I decided to recommend to the regents that the Athletic Department make whatever permanent improvements were needed in the concession facilities, using reserve funds for the purpose, and that McClure's be asked to increase the annual commissions paid to the university by 10 per cent of the cost of the improvements. The regents approved the recommendation unanimously.

I then suggested to the board that within the next year or so the Athletic Department take over the management of concessions at all athletic events on campus and hire students as salesmen. The regents seemed unanimous at the time in tacitly approving the idea, but some were to change their minds later.

The Big Seven Conference met as scheduled on June 30, 1952. The feeling of the group appeared to be that the conference could not live with the NCA's restrictive regulations. It was decided to give special attention to the somewhat more liberal statement of the ACE, and the faculty representatives were asked to prepare a summary of points where the conference rules and policies diverged from those of the ACE. They were then instructed to develop a proposed revision of conference rules and regulations that would be based on the recommendations of the

ACE—a revision that would be as realistic and workable as possible.

It was decided also that the conference should follow through on efforts to persuade the ACE to take steps to harmonize its recommendations with those of the several regional accrediting agencies. Presidents Stearns and Gustavson were named to serve as a committee to meet with the ACE in an effort to reach that goal. Stearns and Gustavson received a sympathetic reception from the ACE, but since the other accrediting agencies had not accepted jurisdiction over athletics in their regions, the problem appeared to boil down to reconciling the conflicting regulations of the ACE and the NCA.

CHAPTER 15

Another Bowl Decision—More on Aid to Athletes

1952

THE Sooners approached the 1952 football season with changed eligibility requirements: freshmen could no longer play in varsity competition because of action taken by the NCAA the preceding April.

The season opened on September 27 with the University of Colorado at Boulder. The Sooners were somewhat less than impressive that day; they lost the ball six times on fumbles, and had to come from behind late in the fourth quarter with a do-or-die touchdown drive to gain a 21–21 tie.

Things went better the next week against the University of Pittsburgh in a game played at Norman. Oklahoma won 49–20. The Sooner offense performed well, rushing for 326 yards and passing for 95. But, as Wilkinson pointed out after the game, the defense was spotty. Many of the boys played well in their own areas but were slow in recovering and supporting when the play went "someplace else"—not good pursuit. As a result, Pittsburgh was able to mount three touchdown drives of 63, 45, and 52 yards. The coaches needed to work on developing greater consistency in the defense. Superb defensive efforts by Doc Hearon, Tom Catlin, and Ed Rowland were evidence that the ingredients for a strong defensive team were present. Each came through with defensive spectaculars that led to touchdowns. On the whole the Sooner coaches were pleased with the team's performance. But they were cautious about the game with Texas the following week. Wilkinson wrote in his football letter: "We must practice hard this week for Texas, which will be on the upsurge after losing a hard-fought game to Notre Dame. Although our defense needs the most work we've got to improve at everything."

As things turned out, any apprehension about the outcome of the annual classic with Texas proved groundless. With less than eleven minutes gone in the first quarter, the Sooners had four touchdowns to their credit, and the score was 28–0. The nearly seventy-six thousand stunned fans stared in disbelief as quarterback Eddie Crowder put on a sleight-of-hand exhibition that kept everyone, including officials and cameramen, in doubt about the location of the football. His favorite maneuver was to receive the pass from center, fake to fullback McPhail, and then retreat with the ball tucked between his left hip and elbow, apparently watching McPhail try to make yardage through the line. When the defense had converged on McPhail, Crowder would pull the ball from his hip and throw a pass, frequently to John Reddell or Buddy Leake. McPhail carried out his part of the fakery in superb fashion. He seemed to run harder and put forth more convincing effort when he did not have the ball than when he was carrying it.

But despite what appeared to be an almost hopeless situation, the Texas team did not quit. In the second quarter they mounted a 74-yard touchdown drive and kicked the extra point. Later in the same quarter they blocked a punt and recovered the ball on the OU 29-yard line. From there they drove to within one yard of a second touchdown, where they were held for downs. The half ended with OU leading 28–7. The third quarter was scoreless, but in the final period a scoring bonanza produced a total of five touchdowns, three by OU and two by Texas. The final score was 49–20.

It had been another great afternoon for the OU offense. McPhail had rushed for 147 yards, Vessels for 106, and Leake for 75. Leake was the leading ground gainer; he caught three passes for 75 yards, giving him a total of 150 yards. John Reddell received two of Crowder's passes for a total of 58 yards.

OU football players, coaches, and fans were in a jubilant mood that evening as they journeyed northward across the Red River to home territory. But the squad and coaches had only a brief time to enjoy the memories of their performance. Attention must be given to the upcoming game with the University of Kansas, to be played the following Saturday at Lawrence.

The Kansas team, coached by Jules Sikes, had compiled an impressive record: nine consecutive victories, including a 21–12 win over Colorado, the team that had tied OU at Boulder. While

OU was playing Texas, Kansas had been busy walloping Iowa State by a score of 43–0. Wilkinson, whose coaching success was due in no small measure to his effective use of psychology in dealing with his squad, was quick to bring KU's record to the attention of the players and fans. He predicted that a "terrific" game was in prospect.

His forecast turned out to be accurate. The Kansas team was keyed up for the occasion and played OU pretty much on even terms during the first half, which ended 21–13.

Early in the third period the Jayhawks launched an 81-yard drive for a touchdown and kicked goal, reducing OU's margin to one point—21–20. On the next series of plays McPhail, lunging to receive a Crowder pass, had the misfortune to deflect the ball into the hands of a Kansas defender on the OU 40-yard line. After two successful pass completions, the ball rested on the Sooner 13.

I remember sitting in the stands, about fifteen rows up, with the line of scrimmage directly in front of me, thinking that if the Kansans were able to push the ball across for a touchdown they would probably gain enough momentum to win the game. This was the turning point. With first and 10 on the OU 13, the Kansas quarterback gave the ball to talented halfback Charley Hoag, who broke through the OU line and headed for the end zone. But Tom Catlin, seeming to come from nowhere, dropped him on the OU 6 for a 7-yard gain. The touchdown had been averted, but the little group of OU fans around me could take little comfort, because coming up was second down and only 3 yards to go. On the next play Kansas gained only a yard before Bo Rowland dropped the ball carrier with a jarring tackle. With third down and 2 to go, Catlin seemed to take full responsibility for stifling the Kansas offense. He moved with a lunge as the ball was snapped, shot through the gap, and dropped the quarterback for a 5-yard loss. I had a great view of this defensive maneuver, and I consider it one of the best plays I have ever seen. On the fourth down, from the OU 10-yard line, the Kansas quarterback threw a pass, but the fired-up Catlin diagnosed the play accurately, sprinted laterally to the rear, and knocked the ball out of play.

OU's great defensive stand seemed to take much of the fight

179

out of the Kansas team. On the next three possessions Crowder engineered three touchdown drives of 90, 73, and 55 yards, and the final score was 42–20.

The next week Wilkinson wrote in his football letter:

I've never been more pleased with a team victory than I was with this one. Kansas is a great football team. All the blue chips were on the table Saturday—national rankings and conference championships were at stake. Our Oklahoma team rose to the heights the occasion demanded and came through to victory.

But, with typical Wilkinson caution, he went on to say: "We will have to fight for our lives each remaining Saturday of the season because each of our opponents will be keyed to play their best game of the year against us."

Actually the two following games were little more than pleasant outings for the Sooners. They defeated Kansas State at Norman on October 25 by a score of 49–6. The following week they ran over Iowa State at Ames by a margin of 41–0. Perhaps the most memorable event in the Iowa State game was when Leake *missed* a try for point after a touchdown; he had kicked twenty-eight consecutive extra points before that miss. Counting Jim Weatherall's contributions of the preceding season, the OU string of consecutive points after touchdowns had reached thirty-five.

Preparations began the following Monday for the long-awaited date with Notre Dame. The squad was in reasonably good physical condition. The Fighting Irish had a splendid football team and, as usual, were in contention for national honors.

Mrs. Cross, our son, Bill, and I flew to South Bend on Friday, November 7, with Bill Warren and his family, of Tulsa, Oklahoma. That evening we attended a dinner given by the Reverend Theodore M. Hesburgh, who was beginning his first year as president of Notre Dame.

The next afternoon the weather was clear, coolish, and with only a slight wind. A record crowd of 57,466 fans pressed into the Notre Dame stadium to see the game, and perhaps 20 million more waited to watch the play-by-play telecast by Mel Allen.

My family and I shared box seats with the Notre Dame party, including Father Hesburgh. Behind us was the Notre Dame faculty, impressive and somewhat sobering in their black habits. As we awaited the opening kickoff, I had an opportunity to discuss with Father Hesburgh some of the problems in the administration of intercollegiate athletics, especially the two that seemed most pressing to me, eligibility regulations and aid to athletes.

Not much of interest happened during the first twelve minutes of the game; each defensive unit was able to contain the opponent's offense, and it looked as if a great defensive battle might be in prospect. But late in the first quarter, with the ball on Notre Dame's 27-yard line, Eddie Crowder, in a manner reminiscent of his performance during the OU-Texas game, faked a pass-off to Buck McPhail so convincingly that the unfortunate Mc-Phail was immediately swarmed by at least half of the Notre Dame defensive unit. With the ball concealed between his left hip and elbow, Crowder watched the pileup and then flipped a pass to Billy Vessels, who was waiting in the left flat zone. Vessels caught the ball and streaked down the sideline to score, almost before the Notre Dame team realized that McPhail did not have the ball. Leake kicked the goal, and the Sooners went into the second quarter leading 7–0.

Midway through the second quarter Notre Dame recovered an OU fumble (the first of five) on their own 40-yard line. In nine plays they drove 60 yards for a touchdown. The try for the extra point was successful, and the score was 7–7.

Two minutes later OU regained the lead when Vessels, aided by perfect blocking by Jim Davis, Max Boydston, and Dick Bowman, slipped through the line, cut quickly to the outside, and streaked 62 yards for his second touchdown. Again Leake kicked goal, and the Sooners led 14–7.

Just before halftime, J. D. Roberts, OU's excellent guard, was jolted from behind by a Notre Dame player after a play had ended. He instinctively threw an elbow around in an apparent attempt to catch his opponent on the side of the head. He missed, but an official who had not seen the beginning of the altercation, expelled Roberts from the game. Lost also for the second half was Ed Rowland, the 225-pound tackle, who had been injured during the second quarter.

Early in the third quarter, following an intercepted pass, Notre Dame tied the score at 14–14. But it took OU only three plays to regain the lead. The first two of these were handoffs to Mc-Phail and Vessels, each of whom carried for a 5-yard gain. In an apparent effort to stop the powerful rushing attack, the Notre Dame defense moved into an eight-man line. Crowder, who had called a handoff to Vessels straight ahead in the huddle, noted the line and checked signals, changing the play to a pitchout to Vessels around right end. Vessels took the pitchout at full speed, and when McPhail took the Notre Dame end out of play with a tremendous block, he was able to turn downfield along the side-line. Then, after eluding some tacklers and outrunning others, he cut back to the inside and crossed the goal line for his third touchdown—a 47-yard run. Leake succeeded in his third try for point of the afternoon, and OU led 21–14, with 4:35 to go in the third period.

Notre Dame countered with a bruising 79-yard drive that ended in a touchdown a few seconds after the opening of the fourth quarter. The try for point was good, and for the third time Notre Dame had come from behind to tie the score at 21–21. Then came the turning point of the game.

Notre Dame kicked off to OU, and Larry Grigg received the ball somewhere within the 20-yard line. He started upfield, but after gaining almost full speed, he was met head on by a Notre Dame tackler named Dan Shannon. Both players were stunned by the collision, and Grigg lost the ball to a Notre Dame player on OU's 25-yard line. Shannon was carried from the field and did not return. From OU's 25-yard line Notre Dame was able to score in four plays. The first of these carried to the OU 7. The second involved a so-called sucker shift, during which the Notre Dame offense shifted in such fashion as to suggest the beginning of a play, causing the Sooner defensive line to lunge offside. After the penalty was assessed, Notre Dame had a first down on the OU 2. The Sooner forwards held the Notre Dame fullback for a 1-yard gain, but the next play brought a touchdown, and the Fighting Irish went into the lead for the first time. Larry Grigg slipped through to block the try for extra point, however, and the score stood 21–27. OU could still win the game by scoring another touchdown and extra point during the remaining 13:20.

The Sooners had three opportunities to do so, but each time

Billy Vessels, whose performance in the 1952 OU-Notre Dame game won him the Heisman Trophy. Courtesy Sports Information Department.

their drive fizzled short of the goal line. Notre Dame was the winner, and OU's chances for a second national championship had gone down the drain.

It had been a very physical contest, characterized by consistently rugged blocking and savage tackling. Sports writers throughout the nation described it as one of the greatest football games ever played. Statistically, the Sooners outgained the Fighting Irish on the ground, 313 yards to 219, but lost the aerial battle, 135 to 44.

Billy Vessels had chosen an opportune time to stage what surely was the finest performance of his career. He carried the ball seventeen times and gained 195 yards, including three carries for touchdowns. He played with an abandon seldom seen in any athletic contest. Whenever he saw that there was no way of avoiding a tackler, he would throw himself forward to a horizontal position, using his body as a sort of projectile to gain additional yardage. His great playing convinced the nation's leading sportswriters that he should receive the Heisman Trophy, and he was selected for the honor two or three weeks later.

The following week Wilkinson wrote in his football letter:

I believe the story of the contest is wrapped up in the physical element. Football is a hard, tough driving game. Notre Dame was able to play tougher physically. They beat us with their superiority in this phase of the game. Only one of our fumbles was mechanical. On the others, Notre Dame just knocked us loose from the ball. A lot of people criticize that kind of football, but they aren't justified in doing so. The willingness to hit harder than the other fellow, to go all out for something you want and believe in is one of the great lessons of the game.

As the crowd poured out of the stadium, I visited both dressing rooms with Father Hesburgh and a few other members of the Notre Dame party. No one could have been more gracious in victory than Father Hesburgh and Frank Leahy, a fellow South Dakotan. Leahy was generous in his praise of several of the Oklahoma players but naturally singled out Vessels for special attention; he said that Vessels certainly would win the Heisman Trophy that year. He invited Mrs. Cross and me to his home for dinner that evening, but Father Hesburgh assured me after we had left the dressing room that Mrs. Cross and I would be "more comfortable" at a dinner he had planned for a few guests. I suspect he was right. In any event, we were treated so tactfully that evening by the good father and his associates that much— though not all—of the sting of defeat was removed.

After the meeting of the Big Seven Conference presidents and faculty representatives on June 30, 1952, each school had been, in effect, left on its own to cope with the problem of athletic subsidy within the limits of the regulations. The institutions decided independently to continue awarding aid to athletes on the basis of athletic ability, and when this became apparent, President Middlebush, of the University of Missouri, sent a letter to

184

the NCA stating that no school in the Missouri Valley Conference was abiding by the rules of the association. In response the presidents of the seven schools received from the association stern letters expressing surprise and disapproval. When I returned to my office after the Notre Dame game, my letter, signed by Manning M. Patillo, Jr., associate secretary of the association, was on my desk. It read in part:

If, as President Middlebush implies, the University of Oklahoma has rejected the conception of inter-collegiate athletics as an amateur, educational activity, this would, of course, be a matter of serious concern to the commission. The revised clear and specific criterion on subsidization which reads in part as follows: "Since colleges and universities exist to educate students, and not to sponsor athletic contests or entertain the public, the subsidization of athletes is disapproved. By this statement the commission means quite literally that the possible contribution a student can make to the winning of athletic contests should not be taken into consideration at all in the granting of financial aid of any kind."

Before the Board of Review considers the possibility of authorizing a comprehensive investigation of the University of Oklahoma, it would like to receive from you a full statement on the present policy of the University with respect to financial aid to athletes.

Pondering the letter, I thought I could see real trouble in the offing. I included the letter in a report to the regents on November 13, 1952. Some regents shared my concern about possible difficulty with the NCA, but others, especially Regent Little, were inclined to take the matter lightly. It was agreed that the university had no choice but to make a report of its athletic situation to the association and then cooperate with other larger universities in the north-central region in an effort to convince the officials of the association that the regulations were unrealistic — that they would place the north-central institutions at a crippling recruiting disadvantage.

After introducing Patillo's letter, I told the regents that there had been talk statewide that the university might change its policy and accept a bid to play in a bowl game. I suggested that pressure to do this would surely develop if OU should win the Big Seven championship. I reviewed the action taken at the May meeting and warned the regents that there might be difficulty ahead, because I had heard that the football team and coaches wanted very much to play a postseason game. I told the board that the problem was intensified in that, if things went well for the remainder of the season, OU might receive invitations to all postseason bowls except the Rose Bowl. I reminded them that, after their May meeting, it had been announced that OU would abide by conference regulations and that these regulations prohibited postseason contests.

In the discussion that followed, it became obvious that several of the regents had changed their minds about the bowl restriction. They now took the position that if the team and coaches wanted to play in a bowl game they should be allowed to do so. I then asked if they would permit the team to play in a bowl game even if it meant that Oklahoma would be dropped from the Big Seven Conference. It would take the votes of five institutions to discipline a member school, but I had little doubt that five of the six would do so if there was any extensive violation of conference regulations.

My argument had little impact. Almost immediately Regent Little moved that "the playing of a bowl game be left to Coach Wilkinson and his staff and the boys." Regent Short seconded the motion, and six members of the board voted in favor. Only Regent McBride voted no.

I was surprised and depressed by the action. It seemed dangerously close to permitting a football program to determine basic university policy. If that could happen in this situation, it could happen in the determination of other policy. I was also disturbed that the regents had taken important action without a recommendation from the president; this seemed a dangerous precedent. I decided not to protest at the moment, however, but to await a more favorable time to try to get the board back on the right track in its decision making.

After Notre Dame three games remained on its schedule, the University of Missouri at Norman on November 15 (Dad's Day), Nebraska at Norman the following week (Homecoming), and the season's windup with Oklahoma A&M. Missouri was defeated handily by a score of 47–7, and Nebraska fell 34–13. The outcome of the final game with Oklahoma A&M was in doubt only momentarily, when Bill Bredde, A&M halfback, returned the opening kickoff 98 yards for a touchdown. But the successful try for point following his caper was the last bit of scoring the Aggies could muster. OU went on to win 54–7.

The blazing three-game windup of the season naturally led to increased pressure for a postseason game. The students had begun promoting it during the Missouri game, when shouts of, "Let's go south!" emerged from the student section of the stadium. The next day, Sunday, I had received several calls at home urging me to take steps either to persuade the conference to lift its ban on postseason contests or to accept a bid anyway and take the consequences. The calls were from students, fans, and alumni from within and out of the state.

On Monday, November 17, I called the president of the board, Dr. Oscar White, of Oklahoma City, and told him about the weekend pressure. We discussed the possible consequences of announcing publicly the action taken by the regents on November 13—that the decision would be left to Coach Wilkinson, his staff, and the players. Since the regents had taken this action, Dr. White saw no alternative but to follow it.

I called Wilkinson and asked him and the squad to consider the matter and vote on it as soon as possible. Wilkinson agreed, but with obvious reluctance. He said he thought it unwise "to base a policy decision of such magnitude on the vote of a group of young students, most of them scarcely out of their teens." But he went on to predict that, after the issue had been made clear to the team, the members would vote not to accept a bowl game if it meant endangering the university's affiliation with the Big Seven Conference.

Wilkinson called the players together on Wednesday, November 19, and explained the situation to them. Then he left the room so that the boys could discuss the problem in privacy and conduct their own voting. After the meeting Eddie Crowder, the co-captain, reported the team's decision: "The team wants to go, naturally, but we don't think the team should make such an important decision affecting the school and the conference. The rules should be changed. We'd like to go, but the decision should not be in our hands." The voting, he said, had been unanimous. Thus the athletes quite properly passed the decision back to the Board of Regents, where it belonged.

In the meantime, the regents, aware that they must take some action regardless how the vote turned out, had arranged to meet in special session the following morning, Thursday, November 20. Regents White, Benedum, Short, Morgan, and Little were present for the session; Foster and McBride were not able to come. They asked Wilkinson to report on the team's attitude. He said that the boys would like very much to play in a bowl game but did not want to do anything that would "jeopardize the athletic program or in any way be against the best interests of the university." Finally Regent Morgan moved that, "since we have always followed the regulations of the conference to which we belong, we shall continue to do so." When the vote was called, all the members voted aye except Regent Little, who asked to be recorded as voting no.

Morgan's motion settled the question whether the OU football team would play in a bowl game, but it led speedily to another question: Could the team be sent to a bowl game as spectators? This possibility was suggested by Regent Little and received quick support from Regent Short. I protested that that would be in violation of the regulations of both the conference and the NCAA prohibiting gifts of any kind to athletes. But to my surprise Wilkinson disagreed. He said that he did not think that sending the team to Miami would violate conference or NCAA regulations. While the regents took no action that day, it was clear that all of them supported the idea of a holiday junket for the team.

The regents' decision to let the team and coaches decide whether to accept a bowl bid led to an extraordinary amount of unfavorable publicity, both local and national. I received a veritable flood of clippings—critical articles and editorials from major newspapers. Most of them were accompanied by caustic comments about the deterioration of judgment and ethics in the administration of the university. I was blamed for the decision to let the football team vote on the playing in a bowl game. Writers generally took the position that the regents had referred the problem to the president of the institution, and he in turn had referred it to the coach and team, called by one sports writer "adroit buck-passing which backfired."

My multiple frustrations were eased somewhat late in November, when the more than twelve hundred sports writers and sportscasters of the nation voted Billy Vessels winner of the 1952 Heisman Memorial Trophy. The Downtown Athletic Club of New York invited Wilkinson, Gomer Jones, and me to be guests for the award banquet on December 2. The trip to New York allowed me to put aside temporarily the worrisome problems of the president's office. We stayed in the New York Athletic Club, where we enjoyed excellent food, steam baths, and relaxing rubdowns. The dinner on December 2 was a big success in every way. Vessels made a splendid response when the Heisman Trophy was presented to him. He captivated his audience and received a standing ovation following his appropriate remarks of appreciation, wherein he referred especially to his teammates, the coaches, and the university.

Shortly after I returned from New York, Walter Kraft, OU's faculty representative to the Big Seven Conference, discussed with me the instructions he had received from Quintin Little, chairman of the regents' committee studying the possibility of transferring to the Southwest Conference. Little told Kraft that the faculty representatives of the Southwest Conference would meet on December 12, and the committee wanted him to attend the meeting and explore the possibility of being invited to join the conference. Kraft told me that both he and Wilkinson were opposed to changing conferences but that the regents' committee nevertheless wanted to explore the possibility. Little suggested to Kraft that he might talk with the conference members off the record and thus avoid publicity. We both knew from past experience that this would be impossible, but Kraft followed instructions and went to Dallas for the December 12 meeting.

Several Texas reporters got word of what had happened, and the following day the university received another blast from the news media. But there was one favorable result: Kraft was treated courteously at the meeting, but it was made clear to him that entrance into the conference was by invitation only and that conference officials had on several occasions successfully re-sisted pressure to issue invitations to other schools, even some Texas schools—especially the University of Houston and Texas Technological College at Lubbock. The Texans were not likely to respond favorably to pressure exerted by OU alumni living in their state.

Soon afterward Wilkinson again took up with me the possibility of sending the OU team to the Orange Bowl as spectators. He spoke of the team's disappointment at not being able to play in a bowl game, and he stressed his pride in the good judgment they had used when they voted on the postseason contest. He said that it would cost only a little over ten thousand dollars to send the team to Miami, and he asked me to request of the regents an increase in the travel budget of the Athletic Department to pay for the trip. I told him again that I thought the trip would be a violation of conference regulations. He said that, as he interpreted the rules, there would be no violation and asked me again, with a slight note of impatience, if I would present the request to the board. I agreed to do so, but I told him that I would warn the board that a violation of regulations would surely be involved.

A day or so later I received a letter from Kenneth Farris with an itemized list of the expenses for the trip. The total amount was $10,463, and Farris asked for a supplement to the travel budget in that amount. I placed Farris' request on the agenda for the December 11 meeting but also attached a list of the specific Big Seven Conference regulations that would be violated if the football team was sent to Miami. I ended the list with the statement that "this information is submitted to you, not with the thought that we should at this late date prohibit the football squad from making a trip to see a bowl game, but to place on record the information I presented to you orally when the board met last."

When the regents assembled on December 11, they faced the dilemma of having, in effect, contradicting recommendations from the Department of Athletics and the Office of the President. After considering their problem for some time, Regent Benedum moved that "the communication of President Cross, under date of December 9, be made a matter of record in the minutes of this meeting, and that the letter from Kenneth Farris, itemizing the expenses of the team to the Orange Bowl game, and requesting an allocation of $10,463 as a supplement to the travel budget of the athletic department, be approved." However, Regent Mc-Bride, worried about the situation, requested that the vote on the motion be delayed until after lunch. He thought that, since Wilkinson and Kraft had been invited to lunch with the board, it might be well to get their views about possible rule violations. During lunch Wilkinson assured the board that there would be no violation. Kraft, perhaps not wanting to get caught in the crossfire, did not express an opinion.

When the board resumed session in the afternoon, all the members voted in favor of the Benedum motion except Regent Mc-Bride, who asked to be recorded as voting no. Regent Short, who had become somewhat concerned by the seriousness of the issue moved that "the record show the foregoing motion was adopted by the Board of Regents despite the recommendation of President Cross to the contrary." His motion was passed unanimously.

Reflecting that evening on the events of the day, I tried to analyze my failure to convince the regents that sending the football team to the Orange Bowl game as spectators would violate the rules. The issue seemed so clear to me that I could not understand the failure of the board to accept my opinion—even allowing for Wilkinson's magnetic charm in presenting his opposing one. I knew that to send the team to Miami would almost certainly have disastrous consequences. With such blatant violation it was almost certain that the whole team might be declared ineligible for future competition. I wasted a lot of time wondering why Wilkinson and the regents could not understand this—why they seemed so willing to take the risk. Finally, in the early hours of the morning, I reached a decision. Though the regents seemed impervious to logic, they might be susceptible to pressure. I thought I knew a way to apply the pressure.

After an early breakfast I called the presidents of the other Big Seven institutions and discussed my problem with them very frankly. I found them surprisingly well informed about what had been going on at OU. Each of them had already reached the conclusion that the rumored trip would be a violation of conference regulations, and each had become impatient with the seemingly never-ending problems caused by the southernmost member of the conference. At least two of them had received protests from their head football coaches, alleging that Oklahoma was using the gift of the trip as a recruiting measure. All expressed friendly relief when I explained that the governing board at OU had taken the action against my advice. All agreed to go on record as saying that the University of Oklahoma would receive severe disciplinary action if conference regulations were violated—disciplinary action that could range from declaring those who made the trip ineligible for future athletic competition in the conference to the expulsion of the university from the conference and the cancellation of future games.

I then called Reeves Peters at the conference headquarters in Kansas City. He too had been disturbed by what he had heard from the Sooner State, and he assured me that the NCAA certainly could be expected to deal harshly with a member school that gave an athletic team a postseason gift of any kind.

Fortunately, the Oklahoma press took a decidedly dim view of what the regents had done. The December 11 edition of the *Oklahoma City Times* carried the story with a headline "Christmas Gift! Regents Give Big Red Orange Bowl Junket." The first paragraph began: "University of Oklahoma football lettermen get an Orange Bowl trip for Christmas Thursday, tagged 'With Love from the OU Regents.'" The article went on to say that twenty-eight players would make the trip in a fifty-two passenger chartered plane, which would leave for Miami the morning of December 31 and return January 2. The other major papers of the area came up with almost daily analyses of "what had gone wrong" with the management of athletics at the University of Oklahoma. One writer (Bill Sampson) said:

Sometimes the logic of the regents is a bit hard to understand, but they must know what they are doing. As long as they have decided to break the Big Seven and North Central Association rules and send the Big Red to the Orange Bowl as spectators, why did they hesitate on sending them as players?

A Fort Worth writer commented:

192

Each day it looks more and more as if the University of Oklahoma is asking for it—asking for trouble with both the Big Seven and the NCAA. It is obvious Oklahoma is talking one way and acting another. Maybe the Sooners don't want to jump but would love to be pushed out of the Big Seven.

Another writer, in Omaha, referred to the bowl trip as a "pleasure jaunt." He suggested that the conference would be justified in ousting OU and that other leagues might well think of dropping the Sooners from their schedules.

These, and dozens of similar comments, were not lost on at least a few of the regents. When I called the president of the board early in the third week of December, suggesting that a special meeting to reconsider the Orange Bowl trip might be in order, he was quick to agree. He asked me to send out notices of a special meeting on Friday, December 19, at 3:00 P.M. in my office.

At the meeting I reported in detail the attitudes of the conference presidents and alluded to the very unfavorable reactions that had been expressed in the newspapers. I also reminded the board of the possibility that the NCA might become concerned, a development that could lead to disaccreditation of the university's academic programs.

Regent McBride asked me if I wanted to make a recommendation. Somewhat miffed by all that had happened, I replied that I did not care to make a recommendation "at this late date" but that my position was the same as it had been at all previous meetings—that the university would be in violation of conference and NCAA regulations if it sent the team to a bowl game. Regent McBride then made the following motion:

In the light of the facts presented at a special meeting called, and because of the evidence as stated and unstated, I move that the president's advice as of that meeting be upheld, and that we rescind the previous action, otherwise this school will suffer irreparable injury.

The motion passed, with only Regent Little voting no.

Earlier in the meeting the extremely generous Little had placed on the table a check for fifteen thousand dollars to pay the team's expenses in case it was decided that the university should not do so. We explained to him that this also would be a violation of conference regulations. He then said that when he voted no on the motion not to send the team he did so because he had given his word to the team and would stick by it. He said he wanted it made a matter of record that he had offered to send the team at his own expense but that under the rules, this would not be possible. It was agreed that the gist of his statement would appear in the minutes of the meeting.

As they left my office after adjournment, several members of the board assured me that in the future no action of any kind concerning athletics or any other university activity would be taken without first considering my recommendation.

As I walked along Parrington Oval toward home, I reflected with relief that what might have been a major disaster for the university had been averted. I was pleased also with the reaction of the news media, especially that of John Cronley, sports editor for the *Oklahoma City Times,* whose column in the December 21 issue, included the following comments:

Congratulations are in order for President George Cross and the University of Oklahoma Board of Regents for wisely and resolutely restoring to order the Sooners' athletic affairs. . . .

There was a wave of resentment when the Big Seven reaffirmed its anti-bowl stand which cost the Big Red an Orange Bowl appearance. . . .

However when the riled regents declared that the team would go as spectators, at a cost of some $10,000 to the athletic fund, the drastic decision brought forth sharp criticism and unfavorable publicity. . . .

As Dr. Cross so strongly and clearly pointed out, there was little sense in attempting to describe an outright gift in any other terms; the Sooners were vulnerable, if the Miami jaunt was allowed to stand, just when some of the reformers and de-emphasizers may be itching for exactly such an opportunity to crack a few heads. . . .

The regents muffed one, all right, but they're to be roundly applauded for yielding to the Cross influence and patching up the first serious athletic breach they've ever had with the school's president.

Despite the many problems that had arisen before and during the season, I took satisfaction in what OU's fine team had accomplished. They had won the Big Seven championship, had been rated fourth in the national poll (behind Michigan State, Georgia Tech and Notre Dame), and had led the nation in scoring, with 407 points.

Billy Vessels, Tom Catlin, Eddie Crowder, and Buck McPhail

The 1952 team. FIRST ROW (FRONT ROW), LEFT TO RIGHT: Merrill Green, Buck McPhail, Eddie Crowder, Auston Ingram, Billy Vessels, Jennings Nelson, Dick Ellis, John Reddell, Jerry Ingram, Juel Sweatte, Gene Calame, Buddy Leake, Gene Mears. SECOND ROW: Chet Bynum, Ross Ausburn, Merle Owens, Carl Allison, Don Brown, Raymond Powell, Jack Ging, Ed Rowland, Bob Gaut, George Cornelius, Roger Nelson, Sam Allen. THIRD ROW: Mickey Imel, John Washington, Maurie Delhotal, Bob Herndon, Ron Thompson, Steve Champlin, Kurt Burris, Doc Hearon, J. D. Roberts, Dave Shelton, Tom Catlin, Jim Davis, Melvin Brown. FOURTH ROW: Max Boydston, Jerry Donaghey, Bob Berendsen, Chuck Baker, Bob Santee, Dale Lawyer, Lester Lane, J. W. Mashburn, Milton Simmons, Von Worten, Wray Littlejohn, Jack Van Pool, Jerry Wilkes. FIFTH ROW: Kent Braden (student manager), Bob Pyle, Gene Cook, Bob Ewbank, Bill Coffman, Reece McGee, Jerry Cross, Tom Carroll, Kay Keller, Bob Santee, Dick Bowman, Don Ellis, Jim Acree. Courtesy Sports Information Department.

had been named to All-America teams. Vessels had ranked second in national rushing with 1,072 yards, and McPhail was third with 1,018 yards. Vessels, McPhail, Buddy Leake, and Merrill Green, in that order, finished first, second, third, and fourth in Big Seven scoring. Despite the tie with Colorado and the loss to Notre Dame, 1952 had been a remarkably successful season.

The North Central Association—The Stadium Concessions

1953

THE membership of the North Central Association of Colleges and Secondary Schools was scheduled to meet the last week in March, 1953. Included on the agenda for the meeting almost certainly would be an item concerning athletic scholarships. Those involved with the athletic program at OU and others throughout the state who knew of the association's recently adopted policy prohibiting financial aid to any student because of athletic ability awaited the meeting with a great deal of interest and concern. Norman Burns, secretary of the association, was well informed about athletic scholarships in the area, and he took a dim view of what was going on. It was generally thought that some sort of critical action would be taken at the meeting with regard to OU and possibly other institutions of the conference.

But to the very great surprise of nearly everyone, and the mixed emotions of several, the association's commission on colleges and universities, in session on Wednesday, March 25, gave no attention to institutions in the Big Seven Conference but instead leveled a blast at Oklahoma A&M College. The commission recommended that the Stillwater institution be dropped from the list of accredited institutions effective July 1. The recommendation was based on several charges brought before the commission, including strong criticism of A&M's athletic policies.

University of Oklahoma officials and partisans were frankly mystified by what had happened. The reasons given by the commission for recommending that A&M be dropped from accreditation may have been sound enough as far as the school's athletic program was concerned, but surely a number of other schools within the North Central area, including OU, were equally vulnerable. Why had Oklahoma A&M been chosen?

A possible explanation developed when an A&M representative to the North Central meeting pointed out that the chairman of the association's commission on colleges and universities was

Henry G. Harmon, president of Drake University. Drake had broken off athletic relations with Oklahoma A&M College back in 1951, following an unfortunate incident in a game when an A&M player allegedly slugged one of Drake's star players and broke his jaw. This caused a great furor in the sports world—in part because the Drake player was black—and much interinstitutional bitterness developed when A&M officials reportedly declined to discipline the offending athlete. The A&M people thought the incident might have been a factor in reaching a decision to recommend dropping their institution from the association.

State reaction to the news from Chicago was vigorous. Oliver Wilham, president of A&M, sent a telegram to the North Central Association pledging that his college would comply with all the association's criteria governing intercollegiate athletics. Several members of the Oklahoma legislature conferred with the state attorney general, Mac Q. Williamson, and Williamson sent a telegram to the association in which, according to newspaper accounts, he urged that action on the accreditation of A&M be taken "only after mature consideration." Governor Murray spoke of the possibility of filing a suit against the association to prohibit the organization from disaccrediting A&M College.

As a result of this activity—or perhaps in spite of some of it— P. N. Ball, president of the association, said that the executive committee would defer final action on A&M's status pending receipt, within thirty days, of documentary evidence that the institution had conformed with the North Central athletic program. The evidence apparently was provided, and things finally worked out satisfactorily.

One interesting result was likely if the North Central Association insisted on enforcing its rigid rules prohibiting athletic scholarships at its member institutions. The University of Houston would surely emerge as the athletic powerhouse in the Missouri Valley Conference, because Texas was not one of the nineteen states under the jurisdiction of the North Central Association. Thus Houston, the only university in the Missouri Valley Conference not subject to North Central regulations, would be free to provide scholarships in all sports; this would almost immediately assure Houston dominance in athletics.

198

The North Central regulation was of concern, of course, to all the athletic conferences within its area. In addition to the Big Seven and the Missouri Valley, the Skyline and the Big Ten conferences were affected. Even before the news broke about A&M's difficulties, the schools of these four conferences had arranged for a meeting at Chicago on April 27 to discuss their mutual problems. It was hoped that representatives from the North Central Association could be persuaded to attend this meeting and gain a better understanding of the problems the schools faced.

In the meantime, it was learned that alleged lack of faculty control over athletics at Oklahoma A&M had been a factor, perhaps an important one, in the association's decision to take action against the college. Reflecting on this, I was pleased that OU had taken steps several weeks earlier to develop a plan for greater faculty control at OU.

Early in January, 1953, the Faculty Senate of the university had been invited to make a thorough study of intercollegiate athletics at OU. The request was largely the result of two specific factors. The first was the prolonged controversy over whether the OU football team would play in or attend a bowl game following the 1952 season. The other was the undesirable publicity stimulated by the efforts of a few well-meaning individuals to transfer the institution's membership from the Big Seven to the Southwest Conference. In regard to the report, the senate was asked to devote special attention to two questions:

1. What should be the purpose of the athletic program at the University of Oklahoma and its relation to educational policy?

2. What action—involving possible changes in policy and organization—should be taken to put into effect such purpose?

By interesting coincidence, the senate's report, prepared by a committee chaired by Lawrence Poston, Jr., reached my office at approximately the same time news of Oklahoma A&M's difficulties with the North Central Association appeared in the newspapers. The gist of the committee report was as follows:

1. Since it is the major purpose of the university to provide

199

the opportunity for all students to develop to the fullest possible extent all desirable abilities and skills, it shall be the purpose of intercollegiate athletics to provide the opportunity for each student to attain proficiency in athletic endeavors. The program shall be conducted in the realization that athletics is not an end in itself, but merely one of the contributing factors in the total education of the student.

2. A policy of providing financial aid to students who participate in athletics, when carefully regulated and limited in extent, is approved. Such a policy, when so regulated and limited, is not inconsistent with the amateur status of college athletes nor with the proper aims of intercollegiate athletics. Under ideal circumstances, the granting of scholarships to athletes might be administered differently from present prevailing practices. Such circumstances, however, do not now exist. It seems necessary to assert that the elimination of abuses in intercollegiate athletics cannot be expected to follow from any policy which is blind to the subterfuges which are readily at hand to subvert it. And no expedient has yet been proposed which ensures that such subterfuges can effectively be prevented or controlled. Under such circumstances, it is believed that an open and honest policy in this regard is preferable to one which is essentially hypocritical. A pretense of purity is scarcely justified in the face of almost universal practices, which inevitably appear when a university washes its hands of this matter, and the existence of which is conceded by all except those who deliberately choose not to see. Under-the-counter transactions corrode the moral fiber and distort the sense of values of the students affected thereby, and produce the further evil, mentioned above, of withdrawing from the university administration, where it properly belongs, the ultimate control and responsibility for a university's athletic program. To proclaim that financial aid to athletes will not be countenanced in any form, when such aid inevitably will be forthcoming from some source or other, is, therefore, not only hypocritical, but tends to promote the very moral evils which the several regulatory agencies are most anxious to prevent.

3. Appropriate steps should be taken as soon as possible toward the dissolution of the Athletic Council as a corporation, and

beginning on June 1, 1953, the Athletic Council shall be composed of nine tenure-holding members of the faculty, one undergraduate student, one alumnus, the director of athletics (ex officio, nonvoting), and the athletic business manager (ex officio, nonvoting), who shall serve as secretary of the council.

The report provided that the faculty members would serve three-year terms and would be appointed by the president from a list of nominees provided by the Faculty Senate; that the student representatives would be chosen annually by the Student Senate; and that the alumni member would be chosen annually by the Alumni Association. The chairman of the council would be chosen annually by the members of the council from the nine tenure-holding members of the faculty.

The report further provided that all questions of athletic policy relating to intercollegiate athletics should be referred to the Athletic Council for consideration and recommendation and that the council could on its own initiative bring up matters of policy for consideration. Recommendations developed by the council were to be submitted to the president of the university.

The senate's recommendations were presented to the regents at the monthly meeting on April 9; they were approved unanimously. The senate report was significant in that it represented the first time that an agency of the faculty had made a recommendation to the administration or the regents of the university about intercollegiate athletics.

Dissolving the Athletic Council as a corporation was a long-needed reform but really was more a matter of "tidying up" than anything else, because control of athletic funds, as well as all other matters pertaining to athletic policy, had long since been taken from the council by action of the regents.

The regents welcomed a new member of the board at their meeting on April 9: W. D. ("Dick") Grisso had been appointed by Governor Murray to succeed Dr. White, whose term was expiring. Grisso, an Oklahoma City lawyer with oil interests, was the son of a well-known pioneer physician and oilman of Seminole, Oklahoma. He was an alumnus of the university, and he had served two terms in the Oklahoma legislature.

After the close of the season I had had two or three visits with

201

Farris and Wilkinson about the concessions at the games. We discussed the continuing deterioration of the equipment used in providing the sandwiches, coffee, and cold drinks and the increasing complaints about the appearance of the vendors who circulated through the stadium during the games. We finally decided to recommend to the regents that the university operate its own concessions, that the Athletic Department be given managerial responsibility, and that new equipment be provided—food-handling equipment, seat cushions, stadium chairs, and other accessories.

At the April meeting of the board I recommended that the university take over the stadium concessions for the 1953 football season. The board approved without a dissenting vote, although the members expressed some doubt that the Athletic Department had the "capability" of operating the concessions profitably.

Any doubt about the profitability of the concessions was dispelled shortly after word of the board's action got out. Jake McClure, of McClure Concessions, Inc., protested to T. R. Benedum, who had succeeded Dr. White as president of the board. He asked the board to reconsider its action and let his company continue to operate the concessions. He enlisted the support of Governor Murray in his efforts and subsequently exerted enough pressure on the regents that when Roy C. Lytle, an Oklahoma City attorney acting on behalf of McClure's, asked for a special meeting with them to discuss the concessions problem, it seemed advisable to agree.

At this meeting, at which all members of the board plus Wilkinson and Farris were present, McClure spoke about his operations during the past several years. He assured the board that he had tried to provide the best possible service at prices comparable with those charged throughout the country. He asked the regents to rescind their action and give McClure Concessions a long-term contract.

Wilkinson was then asked to give his opinion about the advisability of OU managing its own concessions. He said that he had been skeptical in the beginning and that he was still not sure that the Department of Athletics could operate the concessions successfully. But, he pointed out, Farris, the athletic business manager, had made a thorough study of the possibilities, and was in a better position to predict what might happen.

Farris was armed with a comprehensive written plan outlining the steps that were to be followed in implementing his concessions program. He had made a list of the equipment that would be needed to launch the program. The cost was $14,190 plus $7,500 for the remodeling of old stands and the construction of some new ones under the stadium.

After Farris had spoken, he and Wilkinson left the meeting, leaving the regents to come to a decision. Regent Morgan almost immediately moved that the prior action of the board be reaffirmed. However, Regent McBride offered a substitute motion: to defer taking over the concessions for one year because "the statistical report is not sufficiently complete, and we do not at the present time have enough information to justify taking over the operations this fall."

Before the vote on the substitute motion I was asked if, in the light of the discussions I had heard, I wanted to change my recommendation. I said no.

When the vote was taken on the substitute motion, Regents Short and McBride voted aye; Morgan, Foster and Little voted no; and Grisso abstained. Benedum said that he was in favor of the McBride motion, but declared it defeated.

A vote was then taken on the original motion, to reaffirm the board's previous action. Regents Morgan, Foster, and Little voted aye; Short and McBride voted no; and Grisso did not vote. Regent Benedum reported that he opposed the motion but declared it passed. OU would manage its own concessions.

I then reported to the board the outcome of the meeting of the presidents of the universities in the Big Seven, the Big Ten, the Skyline, and the Missouri Valley Conferences which had been held in Chicago on April 27 and 28. The purpose of the meeting, as I have mentioned earlier, had been to discuss the NCA regulation passed the preceding September prohibiting the awarding of scholarships on a basis of athletic ability. Norman Burns, secretary of the North Central Association's Commission on Colleges and Universities, accepted an invitation to appear before the presidents and discuss the problem with them. He pointed out that the troublesome regulation had been passed unanimously at an NCA convention and that the schools of the four athletic conferences had been represented there. He responded courteously to several sharply worded questions, but it was obvious that he strongly favored the rule and had no intention of backing down.

After Burns had left the meeting, the presidents composed a telegram to the North Central Association requesting reconsideration of the regulation. Included in the telegram was a request for a suspension of enforcement until the presidents had an opportunity to meet with officials of the association.

The presidents then discussed action that might be taken in case the NCA refused to modify its regulation. It was decided that, in such case, the institutions of the four conferences might withdraw from the association and organize a new accrediting group.

I explained all of this to the OU regents and asked for authority to commit the University of Oklahoma to membership in a new accrediting group if it should be necessary; the board gave quick, unanimous approval.

Fortunately this authorization turned out to be unneeded. Within the next few weeks arrangements were made for representatives of the member institutions of the four athletic conferences to meet in Chicago on June 12, 1953, with the NCA's Commission on Universities and Colleges. At that meeting the NCA commission was persuaded to recommend to the association that the athletic code be rescinded and replaced with the policy adopted by the American Council on Education in 1952—that institutions should award scholarships and financial aid to students on the basis of academic ability and economic need and that athletes holding scholarships or grants-in-aid must meet the same academic and financial standards as those required of other students.

While the commission was only a recommending agency and the change in policy would have to be reviewed later by the executive committee of the NCA and finally by the entire membership at an annual meeting, no one doubted that the problem had been largely solved.

As a matter of fact, the Executive Committee of the association approved the commission's recommendation late that month, and I received a telegram from Burns dated July 3, telling me that, in the light of what had happened, it would no longer be necessary for the University of Oklahoma to file reports on its athletic policies requested by the association.

In the meantime, the concessions problem erupted again. Political pressure exerted on the governor and his appointees to the OU Board of Regents forced reopening of the matter when the regents met for their regular monthly session on May 13. At that meeting Regent Grisso spoke as follows:

> I would like the matter not to be closed. It was brought up at my first meeting as a member of this board and I did not know anything about it. I am not convinced the right policy has been arrived at. I would like to study the matter another month. I think I can come up with a better solution and I do not want to vote for or against the Farris plan. I would like to have it brought up at the June meeting.

After a brief discussion it was decided to grant Grisso's request. That decision caused me great concern in the days that followed. Perhaps it did not make any significant difference whether McClure or the university handled the concessions, but a question of principle seemed to be involved. If political pressure could be used to determine university policy, great damage to the university might occur in the future when a really important issue was involved. At the least, the confidence of the faculty, students, and public in the integrity of the university administration would be shaken.

In the meantime, the concessions issue had reached an impasse. I believed that I could depend on only Regents Morgan, Foster, and Little to vote for the university to take over the concessions. I was somewhat surprised by Little's attitude. Usually gruff and truculent in his relations with me from the time of the controversy over the bowl game, he was equally gruff and positive in his support of my recommendation on the concessions. Though comparatively uninformed about university operations, he was extremely honest and well-meaning in his approach to the solution of university problems. He was compassionate and generous. He was not concerned about political pressure; his position in political circles was secure. It was rumored that he had contributed substantially to the campaigns of several influential members of the state legislature, and having justifiable confidence in the influence money could command, he had little concern for what politicians might think of his actions as an OU regent. Morgan and Foster had always been completely nonpolitical in performing their duties as regents, but the other four members of the board were politically oriented to a high degree and might honestly take the position that it would be in the university's best interest to keep the good will of the governor of the state, even if it meant reversing their action on the concessions issue. After listening to them at the meeting, I was sure that they were inclined to that position. I was apprehensive that at the next meeting the regents would vote 4 to 3 to rescind their previous action.

At the June meeting Grisso proposed that the university enter into a five-year contract with McClure. He believed that the year-to-year contracts with McClure had been one reason for the poor condition of the equipment and that it was the university's responsibility to clean up the facilities. It was his view that the university should provide outlets for gas and water and purchase some of the equipment. He suggested also that the university might provide special uniforms for the vendors and other personnel.

Farris was called to the meeting and he reported on a trip he had made to other middle-western institutions to gather information about the management of concessions. After he left the meeting, I commented as follows:

This is probably a good time for me to remain silent. However, on another occasion a regent remarked that I had not expressed my views forcefully enough. I have the greatest respect for the ideas expressed by Mr. Grisso, and I appreciate his sincerity. The disapproval of the way McClure has handled the concessions has been from slight to severe. There has been widespread approval of the athletic department taking over the concessions. It is the opinion of the faculty and most people in this area that political pressure has been applied in this matter. I am not concerned about this, but if the faculty gets the idea that political pressure may determine policies of the university, we will soon be in serious difficulty. We will lose the confidence of the faculty in the integrity of the president and board of regents. I want to make

After coming to grips with some confusing political maneuvering, OU finally began operating its own concessions at athletic contests. Regents Quintin Little, of Ardmore (left) and Dave Morgan, of Blackwell.

my position in this matter perfectly clear. You will make a mistake if you rescind your previous action. It would be better for us to give it a trial even if we fail.

Little then moved to table the Grisso proposal. He, Foster, and Morgan voted in favor of the motion; Short, McBride, and Grisso voted against it. Benedum, president of the board, broke the tie with a negative vote and announced that the motion had failed.

Regent McBride then moved, in lieu of the Grisso proposal, "to enter into a one-year contract with McClure on an audited basis of thirty per cent of gross, plus one thousand dollars and that the athletic department prepare to take over the concessions on the first of July, 1954." The motion failed, with only Short and McBride voting aye; the rest of the board voted no.

The chair then called for a vote on the Grisso proposal. Only Grisso and Short voted for it.

I then waited for a member of the board to move that a one-year contract to operate the concessions be given to McClure with the provision that the question of the university operating its own concessions be studied during the year. I was certain that such a motion would receive a tie in the voting, with the president of the board breaking the tie in favor of the motion. But to my surprise no such motion was made, and the president of the board got underway with the remainder of the agenda.

All of this puzzled me a great deal. As if by design, Grisso had made a proposal which, because it included a five-year commitment to McClure, could not be approved. On the other hand, McBride had made a motion unacceptable to Grisso, because of its provision that the university take over the concessions after one year. Thus proponents of the idea that the university should operate its concessions apparently won through a failure of the opposition to get together and come up with a satisfactory alternative. At first I could not understand why all the regents seemed reasonably satisfied with what had happened. Then it occurred to me that those on the board under pressure from the governor may have achieved their objectives by going on record in favor of contracting with McClure while not really wanting to come up with a plan that would accomplish this—most subtle political maneuvering.

CHAPTER 17

Television—The Orange Bowl—
The NCAA Inquiry

1953–54

WILKINSON and his staff accepted the decision about the Orange
Bowl trip in good grace and turned their attention to recruiting
and planning for spring practice. The staff—Gomer Jones, Pop
Ivy, Bill Jennings, Pete Elliott, and Dee Andros—was unchanged
from the preceding year, but a new athletic trainer, Ken Rawlinson, came to work in February, replacing Joe Glander, who went
to the University of Idaho.

Rawlinson came with impressive credentials. He had had nineteen years of experience: six years as assistant trainer at the
University of Illinois; four years at Casey Township High School,
Casey, Illinois; five years as head trainer at William and Mary
College; and four years as head trainer at Lafayette College.
He quickly demonstrated his competence in diagnosing and treat-
ing athletic injuries at OU's spring football practice in 1953, and
at the time of this writing he continues to supervise the training
room effectively.

The big question confronting the coaches during spring practice was who would succeed Crowder as quarterback for the
1953 season. Prospects were Buddy Leake, who had played right
halfback on the 1952 team; Gene Calame, who had played behind
Crowder the previous season; and Joe Mobra, a sophomore facing his first varsity competition. None of the trio had ever started
at quarterback in collegiate competition.

The opponent for the first game, Notre Dame, was of such high
quality that the coaches would have little opportunity to experi-
ment with quarterbacks—or other players, for that matter. Because of what many regarded as implausible scheduling, the university would open its 1953 season with a team that sports writers
gave a good chance to win the national championship. The one
cheerful thought was that the game would be played on Owen
Field in the friendly confines of the OU Stadium. But as things
turned out, that could be a cheerful thought only for the coaching

staff and the squad. In midsummer ticket buyers learned that the game was sold out. As soon as it became apparent that there were too few tickets to go around—about twenty-five thousand too few—the Athletic Department asked the NCAA for permission to televise the game. Permission was forthcoming to televise in the Oklahoma City area, where WKY-TV would originate the telecast under what was known as the home-station rule, but not elsewhere.

Citizens in other parts of the state with TV stations, such as Tulsa, were, of course, irked by this ruling. They knew that the NCAA regulation had been devised to prevent a televised game from interfering with attendance at other games in the area, but there was no intercollegiate football game scheduled for that Saturday within the range of the Tulsa station. The fans' discontent over what they considered to be an unfair ruling grew to huge proportions during the first weeks of September, and the regents were besieged with requests to televise in defiance of the NCAA's regulations. Governor Murray received so many phone calls, letters, and telegrams that he, too, asked the board to permit telecasting from all stations in the state. Senator George Miskovsky, long a critic of NCAA television policies, demanded that the governor declare martial law on the day of the game, exercise his sovereign right over the stadium press box, and allow any TV crew to broadcast from it.

But the regents, now somewhat experienced in matters having to do with defiance of conference and NCAA regulations, were cautious. After a special meeting on September 23 they issued a statement that the university would abide by the regulations of the NCAA. Oklahoma fans were somewhat sullen about the decision, but they began organizing viewing parties within the limits of the area served by WKY-TV.

The day of the game dawned bright and clear, with promise of 90-degree weather—a promise more than realized, for the thermometer registered 94 degrees at game time. Notre Dame's official party included the president, the Reverend Theodore M. Hesburgh. After lunch in the Student Union Building we walked to the stadium and sat together in the president's box.

The hot weather was especially trying for the players, because

210

The Reverend Theodore M. Hesburgh, president of Notre Dame, President Cross, and Governor Johnston Murray of Oklahoma discuss the merits of their teams at the OU-Notre Dame game, 1953. Courtesy Sports Information Department.

the two-platoon system of prior years had been abolished. Playing two-way ball, with no opportunity for rest except for occasional individual substitutions as the coaches could manage, promised to be an exhausting experience. Even the fans, as they gradually filled the stadium, realized that they were in for an uncomfortably warm afternoon.

The coaches had finally decided to start Buddy Leake as quarterback. Diminutive (157 pounds) Jack Ging was the left halfback, Larry Grigg ran at right halfback, and Max Boydston played fullback.

It was a close, well-played game. The statistics—first downs, yardage gained, and so on—were very close. The difference was in the number of errors. Two OU fumbles, a blocked punt, and an intercepted pass each led to a Notre Dame touchdown followed by a successful try for point. OU scored three touchdowns, only one of which followed a good break—a recovered fumble on the Irish 23-yard line.

The final score, 21–28, was, of course, a disappointment to the OU fans. But no one could criticize the quality of the play of either team. Perhaps the outstanding performance by an OU athlete came in the fourth quarter, when Merrill Green replaced Larry Grigg, who left the game with an injured ankle. With the score 14–28, Green quickly brought new life to what appeared to be a dying cause when he dashed 34 yards to the Irish 14-yard line on a Statue-of-Liberty play. But OU was unable to take the ball in for a touchdown, and the Irish took possession. Green then displayed his defensive ability by slipping through the Notre Dame line and throwing a passer for a 3-yard loss. When it came time for the Irish punt, Green raced back up the field and received the ball on the OU 40-yard line. From there he traveled 60 yards for a touchdown, aided on the Irish 30 when Jack Ging eliminated a Notre Dame linebacker with a beautifully thrown body block. As he passed the Sooner bench at midfield, Green yelled to the occupants, "Get out the kicking tee!" Leake's successful try for point made the score 21–28, and, with a little over five minutes left, OU was back in the ball game.

Green, playing once again on the defense, gave OU an opportunity to launch what could have been a tying touchdown drive when he made a leaping interception of a Notre Dame pass on the OU 40-yard line. But two plays later Notre Dame intercepted an OU pass, and the game was as good as over.

The only other incident about the game that I remember clearly involved our son Bill. He had been squeezed out of the box section because of the large number of guests. But he had talked briefly with Father Hesburgh at the Student Union Building before the game and had asked him if he would bless a Saint Christopher medal that had been given to him by a Roman Catholic friend of ours. Bill had always been a little accident-prone, and apparently he thought that a Saint Christopher's medal blessed by the president of Notre Dame might be effective in warding off misadventures. Father Hesburgh expressed his willingness, and Bill hurried home to get his medal, planning to bring it to

212

the box between halves. But he forgot all about it until late in the fourth quarter, when, realizing that Father Hesburgh would join the Notre Dame party right after the game, he decided to come to the box and have his medal blessed between plays during the waning moments. As Father Hesburgh held the medal for the blessing, the OU team came out of a huddle for one of its final offensive efforts. It seemed to me that the ceremony, while doubtless adequate, was somewhat hurried. But Bill was satisfied, and Father Hesburgh smiled later when I mentioned the haste with which he had said the blessing.

After the game ended, the two teams met briefly in the center of the field and shook hands. The Notre Dame players had some difficulty getting to their dressing room through the crowd of well-wishers that blocked their way. They did not carry their coach off the field; they gave the impression of accepting victory as a matter of course.

The following week the Sooners journeyed to the University of Pittsburgh for a game on October 3. It was a lackluster contest that ended in a 7–7 tie. Especially disappointing to Sooner supporters was the ineffective OU offense—only 63 yards rushing and 100 yards passing. Of concern also was the fact that Jackie Ging suffered a severe shoulder separation during the second quarter of the game, an injury that everybody but Jackie thought would end his football career. He insisted to the coaches that he "healed fast" and would be ready to play again in two or three weeks.

Flying home from Pittsburgh, the Sooner coaches discussed ways and means of improving their squad's offensive game. By the time the plane landed in Oklahoma, they had decided to put Gene Calame at quarterback and return Leake to his old position at halfback, where he had performed so well in the past.

The decision paid off in fine fashion in the third game of the season, the annual encounter with the University of Texas. Calame's play at quarterback was outstanding in every way—play calling, ball handling, faking, and running. His teammates accepted their new leader with confidence and played together so effectively that they led Texas 19–0 at the beginning of the fourth quarter.

The most spectacular scoring effort during the first three quar-

213

ters certainly must have been the 80-yard punt runback by Merrill Green. It came halfway through the second period, when Wilkinson inserted Leake and Green as double safeties to receive a kick from the Steers' punter, Dougal Cameron. The OU fans knew that if either of the safeties received the ball they would see an exhibition of OU's famed crisscross pattern, wherein the two safeties would crisscross and head for opposite sides of the field, faking in the process so that the defensive team would not know which one had the ball until the line of blockers began to form. OU had had good success with the play several times in the past.

Green caught Cameron's punt on the OU 20 and then faked a handoff to Leake so realistically that the Texas team was fooled momentarily. The blocking on the runback was superb. Wray Littlejohn, OU fullback, got the play underway by cutting down two Texas defenders as Green turned upfield. J. D. Roberts also helped clear the way with a beautiful downfield block, and Dick Bowman contributed a critical block that left only the Texas quarterback, Bunny Andrews, in a position for a possible tackle. But Green outran Andrews and completed his 80-yard dash, crossing the goal line standing up.

The fourth quarter was a nerve-wracking experience for the OU fans. Midway through the period the Texans drove 78 yards for their first touchdown of the day and with a successful conversion brought the score to 19–7, with 6:14 left. Shortly afterward OU fumbled on its own 40-yard line, and the rejuvenated Steers punched the ball to within 4 yards of a second touchdown before losing it on a fumble.

With 2:35 remaining, OU began using up time. Things went well for five plays, but on the sixth the Sooners were penalized to the one-half-yard line for delay of the game. At this point the Sooners decided to give Texas an intentional safety, worth two points, to get some room for a free kick from the OU 20-yard line. Calame took the snap from center and retreated into the OU end zone, running laterally back and forth to use up as much time as possible. But in the course of his maneuvering he thought he saw an opening down the west sideline and decided to take it. His decision turned out to be a mistake; he was tackled on the OU 3-yard line, and Texas took over. It took the Steers only one play to score, and after a successful try for point the score for the afternoon stood at 19–14.

With 29 seconds left, the fired-up Steers tried an onside kick, but they were too eager and were penalized 5 yards for being offside. The next onside kick did not travel the required ten yards, and Oklahoma gratefully took possession for the remaining five or six seconds.

In his football letter following the game, Wilkinson paid special tribute to Tom Carroll, who had played extremely well as a replacement for Jack Ging. Carroll was a veteran of the Korean War. He had served as communications sergeant in an all-vehicle company and had done all of his traveling in a jeep. When he returned to the university, his legs were so out of shape that he could not quickly recover his speed. But he spent a year running daily to regain the snap and speed that he had once had — effort that paid off well when he replaced Ging. Wilkinson also mentioned Carl Allison, the left end from McAlester, who played the full sixty minutes against Texas in 91-degree heat.

On the whole, OU partisans were well satisfied with the outcome of the game. The consensus seemed to be that the team had jelled and that the rest of the season would be a winning one. But even the most optimistic of fans would not have predicted that the Texas game was the first in a series of forty-seven continuous wins that would establish a new record for consecutive victories in modern football. OU would not be defeated again until Statehood Day in 1957, when Notre Dame, the last team to turn the trick at the beginning of the 1953 season, would win again by the same margin — 7 points.

After Texas the Sooners had two games at home, the University of Kansas on October 17 (Dad's Day) and the University of Colorado on October 24 (Homecoming).

The Kansas Jayhawkers were not able to provide much competition. Before a crowd of 42,500 four OU teams ran up a score of 45–0, setting a modern school rushing record of 537 yards. To demonstrate the versatility and depth of the offense, the first team scored the first three times it had the ball, and the third and fourth teams scored the last three times they had possession. As V. L. Nicholson put it in his story to the *Topeka Capitol,*

"Owen Field was a one-way street and the traffic got a trifle heavy around the Kansas goal line."

The game with Colorado was a different story, as might have been predicted, because Colorado had tied OU 21–21 at Boulder the preceding year. The excellent performances against Texas and Kansas had made the OU fans—and probably the team too—overconfident. Wilkinson warned about the dangers of this in his football letter of October 20:

I know that a lot of you think we've got pretty much of a cinch in this game. When you think something's going to be easy, that's when the going really gets tough. Our squad will either continue to improve or start to deteriorate this coming week. Our problem is to keep trying to improve. A good football squad will work hard to grow a little better and learn a little more each Saturday it plays.

The fans were unconvinced; the game was played before a surprisingly small Homecoming crowd of 34,000. Those who went saw a close contest. Inspired by an early favorable break in the game, the Coloradans thoroughly outplayed the Sooners during the first half and led 7–13 when the two teams went to their dressing rooms at half time.

After a punt blocked by J. D. Roberts on the Colorado 28-yard line in the third quarter, OU tied the score at 13–13 and took the lead, 20–13, midway in the fourth quarter. With only 7:11 left, the Oklahoma partisans in the stands settled back with some relief.

But the Coloradans were far from ready to concede. They received the kickoff and drove 80 yards for a touchdown and extra point, tying the score for the second time, with 1:30 left to play. Oklahoma's starting line had tired during the fourth quarter, and Wilkinson had sent in the alternate forward wall. The depth of the OU squad was demonstrated well during the final seconds of the game. Larry Grigg received the Colorado kickoff, and two plays later OU had the ball on its own 49-yard line with 44 seconds left. At that point the alternate line, blocking crisply on a trap play, opened a hole for Green to pass through with the ball. In a beautifully coordinated effort end Kay Keller trapped the middle guard, Cecil Morris and Doc Hearon teamed up to eliminate a tackle, Bo Bollinger inactivated the middle

216

linebacker, and Don Brown took care of another linebacker. Green spurted, faked, and cut downfield with only two defenders left between him and the goal line. Carl Allison helped him past the first with a well-placed block, and Green managed to out-maneuver the final man himself. Leake's successful try for point placed Oklahoma in the lead, 27–20, sealing the victory with 36 seconds left.

In his football letter the following week Wilkinson made an interesting analysis of the game:

> The thought occurs to me that this game, and also several others played around the nation the same day, illustrates so eloquently a point that many fans overlook. If you were to grade a perfect college football team at 100%, everybody we play would rate above 90. The grade varies from Saturday to Saturday. If we are playing at the top of our game, we might score 94. If our opponent were only 92% efficient we should win. But if we play a little off our usual form and our opponent, sharp and ready, goes after us like Colorado did Saturday, we can lose to any team we play. Every team has good players, fine coaching and the desire to win. Victory usually goes to the team that is "ready" physically and mentally when the game begins.

The sixth game of the season was against Kansas State at Manhattan. The Sooners won it decisively, if not easily, by a score of 34–0. The team effort was excellent, characterized by hard blocking, tackling, and running. The outstanding individual effort was by Larry Grigg, who displayed durability, carrying the ball twenty-five times for a gain of 177 yards. Noteworthy also was the fact that Jackie Ging, as he had predicted, had healed rapidly and, to the surprise of the team's physician and the trainer, was ready for action. He was used sparingly, however, carrying the ball four times for a gain of 12 yards.

Next on the schedule for the steadily improving Sooners was the University of Missouri at Columbia on November 7. Missouri had to be considered a strong contender for the Big Seven championship, with victories over two Big Ten teams and a decisive win over Nebraska, 23–7. Missouri did indeed prove a severe test of OU's claim for preeminence in the conference and a high national rating. The two teams were evenly matched, played in spirited fashion, and ended the third quarter with the score tied 7–7.

Early in the fourth quarter Missouri had the ball on OU's 17-yard line, with a third down and 10 yards to go. Though the Sooners must have been expecting a pass play, nevertheless a Missouri receiver managed to get free in the OU end zone, where he waited to receive a perfectly thrown ball from the Missouri quarterback, Vic Eaton. For a brief moment it looked like a certain touchdown, but just as the ball was settling into the receiver's arms, Larry Grigg, who had been racing to the scene, ended his sprint with a leaping stab that knocked the ball beyond the clutches of the receiver. Later Wilkinson characterized Grigg's effort as one of the finest defensive plays he had ever seen. With fourth down and 10 yards to go, Missouri elected to try for a field goal, but the attempt was short, and OU took over on its own 20-yard line.

With only about 7 1/2 minutes left, it was up to the Sooners to take the ball 80 yards for a touchdown without a fumble, penalty, or failure to gain yardage. Any mistake resulting in loss of possession almost certainly would cost them a victory. As Wilkinson put it later, "It was the hour of decision for our team."

Slowly, carefully, and methodically the Sooners started their offensive drive. Behind perfectly executed blocking Calame and his teammates in the backfield brilliantly moved the ball upfield to a first down on the Tigers' 3-yard line. There, the Missouri defense dug in and stopped three plays, leaving OU with a fourth down a short yard from the goal line. Then Calame, noticing that the Missouri defense was bunched to stop an OU power play, called a sweep to the left, faked the end in, and pitched out to Grigg, who crossed the goal line untouched. Leake's try for point was successful, making the final score 14–7. Looking back through the years, I recall that 80-yard drive as one of the best offensive series in OU football.

The following week Wilkinson, concerned about overconfidence, wound up his weekly football letter with these words of caution:

Everyone seems to think our season is over now that we have defeated Kansas State and Missouri. Nothing in football could be so wrong. The minute a team and its supporters think the rest of the season is a coast downhill, the road instantly starts uphill. I hope our fans and our players

218

will realize this. Right now there is only one game left on our schedule. It's against Iowa State here Saturday.

Despite Wilkinson's apprehension the football team had little difficulty with any of the remaining games. The entire squad (forty-five players) helped defeat Iowa State 47–0 at Norman. The win clinched the Big Seven Conference championship and a bid to the Orange Bowl, with the University of Maryland as the probable opponent.

Nebraska fell before the onslaught the following week, in a game played at Lincoln, where the thermometer stood at 32 degrees at kickoff. The final score, 30–7, was scarcely indicative of OU's superiority. A better measurement would have been the 406 yards Oklahoma gained rushing, compared with Nebraska's 80 yards.

Only Oklahoma A&M at Stillwater remained on the schedule. The Aggies, coached by J. B. Whitworth and his able staff, had had two weeks to prepare for the contest because of an open date the preceding Saturday.

The first quarter of the game ended in a 7–7 tie, giving OU fans some cause for concern. But the Sooners took over at the beginning of the second quarter, and again all forty-five players ran up a final score of 42–7, before a crowd of fifty thousand.

An interested spectator that day was Maryland coach Jim Tatum. Tatum's remarks, as reported by the press, gave no indication that he had been especially impressed by what he had seen. He was quoted as saying that his Maryland squad was the greatest team he had ever coached. The fact that the Terrapin team was voted number one in the nation by the Associated Press gave some weight to his remarks. Behind Maryland in the national poll were Notre Dame, Michigan State and Oklahoma, in that order.

When the final statistics were compiled for the regular season, the University of Oklahoma led the nation in rushing with an average of 306.9 yards for the ten games. J. D. Roberts, Oklahoma's great guard from Dallas, Texas, was All America by almost unanimous choice. In addition he won the Outland Trophy, given to the nation's outstanding guard or tackle, and he was named lineman of the year by both the Associated Press and

J. D. Roberts, All-America, Outland Trophy winner, and AP and UP Lineman of the Year, 1953–54. Courtesy Sports Information Department.

the United Press. Buddy Leake had been successful in 50 of 52 extra-point attempts, and Larry Grigg was the leading rusher in the Big Seven conference—790 yards in 130 attempts.

During December two factors heightened interest in the upcoming Orange Bowl game: Oklahoma's only previous appearance in the bowl, against Tennessee, had been a disaster, and the Maryland team was coached by Wilkinson's predecessor at OU.

Mrs. Cross and I flew to Miami with the team on Christmas Day. From the evening newspapers we learned that the Maryland team was a one-touchdown favorite. That pleased Wilkinson; he always preferred to have his team enter a contest as underdogs.

While the team prepared for the game, the rest of us had plenty to occupy our attention. Bruce MacIntosh, president of the Orange Bowl, and his associates had planned an elaborate program of events that included several cocktail parties, a formal dinner

220

Bud Wilkinson and the Sooner squad receive a warm welcome in Miami as they arrive to prepare for the 1954 Orange Bowl game with Maryland. Courtesy Sports Information Department.

followed by an Orange Bowl ball, the Orange Bowl Parade on New Year's Eve, a New Year's Eve party after the parade, and a kickoff brunch the morning of the game. I had not taken a tuxedo with me and had to rent one for the dinner and ball. It did not fit very well, and I was rather uncomfortable during the evening. However, all the other Oklahomans present agreed that it was a splendid occasion.

The kickoff brunch, at the McAllister Hotel, in downtown Miami, was also an impressive occasion. About seven hundred attended, and several hundred more had to be turned away because there was no place to seat them in the huge dining room.

Boyd Gunning was master of ceremonies at the brunch, and among the guests were Bruce MacIntosh, president of the Orange Bowl; Evelyn Ay, Miss America of the year; and Governor and

Harold Keith, sports information director, and Bud Wilkinson discuss a release.
Courtesy Sports Information Department.

Mrs. Murray. Harold Keith, Sooner sports publicity chief, wound
up the program with a brief description of the players on the
OU team, liberally seasoned with his special brand of humor.

Afterward the guests piled into special buses for the trip to
the stadium. There Mrs. Cross and I made our way to the box
seats provided by the Orange Bowl officials. We found to our

222

Jim Tatum and Bud Wilkinson pose for newsmen before the 1954 Orange Bowl game. Courtesy *Oklahoman and Times.*

dismay that the boxes were at midfield at ground level. We knew that we would see very little of the ball game from there.

After an impressive pregame show, with several floats and bands, the main event of the day finally got underway. Sooner fans watched with particular interest as the national champions from Maryland trotted onto the field, because it had been rumored that Maryland's great quarterback, Bernie Faloney, had been injured in the final game of Maryland's all-victorious regular season and would not be able to play. He had been an important factor in his team's success, and, according to Tatum, his loss would give the University of Oklahoma an enormous advantage. Oklahomans were inclined to discount Tatum's statements; "Big Jim" had been known to put out misleading information about

223

the condition of his squad. But sure enough, Faloney did not appear with the starting unit; Charley Boxold, reserve quarterback, was at the quarterback slot.

During most of the first half it looked as if OU might be overmatched. The first threat came almost as soon as the game got underway. Maryland had the ball and, after failing to gain the required yardage in three downs, managed to get off a punt that rolled out of bounds on OU's 1-yard line, a most unfavorable place to take possession against a national-championship team. OU, with Gene Calame at quarterback, unable to run the ball out of the dangerous area, was forced to punt to a Maryland receiver, who was tackled on the Sooner 39-yard line.

The Terrapins then started a drive, moving the ball with the power and precision that had characterized their play all season, and finally found themselves with a first down, approximately 3 1/2 yards from the Sooner goal line.

Probably no one had the faintest hope that Maryland could be held short of the goal line. But OU's starting forwards—ends Carl Allison and Max Boydston, tackles Don Brown and Roger Nelson, guards Melvin Brown and J. D. Roberts, and center Kurt Burris—braced for what certainly was one of the greatest defensive efforts by any team in history.

Maryland used four ball carriers in a futile effort to reach pay dirt. Chet Hanulak wormed his way to the 2-yard line on the first play, Dick Nolan was stopped without gain on the second, Charley Boxold kept the ball on the third and squirmed to within inches of the goal line, and Ralph Felton was held without gain on the fourth and final attempt.

There was a great roar from the Oklahomans as OU took possession on about the 3-inch line. There were looks of disbelief on the faces of those around us.

The Sooners did not try to run the ball out but punted immediately. In the following series of downs they managed to hold the Terrapins, who elected a field-goal attempt from the 43-yard line. The ball went wide of the goal post, and for the first time in the game the Sooners had possession with reasonably good field position, on their own 20-yard line.

But the respite was short-lived. Almost immediately a Sooner offensive back fumbled the ball, and the Terrapins recovered. Once again the powerful Maryland machine drove goalward and shortly came up with a first down on the OU 9-yard line.

In the meantime, Wilkinson, concerned that his first-string line had been worn down by its brilliant goal line stand, had sent in his relieving forwards—ends Joe Mobra and Cal Woodworth, tackles Dick Bowman and Doc Hearon, guards Bo Bollinger and Cecil Morris, and center Gene Mears. His decision about which line to use for the second goal-line stand must have been a difficult one, and many OU fans disagreed with it. But the reserve forwards quickly proved that Wilkinson was right. Three vicious thrusts by the Maryland offense gained a total of only 3 yards, and, with fourth down and 7 to go, Tatum decided to make a second attempt for a field goal. Ralph Felton's kick went to the right of the goal post, and once again the Oklahomans received the ball on their 20-yard line.

The Sooners then displayed the offensive poise they had demonstrated so many times during the season, and in ten brilliantly executed plays carried the ball to the Maryland 28-yard line. There Calame pitched out to Larry Grigg, who, with timely blocks by Calame and Bob Burris, went in for the touchdown. There was plenty of drama and suspense in the remainder of the half. Shortly before it ended, Calame and Bob Burris, covering a pass receiver, ended a play in a three-man collision, and Calame left the game with what appeared to be a collarbone injury.

Sooner fans spent the intermission wondering what would happen during the second half if Calame was unable to play. Jay O'Neal, number-two signal caller for the Sooners, was out with an injury. Next in line for the job was Jack Van Pool, a capable but unheralded athlete from Oklahoma City.

When the team came onto the field for the second half, Van Pool was at the quarterback position with instructions to stick to bread-and-butter plays—nothing fancy. Van Pool turned in a brilliant performance under extraordinary pressure and even brought the team to potential scoring positions on a couple of occasions. OU's defensive units contained the Maryland attack during the last half, and in Maryland's final drive of the game Larry Grigg intercepted a pass in the Sooner end zone to clinch

225

OU's first Orange Bowl victory at 7–0. Grigg played one of the best games of his career that afternoon, figuring prominently in OU's 80-yard touchdown drive and operating brilliantly on defense. He and his associates in the secondary helped establish a defense that held the powerful Maryland aggregation at bay throughout the game. Five times during the afternoon Maryland had possession of the ball within OU's 30-yard line but were unable to score. It was the first time in fifty-one games that the Terrapins had failed to score, and it was only the fourth time in Tatum's seven years of coaching at Maryland that one of his teams had been shut out.

While the approximately seventy thousand spectators were filing out of the Orange Bowl, there was wild celebration in the Sooner dressing room. Quick to arrive on the scene with congratulations was Notre Dame's Frank Leahy. Various Oklahomans soon appeared, including Governor Murray. After several minutes of noisy congratulations, backslapping, and handshaking, the Oklahoma athletes and their coaches showered and dressed for the cocktail party and dinner to be given that evening for the two squads and the official parties at the Latin Club.

Mrs. Cross and I arrived at the party a short time before the other guests, and the dimly lighted, extravagantly appointed club was all but deserted. An Orange Bowl official escorted us to a table occupied by a lone gentleman, who turned out to be a Maryland partisan. The man kept his seat, and I sensed that he was feeling the effects of the bourbon and water he was drinking. I explained that we were "Mr. and Mrs. Cross, from Oklahoma." He made no acknowledgment but launched into a lamentation that was to continue for some time.

"I just don't understand it" he began. "We're supposed to be the greatest team in the nation, and we get beat in the Orange Bowl." I suggested that when two such outstanding teams were playing either might win on any given occasion.

He ignored my comment and continued his original theme. "They told me we had the best team in the nation. I bet my money, and then they lost the ball game." I suggested once again that there were many unpredictables in an athletic contest and that it was always possible for a good team to lose, but my comments seemed only to irritate him.

226

He looked at me almost belligerently and said, "Why can't the best team in the nation win an Orange Bowl game? They let Curly Byrd continue as president four months beyond the time he was supposed to retire so he could be president of Maryland when his national champions won the Orange Bowl game. Why couldn't the best team in the nation win today?"

Realizing the futility of trying to pacify him, I tried to change the subject. But he broke in with an insistent, "Tell me why." I replied that perhaps it was because Maryland didn't really have the best team in the nation. While he was struggling with that idea, Mrs. Cross and I excused ourselves and found another table.

Soon the team and the other guests arrived, and the festivities got underway. After an excellent dinner the head coaches, school presidents, and Governor Murray made short speeches. Jim Tatum was especially gracious in his remarks. He said, "Bud outcoached me." He made no excuses—no mention that if Bernie Faloney had been able to play Maryland probably would have won. The last event of the evening was the presentation of trophies— Orange Bowl watches to the players and a permanent Orange Bowl Trophy to the University of Oklahoma. The trophy, a some- what cumbersome two-foot-tall bowl fitted with molded oranges and topped with the figure of a football player, was presented to Wilkinson, but it was too heavy for him to carry, and he called on his co-captains, Larry Grigg and Roger Nelson, to transport it to the team bus.

It was a satisfying evening in most respects, but as I watched the proceedings, my thoughts returned frequently to the Maryland fan who had had such difficulty understanding or accepting de- feat. I had the disquieting thought that probably both teams had too many fans of this kind—that they were the major cause of the problems that bedeviled intercollegiate athletics.

The next day the football teams and their coaches went deep- sea fishing for additional competition. As I recall the Mary- landers proved to be the superior fishermen.

The Oklahoma party flew home on Sunday, January 3. As our plane touched down at Westheimer Field, I remember thinking with some relief that we could forget about football for a while at least and hoping that the students would turn their attention to classroom activities. But it was not to be. During the following

227

The 1953 team. FIRST ROW (FRONT ROW), LEFT TO RIGHT: Bob Hillis, Kenneth Arms, Bob Herndon, Larry Grigg, Harold Powell, Merrill Green, Jerry Cross, Pat O'Neal, Don Brown, Dick Bowman, Emery Link, Jerry Donaghey, Gene Mears, Wray Littlejohn, Milton Simmons, Chuck Baker. SECOND ROW: Bob Santee, Kurt Burris, Jack Ging, J. D. Roberts, Buddy Leake, Max Boydston, Myron Salter, Doc Hearon, Cecil Morris, Ted Rupe, Bobby Darnell, Gene Calame, Bill Cheadle, Bo Bolinger, Carl Allison, Bob Pyle (student manager). THIRD ROW: Ron Thompson, Bob Loughridge, Robert Van Dee, Calvin Woodworth, James Acree, George Nelson, Melvin Brown, Roy Cartwright, Joe Mobra, Tom Carroll, Kay Keller, Jack Van Pool, Duane Goff, Bob Burris, Dale Bryant. Courtesy Sports Information Department.

weeks the ever-recurring question arose: How long would Wilkinson remain at Oklahoma? Wes Fesler, the University of Minnesota coach, had resigned in December, and it was rumored that Minnesota would offer its distinguished alumnus the most attractive contract ever awarded a coach in the history of collegiate football.

Wilkinson and most of his staff members left early in January for the NCAA meetings in Cincinnati. We expected that Minnesota would approach him once again at that meeting. Speculation quieted briefly when he announced in Cincinnati that he definitely planned to remain at Oklahoma. This announcement apparently followed conferences that he was known to have had with Ike Armstrong, the athletic director at Minnesota. The credibility of his announcement was strained a bit, however, when he went on to Minneapolis after the NCAA meetings and, according to newspaper accounts, met with officials of the university, including President J. L. Morrill. On January 28, Reidar Lund, executive sports editor of the *Duluth Herald and News Tribune,* charged in his column that Minnesota had missed the chance to hire Wilkinson because of "treatment accorded him" during his visit to Minneapolis. The article implied that the "mistreatment" had come from the president of the university. Lund went on to report that Ike Armstrong, whom he described as a man of proven capability, had been "hamstrung" by the university administration in his efforts to develop the athletic program at Minnesota. But both President Morrill and Armstrong denied Lund's charges. Armstrong said that a definite offer had been made to Wilkinson but that he had turned it down. Questioned in Norman, Wilkinson said that he had gone to Minnesota by invitation, to help in any way that he could with Minnesota's search for a new coach. Without knowing precisely what had taken place, the Oklahoma fans were relieved that Wilkinson probably would coach the Big Red for at least another year.

During the spring of 1954 I received a rather involved three-page letter from Walter Byers, executive secretary of the NCAA, asking about OU's recruiting procedures. The letter did not suggest that Oklahoma had been guilty of any irregularities, but the carefully couched inquiry implied that wealthy friends of the institution were suspected of being overly active in helping the coaches persuade young men to come to OU. The NCAA wanted to know who was responsible for the development of athletic policies at OU and who had the responsibility of making sure that approved policies were followed. Especially pointed was a question about whether a fund or funds were available for use by the Department of Athletics that were not administered by the university.

There were penetrating questions about the operation of the Touchdown Club. What was its purpose? Was a copy of its constitution available? How were the activities of the club financed? What was its relation to the university? Did it have any members who held positions at OU either as employees or as members of the Board of Trustees? Did it contribute funds to OU, and, if so, how were these funds administered? What was the amount contributed annually during the past five years?

On April 28 I presented the letter to the regents at a special meeting and offered tentative answers. After lengthy discussion a regent asked whether the news media should be informed of the inquiry. I recommended that they should be told, and George Short, president of the board, agreed with me. However, a majority of the members thought that the inquiry should be handled quietly and settled without publicity, if possible.

As had happened on so many occasions in the past, secrecy proved to be impossible. When the regents assembled for their regular monthly meeting in May, Harold Keith appeared with the news that a Texas sports columnist had hinted that a major football school in the Southwest was in trouble with the NCAA, and he said he had received an inquiry from Texas asking whether the school in question might possibly be Oklahoma. He said that he anticipated more inquiries and that he thought OU's involvement probably would soon receive broad treatment in Texas papers. He advised the regents in effect to acknowledge that the questionnaire had been received.

The board decided to provide the newspapers with copies of Byers' letter and apologize for not releasing the story sooner. Queried by reporters, members of the board stated, somewhat unconvincingly, that the special meeting on April 28 had not really been a meeting of the board at all. Six regents had been on campus for the annual observance of Law Day, and, while the NCAA inquiry had been discussed at an informal meeting of the group, no action had been taken and no minutes of the meeting prepared.

The announcement naturally produced headlines in the newspapers of the area, and sports columnists, especially writers in Texas and Colorado, received the news with delight. Jack Carberry, sports editor for the *Denver Post,* speculated in his column "Second Guess" that the NCAA charges had been precipitated by an article in the *Daily Oklahoman* concerning the presence of United States Senator Joe McCarthy at the Orange Bowl game. The article included a picture of McCarthy, the "red hunter" supposedly "rooting for the Reds." At least, Carberry pointed out, McCarthy and his bride were sitting in the "Red Rooting Section," because next to him was seated the entire Muskogee, Oklahoma, high-school football team with their coach, Paul Young. Carberry suggested that probably nobody cared how "Joe the Wind" McCarthy got to Miami, but he suspected that a number of people, seeing Joe's picture as a "Red Rooter," might have wondered how an entire high-school football team got there.

A possible explanation, which Carberry said had been reported to him, brought into the picture Pete Smith, former All-America end at Oklahoma, who was then operating a restaurant in Muskogee. According to the story, charges before the NCAA alleged that Pete Smith was the "agent" for the Touchdown Club, with an office in the First National Bank in Oklahoma City. As agent for the club Pete exercised influence over the use of a $93,000 "war chest" the club had assembled.

Out of this "chest," according to the Carberry report, unusual "aid" to deserving youths seeking an education had been forthcoming. Specifically, the report charged, a number of Muskogee athletes had received not only regular scholarships at OU but, in addition, fifty dollars a month in spending money with an "open account" at clothing stores, and, for staying in school through the sophomore year and making the team, a new Chevrolet. Carberry hinted, however, that the charges were not confined to recruitment at Muskogee but were widespread. He said it had

231

been charged also that a university regent with a "million dollar a year income" had given "personal scholarships" to certain members of OU's 1953 squad. One scholarship had included the use of a Lincoln Capri.

During the following five months a very careful investigation was made of OU's athletic policies, especially those involving aid to athletes, and promises made during recruitment visits. A seventy-six-page report, documented with thirty-two exhibits, was prepared under the direction of Earl Sneed, dean of the College of Law, who had succeeded Walter Kraft as faculty representative to the Big Seven Conference and the NCAA. The report was mailed to Walter Byers on September 1, 1954, and the news media were told about it. The contents were not made public then, because we wanted to give the NCAA Executive Committee adequate time to examine it first. Byers acknowledged receipt of the report, but we did not hear anything more from him until December.

Wilkinson and I had several conferences during the course of the investigation and the preparation of the report. He was undisturbed by the inquiry and assured me that his coaching staff had been following the policies of the Big Seven Conference and the NCAA "to the letter." There was nothing to fear, he said, from any detailed investigation the association might make. Bud proved to be a poor prophet. Soon we would learn that we had much to fear.

CHAPTER 18

The 1954 Season—OU on Probation

1954–55

WILKINSON's main rebuilding problem for 1954 appeared to be strength in the line. Probably the most serious loss was J. D. Roberts, lineman of the year in 1953; but also missing from the 1954 squad would be Roger Nelson, Melvin Brown, Dick Bowman, and Doc Hearon. There were some excellent holdovers, however, including Kurt Burris and Gene Mears at center; Bo Bolinger, Cecil Morris, Emery Link, and Milt Simmons at guard; Don Brown and Bob Loughridge at tackle; and Carl Allison and Max Boydston at end. Some sports writers considered Boydston, Allison, and Burris excellent candidates for All-America honors.

The backfield was more adequately manned with experienced personnel. Gene Calame and Pat O'Neal would be back at quarterback, and there was an untried but promising prospect for that position named Jimmy Harris from Terrell, Texas. Buddy Leake and Tom Carroll, halfbacks, had eligibility remaining, and a capable reserve, Bob Herndon would also be available. A promising sophomore named Tommy McDonald, from New Mexico, had attracted attention during the varsity-alumni game in the spring. Bob Burris was back at fullback, and Wray Littlejohn would return. Tri-captains were elected for the season, Gene Calame, Gene Mears, and Carl Allison. All in all it looked like a promising squad, especially if the coaches could develop some guards and tackles in time for the early games.

There were some new faces on the coaching staff that year. Pop Ivy, Bill Jennings, and Dee Andros had gone on to other jobs; Sam Lyle, Ray Nagel, and John Shelly replaced them.

The first game, on September 18, was with the University of California at Berkeley, a team judged to be among the best in the Pacific Coast Conference. The California Bears were coached by Lynn Waldorf, who while coaching at Oklahoma A&M in earlier years, had led the Aggies to some of their greatest moments. The California game would indeed be a good test of

Sooner quality, a test of whether the team could do what it had not done in two years—open the season with a win.

There was cause for pessimism during the final week of preparation for the trip west. Gene Calame was injured in a practice session on Wednesday. Trainer Rawlinson thought it was a strained muscle on the right side just below the rib basket. Calame spent the night in the university infirmary but was released in time to catch the 8 o'clock flight to Berkeley the following morning. Mrs. Cross and I flew with the team to Berkeley. We were met at the airport by several newsmen. Wilkinson introduced himself and then presented the rest of us. He introduced me as Dr. George L. Cross but failed to add that I was president of the university. Somewhat to my surprise, a reporter asked me whether I thought Calame would be able to play. I was evasive, saying that we would have to wait and see how he felt the next day but that I thought he would probably play. I was a little startled to read later, in one of the local newspapers, that "team trainer Dr. George L. Cross" thought that Calame would be ready for the game.

The Oklahoma party traveled by bus to the Pleasanton Country Club. The club had been one of the homes of William Randolph Hearst. It had been remodeled, enlarged, and turned into a hotel-type club with space for guests. It was several miles from the metropolitan area, in higher, rugged terrain, in keeping with Wilkinson's belief that his team should be housed in an isolated, quiet area.

The club was a very pleasant place. The team worked out on Thursday afternoon and again on Friday, while several of the guests played golf. Everyone was pleased when Jack Ging, halfback on the 1953 squad, appeared at one of the practice sessions. Ging was living on the West Coast, getting a start with what was to be a successful career in motion pictures and television.

At the close of the practice session on Friday it was still doubtful whether Calame would be able to play. It was obvious, from watching him at workout, that he was in pain when he ran or passed the ball.

The day of Oklahoma's first encounter with a Pacific Coast opponent dawned with bright sunshine and a comfortable temperature which at game time was about 65 degrees. The fifty-seven thousand fans who went to the game fell far short of filling California's huge stadium. The OU group had excellent seats on the west side of the field in the midsection, but that was about the only favorable treatment they received. During the introduction of OU players before kickoff, each time the name of an Oklahoman was announced, the California rooting section shouted in unison "Who's he?" Later, when the game was underway, they would periodically shout, "Dirty Sooners!"

California had been favored to win by a touchdown or two, largely because of the exceptional running and passing competence of their quarterback, Paul Larson. Larson had been unusually effective the preceding year in running off rollout-pass plays, and it was predicted that the Oklahomans would not be able to stop both his running and his passing attack.

The question whether Calame would play was answered when the Sooners came onto the field for the pregame warmup. The plucky little quarterback, his torso swathed in several layers of adhesive tape, took part in the drills and, except for a slight stiffness, gave every indication of being ready for the game.

It was a hard, well-played contest between two well-matched teams. The score at half time was 7–6 in OU's favor, which was probably a more accurate measurement of the difference in the two opponents than the final score, 27–13.

The most exciting event of the game came a little past midway through the third quarter, just after Oklahoma had taken possession of the ball on its own 8-yard line following a California fumble. Calame tried two quarterback sneaks and gained 5 yards. When he came behind center for the third down, he noticed that one of the California linebackers had moved up into the line, leaving the Bruins' left flank open behind him. Calame checked his signals and called a forward pass off a pitchout to the right. The pitchout went to Buddy Leake, who after a few steps threw a pass to Max Boydston in the open spot behind the California linebacker. Boydston caught the ball and took off for the distant goal line, pursued by two Bear defenders, one of them Paul Larson. It was an exciting chase, but Boydston managed to outrun his two would-be tacklers and a few seconds later crossed the goal line—a touchdown play that covered 87 yards.

Two plays later California lost the ball again after a fumble on its own 25-yard line. From there the Sooners carried it in for a third touchdown. Each team scored one additional touchdown, and the final score was 27–13.

Against Texas Christian at Norman the following week the OU team was less than impressive. Apparently unprepared, the ball carriers fumbled ten times, and TCU recovered five of the loose balls. One fumble occurred while the player was carrying the ball across the Horned Frogs' goal line; it was recovered in the end zone for a touchback.

Calame was injured during the second period, and Jimmy Harris, his sophomore understudy from Terrell, Texas, took over. Harris handled the assignment well, calling the plays with confidence and poise.

The game was characterized by an act of sportsmanship seldom seen in an athletic contest—or any other human activity, for that matter. In the second quarter TCU appeared to have completed a pass into the OU end zone, and the field judge, Don Rossi, signaled a touchdown. But Johnny Crouch, TCU captain and right end, told Rossi that the ball had bounced on the ground before the catch and therefore had been trapped by the receiver. His account was supported by the head linesman, who had been following the play. Oklahoma players stared unbelievingly as the official signaled an incomplete pass and brought the ball to the original line of scrimmage.

The only scoring in the first half occurred when Buddy Leake was tackled in the OU end zone while attempting a punt, giving a two point safety to TCU. By the end of the third quarter, the Horned Frogs had established a 7–16 advantage and gave every indication that they intended to hold the lead. The 50,000 spectators, who for three quarters had sat quietly in the stands, watched in shocked disbelief as their favorite football team appeared to do everything wrong.

Then the crowd decided to get behind the team and give some vocal encouragement. Stimulated by the cheerleaders, the student body and the fans in the west stand came through, and the Sooner squad responded to the almost continuous roar. The team played its best football of the afternoon, scoring two touchdowns to gain a 21–16 lead and then, during the final six minutes, holding on to contain a TCU drive that had moved to the OU 7-yard line when the clock ran out.

Wilkinson reviewed the problem of team attitude in his football letter the following week:

I don't think that, in their own mind, our boys were prepared to play as well against Texas Christian as they were against California. Much of this was probably our fault as coaches. The problem of getting a football team in the proper attitude for a game is a serious one. The problem of keeping them in a proper attitude week after week during a prolonged winning streak is almost overwhelming.

Facing the Longhorns at Dallas the next weekend was not a pleasant prospect for Oklahoma partisans. The backfield, already weakened by the loss of Tom Carroll, had been dealt an additional jolt with the loss of Calame, who left the Texas Christian game with a fractured collarbone. But Jimmy Harris, although inexperienced, was far better prepared to take over the quarterbacking responsibilities than might have been expected of a sophomore. When Calame was injured in practice the previous spring, the coaches, apparently concerned about his durability, had assigned him to work with Harris on ball handling and faking. When Calame was injured before the California game, he resumed his tutoring of the promising boy from south of the Red River, and the two continued to work together to get Harris ready for the Texas encounter. Harris was an apt student; he gave promise of being able to move the team come Saturday.

Mrs. Cross and I received an invitation from R. W. Thornton, the mayor of Dallas, to be guests of the city during the weekend of the game. We were to be met at the airport and taken to a suite in the Baker Hotel. A babysitter would be provided for our seven-year-old son, Braden. Limousine service and a motorcycle escort would be provided between the hotel and the Cotton Bowl. Mystified by all of this attention, because I had only a very casual acquaintance with Mayor Thornton, I soon learned that Harold Shank, an OU alumnus serving as secretary of the city of Dallas, had been responsible for it.

Mrs. Cross and I flew to Dallas with the team Friday afternoon.

The players went to Fort Worth for the night. But a reception committee from the mayor's office, including Shank, was on hand to meet Mrs. Cross and me (we had decided not to take Braden). Another party from the Dallas Chamber of Commerce was also there to extend a welcome. After an exchange of pleasantries we were loaded into a black Cadillac limousine and whisked to our hotel in Dallas behind a motorcycle escort. Flowers and fruit were awaiting us in the two-room suite near the top of the Baker Hotel. There was a television set in each room, something rather unusual in those days.

The hotel lobby was crowded that evening with individuals of varying ages and degrees of sobriety, all intent on having a boisterously good time. The hotel management, no doubt alerted from past experience, had wisely removed every vestige of furniture from the lobby and mezzanine.

We managed to get through the lobby to the elevators and make our way to our suite. We rested reasonably well, although, until about 2:00 A.M. there were occasional knocks on the door, followed by, "Is this the Delt party?"

We spent the next morning resting and enjoying the fruit and flowers from the mayor's office. The black Cadillac reappeared at noon and, with motorcycle escort, took us to the fairgrounds. There, after wandering around for a bit, we went to the Cotton Bowl and found our seats.

The game was typical of the series, a hard-fought contest featuring two especially good lines. At the beginning it appeared that OU was destined to continue its fumbling ways of the preceding Saturday. Buddy Leake received the opening kickoff and returned it to the OU 26-yard line, where, in response to a jarring tackle, he surrendered the ball to an alert Texas defender on the OU 29. OU stopped the Texas drive on its 5-yard line by recovering a fumble, but in the series of plays Don Brown, senior tackle, suffered a broken leg.

Facing a strong wind early in the game, the Sooners decided to kick out immediately. The punt was returned to the OU 27. From there the Steers were able to score after five well-executed plays, one of them a 21-yard gain on a forward pass off a pitchout. Thus, with only 6 minutes and 28 seconds gone in the game, Texas led by 7 points.

238

But the Sooners kept their poise, and after Leake returned the second Texas kickoff to the OU 27-yard line, they plowed down the field 73 yards in fifteen plays to a touchdown. Two events were noteworthy during the touchdown march, both of them involving OU's sophomore quarterback, Jimmy Harris. The first occurred when the Sooners found themselves on their own 36-yard line with fourth down and 1 yard to go. In such a situation, so deep in their own territory and so early in the game, it seemed that there was nothing to do but try to punt out of danger. But Harris had other ideas. Aware his team was facing a very strong wind, he decided to gamble—a decision perhaps related to a signal from Wilkinson on the sidelines. The gamble was successful beyond the fondest hopes of the OU partisans. Harris called a handoff to Bob Herndon, the right halfback, who, following a path pretty well cleared by the crushing blocks of Boydston, Gray, Burris, and Morris, carried the ball 14 yards to the midfield stripe, where he was stopped by persistent secondary defenders. The second event of special interest in the drive came two plays later, when Harris completed his first forward pass in intercollegiate competition.

It was very hot in the Cotton Bowl, and the energy of OU's first team had been severely drained by the 73-yard drive. Sensing this, Wilkinson sent in his entire alternate team—six of them sophomores who had played very little college ball—shortly before the end of the first quarter.

The alternate team could not move the ball on their first possession and were forced to punt. But the aggressive youngsters held the Longhorns for downs and received the Texas punt on the OU 40-yard line. On the first play of their second possession Pat O'Neal, the alternate quarterback, completed a forward pass to John Bell for a gain of 40 yards and a first down on the Texas 15. After the pass play Wilkinson sent his rested regulars back in to score the second and, as it turned out, winning touchdown; although there were still more than eight minutes left in the first half, neither team scored during the rest of the game. OU dominated the play in the second half but lost the ball four times on fumbles, each time ruining what appeared to be a good opportunity to score, and the game ended 14-7 in favor of Oklahoma.

The OU band, always effective in its between-halves perfor-

239

mances, put on an unusually good show that day. The band, organized in 1904, was celebrating its fiftieth birthday. Much had been accomplished during that half century. In 1904 there were seventeen musicians, including the band director, a freshman named Lloyd B. Curtis. Curtis must have had extraordinary musical ability; during the summer preceding his enrollment as a freshman at OU he had played with a band at the World's Fair in St. Louis, Missouri. At OU that fall he suggested to Henry D. Guelick, director of the School of Music, that it would be a good thing to organize a band. Guelick, recognizing the boy's impressive talent as a cornetist, waived his academic deficiencies and appointed him to the faculty of the School of Music as director of bands. The young man worked hard with his little group during the school year, playing at athletic contests and other university events, and at year's end President David Ross Boyd signed a pay voucher for him in the amount of fourteen dollars for "conducting rehearsals."

Now, in 1954, the band fielded 140 musicians under the direction of Leonard H. Haug, professor of music education and director of bands. Haug had been responsible for the band's activities since 1945. He was innovative and resourceful in the development of his marching bands. He had chosen the works of George M. Cohan as the theme for this anniversary event. Cohan would have been proud to acknowledge the salute. The intricate maneuvers and flawless music brought applause even from the Texas fans.

The Sooners had little trouble with the University of Kansas the next week and only slightly more with Kansas State a week later. The Jayhawks obligingly fumbled five times, and OU recovered the loose balls. Four of the fumbles were close to the Kansas goal line and were speedily turned into OU touchdowns. The final score was an embarrassing 65–0, and Wilkinson fielded the entire squad of thirty-six men (traveling squads were restricted to that number by conference regulations). After the game, with characteristic restraint, Wilkinson said, "I don't believe we are as good as the score indicates, nor that Kansas is that poor a team." Ever sensitive to the feelings of badly defeated opponents, he wrote in his letter the following week:

I think that the game, and the contrasting records of Oklahoma and

Kansas at this point of the season, illustrate what I have always believed so strongly to be true about football. At the start of the season, all teams are fairly close in ability. However, as the season unwinds and one squad begins losing, everyone starts asking "Why?" This continual complaining discourages the losing team. The constant grumbling and fault finding gradually affects the players. Instead of improving, they begin to play with the dull realization that no matter how hard they try, their efforts seem to be unappreciated by those whose support they need the most, their own fans. On the other hand, the team that is fortunate enough to win a few games picks up the other kind of momentum. It is relatively easy to coach a winning team, but exceedingly difficult when things start to break the other way.

. . . I cannot remember our being the recipients of so many good breaks. I wish we could have saved a few for our future games.

It was a somewhat different story when Kansas State came to Norman to face the powerful Sooners on October 23 (Band Day). The weather was cloudy and windy, uninviting to most football fans and very difficult for football players who had the responsibility of estimating the trajectories of punts and passes. But the scene in the stadium was brightened by the uniforms of approximately seven thousand members of the 109 Oklahoma high-school bands that had participated in the parade on the streets of Norman that morning.

Oklahoma scored three touchdowns in the first half—the third just 2 minutes, 14 seconds before intermission. All three attempts for extra points were successful, and the score was 21-0, where it remained for the rest of the game. The Sooner play was methodical, almost plodding, rather than sparkling during the first half, and it was highly erratic during the second. What might have been an omen that the Sooners were not up for the game came on their first play from scrimmage. Harris, the quarterback, gained 18 yards on a keeper and then fumbled the ball to a Kansas State defender. This was the first of seven OU fumbles (K State recovered three of them) that demonstrated lack of sharpness, especially during the second half. The ability to play well was demonstrated near the end of the game, however, when the alternate unit drove 79 yards, only to be stopped on the K State 1-yard line.

The following week Wilkinson wrote a couple of paragraphs for his weekly letter which probably were intended more for the attention of his football squad than for the members of the OU Alumni Association to whom the letters were mailed. He wrote:

I think this game illustrated one of football's oldest and most inflexible principles. No football team can ever stand still from one week to the next. It either gets better or it begins to deteriorate. Most teams improve steadily from game to game, but I don't think we have made much progress the past two weeks.

Unless we practice better in the future, we are going to be caught soon. Other teams are working hard in practice and are becoming better teams. We were probably better than some of our opponents early in the season but unless we start improving at the same rate that they are improving, we won't be as good at the end of the year.

The sixth game of the season, with Colorado at Boulder on October 30, was a crucial one. The Buffalos, coached by Dal Ward, had a record of 5–1 for the season, and, remembering the close, hard-fought contest lost at OU last year, they certainly would make every effort to be ready for the Sooners. The Coloradans operated from a single-wingback formation, with large, powerful backs.

The game had been sold out a full month before the game. The largest crowd ever assembled in Colorado for a football game was waiting at kickoff time with noisy enthusiasm, aware that the winner probably would be the conference champion. If it should be Colorado, the reward would be a trip to the Orange Bowl. Oklahoma was not eligible to return to Miami because, when the Big Seven Conference rescinded its action barring participation in postseason contests, it added a provision that none of its member schools could play in a bowl game two years in a row. I must admit to being responsible for this regulation, because I had successfully urged the presidents of the Big Seven schools to instruct their faculty representatives to enact it. Later the conference had entered into a contract with the Orange Bowl officials that provided that the Big Seven champion would play in the bowl each year. The contract also provided, however, that if a Big Seven team should win the championship two years in a row the team in second place would play the second year.

It was a bright, clear afternoon in Boulder the day of the game

242

—ideal weather for football. OU muffed opportunities to score in the first quarter, fumbling twice, the second time on the Colorado 2-yard line. Colorado scored in the second quarter, but Gene Mears, the OU center, blocked the try for point, holding Colorado's lead to 0–6. Jimmy Harris, the Sooner quarterback, injured his chest early in the quarter and had to leave the game. Gene Calame, who had been out of action for five weeks with the injured shoulder, took over the quarterbacking duties, and, although he moved the team 76 yards to the Colorado 1, the team was unable to put OU on the scoreboard during the first half.

During the second half OU's starting team, with Calame at quarterback, scored a touchdown and kicked goal early in the fourth quarter. Less than ten minutes later the Sooner alternates, with Pat O'Neal at quarterback, scored a second touchdown but missed the try for point. There was no further scoring; OU won 13–6.

The following week the Sooners went to Ames, Iowa, where they took care of Iowa State handily by a score of 40–0. The offense that day was the most consistent and best balanced of the season: 265 yards rushing, 151 yards passing, and 90 yards on punt returns. The kicking game was excellent too: the punts averaged 50 yards.

Shortly after the Iowa State game, singer Bing Crosby came up with a proposal to utilize the talents of the OU football team in raising money to send the United States Olympic team to the 1956 games at Melbourne, Australia. His scheme involved a post-season contest between OU and UCLA, to be played about the middle of December in one of the large California stadiums, probably the Los Angeles Coliseum. UCLA was rated the number-one team in the country, and OU was also highly regarded. Because of conference regulations prohibiting the teams from playing in bowl games two years in a row, UCLA was not eligible to participate in the Rose Bowl festivities and, of course, OU could not return to the Orange Bowl. What, Crosby asked, could be more natural than to have these two great teams play for the national championship, independently of the bowls?

The idea was very popular with the sports writers, especially those on the large West Coast newspapers. There was heavy pressure on Dr. Raymond B. Allen, chancellor of UCLA, to agree to the proposal and try to persuade the University of Oklahoma to participate. Chancellor Allen telephoned me, and we discussed the idea. We quickly agreed that the game would be a sellout at five dollars a seat in the Los Angeles Coliseum and might well bring more than a hundred thousand dollars through sale of television rights. But we agreed also that it would not be in the interest of either school to participate, because the NCAA regulations prohibited postseason contests except for bowl games previously approved by the association. Moreover, the game would be very disrupting to the academic programs of both institutions and not in keeping with the spirit of the conference regulations prohibiting a team from appearing in a bowl game two years in a row.

After our conversation each of us announced that while we would like very much for the two schools to play, the time was too short to get permission from the two conferences and from the NCAA.

For once Oklahomans seemed to understand the situation pretty well, but the Californians would not give up the idea. United States Senator Thomas Kuchel of California called both Chancellor Allen and me, reportedly on behalf of Vice-President Richard Nixon, urging us to make arrangements to play the game. He pointed out that Wilbur Johns, athletic director at UCLA, was also chairman of the NCAA's postseason committee. With Johns's help there should be little difficulty getting approval from the NCAA.

In presenting their arguments, boosters of the game made much of the fact that support for the Olympic team was much greater in the Soviet Union than in the United States. As a result the United States was likely to be seriously embarrassed at Melbourne. It was really a matter of patriotism, they argued. What loyal Americans could possibly oppose scheduling a game that could produce perhaps half a million dollars for such a worthy purpose?

But the regents supported my decision not to try to gain approval from the conference and the NCAA, and the pressures gradually subsided. I had begun to realize that, given time, most things will pass.

In the meantime, Wilkinson and his staff had been preparing for the Dad's Day game with Missouri at Norman on November 13. The Tigers, though plagued at times with injuries, had had a good season. There was a slim chance that they might represent the conference at the Orange Bowl—if they could defeat Oklahoma and if Nebraska lost the two games remaining on its schedule. They had the best rushing-passing offense in the Big Seven, and like all teams they would be up for OU.

The game was played before fifty-seven thousand fans, the third-largest crowd ever to assemble for an athletic contest in Oklahoma. After a somewhat frustrating first half, during which there was no scoring for nearly 29 minutes, Pat O'Neal finally completed a pass to Bob Herndon for a touchdown. Buddy Leake converted, and the Sooners led 7–0 with only 68 seconds left before intermission. Twenty-five seconds later, after Missouri had fumbled the OU kickoff, O'Neal completed another pass, this time to Billy Pricer, who raced from the 10-yard line into the end zone. Leake's try for extra point was good, and the Sooners led at halftime 14–0. Things can happen quickly in a football game, but I do not remember any other occasion when the same team scored touchdowns 25 seconds apart.

The second half was more productive pointwise. OU scored three additional touchdowns and converted twice. The Tigers finally got their passing attack going and produced two touchdowns and one extra point. But the powerful Sooner defense effectively contained the Missourians on the ground, permitting only one first down from rushing during the entire game.

With two games remaining, OU (5–0) had clinched at least a portion of the conference championship. Nebraska (4–1) was in second place and bound for Miami regardless of what might happen when the Cornhuskers met the Sooners at Norman on November 20—Homecoming at OU.

The previous summer a new chancellor had taken over the administration of the University of Nebraska. He was Dr. Clifford M. Hardin, who had been named to the post after a distinguished career as dean of the College of Agriculture at Michigan State College. It had been customary for the institutions of the Big Seven Conference to have as guests on game days the presidents of the visiting schools and their wives. In the beginning hospitality had included luncheon and box seats at the game. For the past year or so, however, it had seemed better—more comfortable and less embarrassing—for the visiting president to attend the luncheon but to sit in the section reserved for fans of the visiting school. Mrs. Cross and I had found this arrangement especially satisfactory since the OU team had come to dominate the conference so completely.

But for the new chancellor at the University of Nebraska it seemed like a good idea to offer a bit more in the way of hospitality, and so we invited Chancellor Hardin, Mrs. Hardin, and their four children to be house guests on Friday evening preceding the game, have lunch at the house, and then go to the game together. Chancellor Hardin accepted the invitation, partly no doubt because Mrs. Hardin's sister lived in Norman. She was a distinguished researcher and writer in social psychology and the wife of an eminent social psychologist, Dr. Muzafer Sherif, who was a member of the OU faculty. It was arranged that the Hardin children would spend Friday night with the Sherifs.

The next day the children came to our home for the pregame family lunch. Afterward we walked to the stadium, and, on the way, I bought Nebraska pennants for the children to wave. As we were going along, Dr. Hardin said to me: "I know that we have little chance to win this afternoon, but I do hope we are not humiliated by a lopsided score. I would like to think of Nebraska as a worthy representative of the conference at the Orange Bowl." I responded with great sincerity, that I certainly hoped so too, and then, with less sincerity, expressed my belief that his team would do well, both that afternoon and at the Orange Bowl.

The Hardin family was given the number-one box; I sat with Mrs. Cross in the number-two box with a pipe railing between me and Dr. Hardin.

Everything went well during the pregame activities, but I was a bit nervous and uneasy as play got underway. I wanted the Hardin family to have a reasonably pleasant time, and I knew it was quite possible that the OU team might ruin everything for them. My fears appeared to be well founded during the first quarter: after Buddy Leake had intercepted a Nebraska pass on the Husker 48-yard line, OU started an eleven-play drive that ended with a touchdown and a successful try for extra point, with nearly eight minutes still remaining in the quarter. A quick calculation brought the dismaying realization that OU could score 56 points if that scoring rate was maintained the rest of the game —an agonizing possibility. Dr. Hardin, apparently thinking along similar lines, leaned over and said, "Your team scored with so little apparent effort, I'm afraid Nebraska is in for a bad afternoon."

But temporary relief came to both of us during the remaining minutes of the first quarter. Nebraska took the OU kickoff and, using ground plays only, drove 44 yards toward the Oklahoma goal line before a jarring tackle (Cecil Morris) caused a fumble that Jerry Tubbs recovered deep in Oklahoma territory.

At this point Dr. Hardin leaned over and said, "Well, things are looking better. But I do wish we could have driven in for a touchdown." I nodded without comment, because OU's quarterback was already calling signals for the first play after gaining possession.

Something went wrong for OU during the course of that play, and when it ended, Nebraska had recovered a fumble on the OU 20-yard line. Then a pass from the Husker quarterback to a receiver in the OU end zone placed Nebraska on the scoreboard; a successful try for extra point tied the score 7–7, with less than two minutes remaining in the first quarter.

An encouraged Dr. Hardin leaned toward me and said, "Well, I suspect that we don't have much chance to win this ball game, but I feel a lot better. No matter what happens now, it looks like we will make a respectable showing."

While Nebraska had indeed done very well during the first quarter, I was still apprehensive about what might happen during the remaining three quarters. I wanted to win, of course, but by as narrow a margin as possible. My concern was justified. After playing on fairly even terms until midway in the second quarter, a Nebraska safety fumbled the ball after signaling for a fair catch, and Buddy Leake recovered for OU on the Cornhusker 25-yard line. Wilkinson then sent in his alternate unit, which, quarterbacked by Pat O'Neal, scored in four plays—the final one a 21-yard touchdown pass from O'Neal to Tommy McDonald. O'Neal kicked goal, and OU led 14–7.

The situation was still reasonably comfortable, because there were only five minutes left in the half, and it seemed unlikely that there would be any more scoring during the second period. I was pleased a minute or so later when a splendid Nebraska punt with excellent punt coverage left OU with the ball on its own 6-yard line. With the excellent defense Nebraska had shown, there seemed little likelihood that OU could drive 94 yards for a touchdown before the half ended. But OU's first unit, now back in the game, seemed determined to prove me wrong. Gene Calame carried four times for a total of 23 yards, getting his team out of the danger zone. He then completed a 50-yard pass to Max Boydston, placing the ball on Nebraska's 19-yard line. Only 43 seconds remained, and it appeared that the situation called for another pass. But instead Calame pitched out to Buddy Leake, who went around right end for a touchdown, aided as he approached the goal line by a block thrown by Max Boydston. The try for extra point was successful, and the half ended with OU leading 21–7.

Although disappointed by this rather sudden development, the Hardin family was not disheartened, and Dr. Hardin expressed satisfaction with his team's performance. He did say that he hoped the Nebraska defense could settle down and prevent additional scoring during the second half.

But the second half was to be a decidedly unpleasant experience for the Cornhusker team and its fans, headed as they were for the Orange Bowl with such high hopes. OU received the opening kickoff, and promptly drove 74 yards, in eleven plays, to score a touchdown, followed by a successful try for point. But this was only the first of five OU touchdowns scored during the final two periods, even though Wilkinson used his third and fourth teams most of the time. Forty-two Sooners saw action, and the eighth OU touchdown of the day was produced by the fourth team, with Jay O'Neal at quarterback. Tom Carroll, a senior halfback who had been sidelined during the season with injuries, was sent in to kick the extra point. Leake had missed a try for point earlier in the second half. The final score was 55–7.

The game was easily the most unpleasant experience I have ever had at an athletic contest. I could think of nothing to say to our Nebraska guests after the OU score had reached the thirties, and after two or three rather feeble attempts at conversation I watched the rest of the game in silence. The Hardin children, who at the beginning of the afternoon had cheered and happily waved their Nebraska pennants, became quiet early in the second half and, with pennants drooping, cast occasional worried looks at their parents. I spent most of my time fervently hoping that Oklahoma would not score again; but although Wilkinson cleared his bench, each new team was as enthusiastic and capable as its predecessor. The walk home from the stadium after the game was a somber journey. But the Hardins were most gracious when they left. Dr. Hardin said that OU had the best team he had ever seen and that surely it must be the best in the nation.

Only Oklahoma A&M College at Stillwater remained on the schedule, a game that Wilkinson faced with the usual misgivings, though OU had not lost to its sister institution since 1945. The Aggies, with an open date the preceding Saturday, had two weeks to prepare for the OU invasion. They had plenty of incentive, because a win over OU would mean a successful season for them regardless of what might have happened in their other games. And playing at Lewis Field had always been a nerve-wracking experience for OU teams. The turf was usually worn down to the bare dirt, and in the event of rain or snow the field certainly would be slippery and muddy because the college had no field tarp to protect it. That would handicap OU's delicately timed split-T offense.

But the field was dry when the two teams met, and the 60-degree weather was favorable, although a strong wind was blowing across the field from the southwest. Thirty-eight thousand fans, an all-time record, were on hand to see the game. Among these as honored guests were a dozen or so Sooner and Aggie players who had participated fifty years earlier in the first Sooner-Aggie football game, played at Guthrie in 1904.

The season's finale certainly was not OU's best effort. The team did not seem to have the spirit and sharpness that had characterized its earlier efforts, but it did manage to score a couple of

The 1954 team. FIRST ROW (FRONT ROW), LEFT TO RIGHT: Jerry Tubbs, John Sain, John Bell, Bob Timberlake, Bill Harris, Wilbur Derrick, Bill Cheadle, Gene Calame, Carl Allison, Gene Mears, Bob Herndon, Pat O'Neal, Milton Simmons, Don Brown, Calvin Woodworth, Robert Van Dee, Bob Wyatt, Jim Harris. SECOND ROW: Bob Gatling, Robert Derrick, Jay O'Neal, Delbert Long, George Nelson, Billy Davis, Wray Littlejohn, Gene Stephens, Buddy Leake, Buddy Cockrell, Bill Brown, Tom Emerson, Tommy Pearson, Dale Depue, Jimmy Duke, Billy Pricer, Bo Bolinger, Myron Salter. THIRD ROW: Woody Wolverton, Bobby Darnell, Max Boydston, Jim Smiley, Bob Martin, Wayne Greenlee, Bob Loughridge, Duane Goff, Edmon Gray, Tommy McDonald, Robert Burris, Joe Mobra, Kurt Burris, Ken Northcutt, Cecil Morris. Courtesy Sports Information Department.

touchdowns, followed by extra points, thus winning the ball game by a score of 14–0—its nineteenth consecutive win and twentieth game without defeat.

This record served to sustain the NCAA's curiosity about the recruiting policies of the University of Oklahoma. After my correspondence with Walter Byers in the fall, I had made a couple of trips to Kansas City in early December hoping to clear up the matter. But Byers had intimated that he was not entirely satisfied with what he had learned, and so I suggested that a committee of the NCAA come to Norman to interview those involved in OU's football program—the football staff, athletes, and others who might have pertinent information. Byers accepted the invitation and arranged for three representatives from the Committee on Infractions of the NCAA to visit OU on a fact-finding mission. The trio, consisting of Byers; Frank H. Gardener, of Drake University; and E. G. Whereatt, secretary of the infractions committee, came to Norman for conferences on December 16 and 17.

Interviews were scheduled with a number of athletes: Tommy Pearson, of Oklahoma City; Henry Bonney, a 225-pound freshman tackle from Yazoo City, Mississippi; Roger Tayler, a freshman back from Kansas City, Missouri; Tommy McDonald, a sophomore back from Albuquerque, New Mexico; Robert Derrick and Willard Derrick, sophomores from Woodward; Bill Brown, a back from Wagoner; Jerry Tubbs, of Breckenridge, Texas; and Byron Searcy, of Fort Worth, Texas.

Scheduled also for interviews were members of the football coaching staff who had held their jobs long enough to be involved in OU's recruitment program: Bud Wilkinson, Gomer Jones, Pete Elliott, and Sam Lyle. Bill Jennings, former backfield coach at the university but then employed by the Noble Drilling Company, was asked to appear also. Jennings had been largely responsible for OU's recruiting program, and the NCAA committee appeared especially eager to question him. Jennings flew up from Fort Worth and brought Byron Searcy with him (Searcy had dropped out of school after an operation).

In addition to those directly involved with the athletic program, Quentin Little, OU regent from Ardmore, was asked to appear before the committee, and Dr. C. B. McDonald, the Oklahoma City dentist who had figured prominently in the "rescue" of Lindell Pearson from Arkansas, received a similar invitation.

Members of the committee did not reveal to the university or to the press the nature of the charges they were investigating. But it was apparent from their questions that OU had been accused of financial extravagance in conducting the program— simply outbidding competing institutions for athletic talent.

The athletes were asked what inducements, if any, had led them to choose OU; what added benefits had been made available to them since they had entered the institution; and what, if any, commitments had been made to them concerning employment after graduation from the university. All the athletes denied that any special inducements had been offered; several of them said that they had received more attractive offers from other schools.

In questioning Regent Little, the members of the committee got down to specifics. Had Little loaned a car to Byron Searcy on several occasions, and had he entertained Searcy in his home over a weekend in an effort to persuade him to play at OU? Little denied this emphatically with the comment that "I knew Searcy's daddy for years, and even went to school with him as a boy in Kingston, Oklahoma, but I sure didn't do any recruiting with him or his son." Searcy confirmed Little's story.

The meetings continued on into Friday morning, but the committee adjourned in time to depart for Kansas City shortly after noon.

One objective of the committee had not been realized, an interview with Buddy Leake. Leake was participating in the annual North-South game, but it was arranged that he would go to Kansas City a few days later for questioning.

We did not hear anything more from the NCAA until April 26, 1955, when the policy-making council of the association, after hearing a report from the infractions committee, voted to place the University of Oklahoma on probation "for a period of two years from that date." The council announced its decision through the following resolution sent to the university and to the news media:

Whereas the NCAA Committee on Infractions has investigated alleged violations of NCAA principles, rules, and regulations by the University of Oklahoma and reported its findings to the Council,

Whereas the Council has found the University of Oklahoma to have been in violation of Article XI, Section 1 of the Bylaws in that University staff members offered prospective student athletes cost-free education beyond the athlete's normal period of eligibility, this practice being in direct violation of Article II, Section 13 (B) of the rules and regulations of the Missouri Valley Intercollegiate Athletic Association in which the University holds membership,

Whereas the Council has found the University of Oklahoma to be in violation of Article III, Section 1, of the Constitution in that it has followed the practice of paying medical expenses for the immediate families of student athletes, specifically the wives and children of such athletes,

Whereas the Council has found the University of Oklahoma to be in violation of Article III, Section 4 of the Constitution in that University patrons have provided student athletes of the University fringe benefits in the form of clothes, miscellaneous gifts of cash and other gifts of relatively nominal value, and in the case of two athletes paid the charges of the periodic use of a rent-a-car vehicle,

Now, therefore, be it resolved that the University of Oklahoma be placed on probation for a period of two years from this date (April 26, 1955), it being understood that the Committee on Infractions shall review the athletic policies and practices at the University prior to the expiration of this probation.

Be it further resolved that the NCAA wishes to record its appreciation of the excellent cooperation and assistance extended to the Committee on Infractions by the University's executive and athletic administration during the lengthy processing of this case.

While I had hoped that the university might get through the investigation without disciplinary action, I was nevertheless pleased that no serious charges against the university's athletic policies had been sustained, and I was pleased also that action taken by the NCAA had not included barring the institution from participation in postseason contests, especially bowl games.

CHAPTER 19

Another National Championship— The Orange Bowl

1955-56

ALTHOUGH deeply concerned, and surely distracted at times by the vigorous NCAA investigation, Wilkinson and his staff—Gomer Jones, Sam Lyle, Ted Youngling, Eddie Crowder (replacing Pete Elliott, who had resigned to become head coach at the University of Nebraska), and Bill Canfield—spent the spring months planning carefully for the 1955 football season. Reports from Harold Keith's office to the media concerning the team's prospects were as usual restrained and tinged with pessimism. Lost from the line would be the three most outstanding players of the preceding season: Carl Allison and Max Boydston at ends and Kurt Burris at center. Gene Mears, the top-flight alternate at center, would be gone also, and the removal of Jerry Tubbs from fullback to center would mean that an entirely new starting backfield must be found because Gene Calame, Buddy Leake, and Bobby Herndon had completed their eligibility.

But despite these losses the sports writers of the Big Seven were almost unanimous in agreeing that Oklahoma would win another conference championship, and writers farther away gave Oklahoma high national ratings, ranging from first to fifth place.

Spring practice gave some cause for optimism. Jerry Tubbs was exceptionally promising at center. Tackles Calvin Woodworth and Ed Gray performed well. Bo Bolinger received occasional mention for All-America honors at guard, and Cecil Morris was almost as impressive. The ends were something of a question mark, but several reserves, including Joe Mobra, John Bell, Bob Timberlake, Tommy Pearson, Fred Hood, and Don Stiller were available.

Who would handle the backfield positions was not clearly established in spring practice, but Jay O'Neal and Jimmy Harris were available at quarterback. Tom McDonald and Bob Burris appeared to be the leading prospects for the halfback slots, although Clendon Thomas and Carl Dodd, from last season's freshman group, seemed likely to provide good competition. Billy Pricer appeared to be the leading candidate at fullback.

In preseason speculation Oklahoma's toughest competition in the conference was Colorado, where twenty-seven of thirty lettermen were returning. Some writers thought that Missouri might be dangerous too, especially because the game would be played at Columbia.

Outside the conference Texas, Pittsburgh, and Oklahoma A&M appeared to have the potential to upset the Sooners. Texas, unimpressive during the past several seasons, had lettermen available for every position, plus a new sophomore quarterback named Walter Fondren, who had been one of the most sought-after high-school athletes in the nation. Pittsburgh, with a new coach, was similarly equipped, with lettermen for every position left over from the squad that had defeated Navy 21–9 in 1954. Oklahoma A&M's new coach, Cliff Speegle, had less-experienced personnel, but the over-all quality of his squad was good, and the needed experience would be obtained for the season's windup with OU. North Carolina, the fourth nonconference team on the Sooner schedule and the opponent for the opening game, was not considered much of a threat. North Carolina's football fortunes had been at a relatively low ebb in recent years, and there were rumors that the institution was trying to lure Jim Tatum back to his alma mater as head football coach.

But when Wilkinson and his squad journeyed to Chapel Hill to start the season, they found that the University of North Carolina had been underrated. The game, played under adverse weather conditions—a temperature of 80 degrees and humidity ranging from 90 to 95 per cent—was not particularly reassuring to Oklahoma followers who were hoping for another undefeated and untied season. The OU team committed a number of errors, fumbling seven times, once in their own end zone with a resultant North Carolina touchdown and once in North Carolina's end zone, where the opponents recovered the ball for a touchback. But the Sooners managed to retain enough poise to dominate the game statistically and win, 13–6.

This unpromising beginning turned out to be in no way prophetic of what was to happen during the rest of the season. The following week, playing at home, the Sooners decisively defeated a good Pittsburgh team, 26–14, in a game characterized by Jimmy Harris' careful and effective quarterbacking and Tommy Mc-Donald's exceptional passing and running. Errors were kept to a minimum, with only one fumble, which turned the ball to Pitts-burgh on the OU 43-yard line. The victory was especially im-pressive in view of the fact that earlier in the season Pittsburgh had defeated the University of California at Berkeley and Syra-cuse University.

Next on the schedule was the annual pilgrimage to Dallas for the meeting with the University of Texas. The Steers had lost a close contest to Southern California the week before. Sam Lyle, who had scouted the game, reported that Texas probably would have won had they not lost their quarterback, Joe Clements, early in the game. At the time of his injury Clements was leading the nation in passing, having completed twenty-two of thirty at-tempts (an almost unbelievable record of 73.3 per cent) for 299 yards, and four touchdowns.

Clements was back at the helm for the OU contest, and Texas dominated the passing game, 191–54 yards. But three intercep-tions by Jerry Tubbs, combined with brilliant quick kicking by Billy Pricer and Clendon Thomas and excellent defensive play, especially by Tubbs, Calvin Woodworth and Cecil Morris, con-tained the Longhorn offense pretty well. OU's offensive effort was well coordinated, and the Sooners came through with a 20–0 victory in a game that many thought much closer than the score indicated. It was OU's fourth consecutive win over the Long-horns and the seventh of the past eight games.

With the preliminaries out of the way the Sooners faced their conference competition. The first of the six opponents was the University of Kansas, at Norman—Homecoming Day. The Jay-hawkers, under Coach Chuck Mather, had shown improvement during the season, and they startled the Homecoming crowd by receiving the opening kickoff and in only eight plays driving 71 yards to a touchdown. But their conversion attempt was blocked by Tommy McDonald, and thereafter it was Oklahoma's game all the way; the entire squad of fifty-one participated in a 44–6 rout. The Sooners came out of the game battered, however; a record twenty-seven players went to the training room for treatment during the following week.

Colorado was next on the schedule, October 22 at Norman, Dad's Day. The Buffaloes, who ran from a single-wing formation under Dal Ward's effective coaching, were unbeaten. Wilkinson, who had regarded Colorado as the primary barrier to another Big Seven championship, was unusually sincere in voicing concern, with so many casualties from the preceding week missing practice. The fourth sellout crowd assembled at the stadium to see the game that most conceded would settle the conference championship. Thousands more were able to see the action telecast to Oklahoma and Colorado fans by two television stations. The teams battled to a scoreless tie during the first quarter, but early in the second quarter a couple of OU fumbles, one on the Sooner 5-yard line, and the other on the 30, led to touchdowns and conversions that gave the visitors a 0–14 advantage with about ten minutes left in the first half. Then, with some brilliant offensive play by Bob Burris and Tommy McDonald, aided by excellent over-all team effort, OU scored three touchdowns followed by successful conversions, giving the Sooners a 21–14 lead at halftime. The Oklahomans retained control during the second half, and all the players who were suited up for the game saw action as the final score grew to 56–21.

In the dressing room after the game Dal Ward commented: "That's the finest football team I have ever seen. Without a doubt, it's the fastest team I ever saw."

Wilkinson was especially complimentary of the Colorado staff and squad. In his newsletter he said that Colorado was the "best prepared team we've played." He followed with the comment: "Although they were bitterly disappointed to lose a battle in which the stakes were so high, and even though so many breaks went against them, they took the defeat as men. I hope that when it comes our turn, as it surely will soon to lose, we can follow their example of real sportsmanship."

With the season half over, national opinion and conference statistics began to take on some significance. The week after the Colorado game the University of Oklahoma placed second in the Associated Press poll, only slightly behind the University of Maryland. The Maryland Terrapins, unbeaten in the Atlantic Coast Conference, moved into first place after a 34–13 win over Syracuse, a highly regarded team that had crushed Army the preceding week. If Maryland and OU could retain their positions in the two top spots during the remainder of the season, a second clash in the Orange Bowl was almost assured.

The Sooners had no difficulty winning their sixth game with Kansas State at Manhattan on October 29. The entire traveling squad played in a 40–7 rout of the Wildcats.

The University of Missouri was the next test, scheduled for November 5, at Columbia. The Tigers, always dangerous at home, had started the season in auspicious fashion, losing to the University of Maryland at Columbia by the narrow margin of 13–12. Later, they were leading Michigan 7–0, when their quarterback, Jim Hunter was injured and lost to the squad. But Hunter, back in the lineup the next Saturday, led his team to a 20–12 win over Colorado at Boulder.

Don Faurot had his squad ready for the Sooners, but the Tigers were not quite able to cope with Jimmy Harris' skillful use of halfback passing—McDonald to Burris and Burris to McDonald —plus an OU recovered fumble on the Tiger 24-yard line, which led to a first quarter score of 14–0 in favor of the Sooners. That score held until well into the fourth quarter, when OU scored again but failed to kick goal, leaving the final tally 20–0.

When the game was over, the two teams met in the middle of the field for what Wilkinson later described as "the most sincere" postgame handshaking session he had ever seen. Later in the dressing room Faurot, whose team had lost to Maryland (13–12), Michigan (40–7), and now Oklahoma (20–0), was asked how he could compare his three opponents. Faurot replied, "Oklahoma, Maryland, and Michigan, in just about that order"—a reversal of the first- and second-place rankings the national polls had given earlier in the week.

In his newsletter, Wilkinson said of the Missouri game:

I've always noticed in college football that after a hard fought game between two fine teams, the players of both teams nearly always have respect for each other and reflect it in their handshakes on the field when the playing is over.

Most of the animosity in college football stems from alumni or followers who have lost wagers or been taunted by friends of the opposing club. If the fans would pattern their sportsmanship after that of the players themselves, the game would come much nearer fulfilling the purpose for which it was created, as a clean robust autumnal sport for college men.

There was little suspense for OU fans in the remaining games of the regular schedule. The Sooners rolled over Iowa State at Norman 52–0, they defeated the Nebraska Cornhuskers 41–0 at Lincoln, and they wound up the season by shellacking Oklahoma A&M 53–0 at Norman. In each of these games Wilkinson swept the bench, mercifully using his first team only sparingly after the issue was decided.

At the season's end the Sooners, who had been in first place in the national polls each week since the victory over Missouri, were voted national champions by the Associated Press for the second time in five years (they had first won the coveted title in 1950). Michigan State had edged into second place over Maryland, thus eliminating the possibility that the first and second teams of the nation would meet in the Orange Bowl.

With conference and national championships tucked away, with a twenty-nine-game winning streak to their credit, and with Bo Bolinger and Tommy McDonald named to several All-America selections, Oklahoma accepted an invitation to meet the Maryland Terrapins in the Orange Bowl at Miami on January 2, 1956.

The Oklahoma squad and coaches had only a few days for rest and relaxation after the game with Oklahoma A&M before beginning preparations for the Orange Bowl game. But they took time off for a social event on December 16 at the Sportsman's Club, in northwest Oklahoma City. The occasion was the presentation of the Reverend J. Hugh O'Donnell Memorial Trophy, an award signifying the national football championship.

It was the second time the Sooners had had possession of the trophy, the first having been the year following the 1950 season. Before handing the impressive plaque to Bo Bollinger, Cecil Morris, and Eldon Loughridge, the OU tri-captains, Joe Abbott, reminded the approximately five hundred guests that Oklahoma could take permanent custody of the trophy by winning one more

Bo Bolinger (left), Wilkinson, and Tommy McDonald hold the Reverend J. Hugh O'Donnell Trophy after winning the national football championship in 1955. Courtesy *Oklahoman and Times.*

national championship. Hinting that that might happen the next year, he speculated that the president of the University of Oklahoma might need a committee to choose a name for the new trophy that would be offered after OU had retired the present one.

As he delivered the trophy to the tri-captains, Abbott remarked that the good wishes of the Notre Dame lettermen, donors of the O'Donnell plaque, "go with you except for one Saturday afternoon in 1956 and one afternoon in 1957"—the dates that OU would play Notre Dame.

260

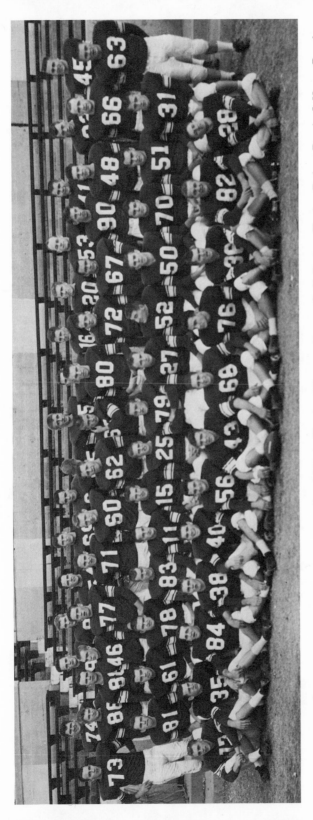

The 1955 team. FIRST ROW (FRONT ROW), LEFT TO RIGHT: Jay O'Neal, Clendon Thomas, Duane Goff, Rodger Taylor, Robert Burris, J. Henry Broyles, Jr., Billy Pricer, Buddy Oujesky, Byron Searcy, Dale Sherrod, Hugh Ballard, Robert Derrick. SECOND ROW: Bob Timberlake, Doyle Jennings, Eldon Loughridge, John Bell, Bill Sturm, Jim Harris, Tommy McDonald, Bo Bolinger, Delbert Long, Chuck Bowman, Jerry Fronterhouse, Barry West, Dennit Morris, Frank Merkt. THIRD ROW: Ed Gray, Bob Martin, Robert Bell, Jim Heard, Ed Parry, Wayne Greenlee, Calvin Woodworth, Ken Northcutt, Bill Krisher, Tommy Pearson, Jim Hagan, Kenneth Hallum, Wilbur Derrick, Gerald McPhail, Henry Bonney, Jim Gafford. FOURTH ROW: Cecil Morris, David Loop, Don Stiller, Bob Darnell, Tom Emerson, Larry Graham, Benton Ladd, Fred Hood, Bill Harris, Joe Mobra, Dale Depue, Jerry Tubbs, Don Nelson, Carl Dodd, Bill Brown. Courtesy Sports Information Department.

Bowl fever, in evidence even before Oklahoma and Maryland signed up to meet for a second time in Miami, continued to mount during December. Orange Bowl officials, until very recent years necessarily resigned to the fact that their attraction ranked third behind the Rose and Sugar Bowl games, were now basking in the certainty that theirs would be the number-one event of the football holiday season. The game appeared to have everything that could be desired. The only two undefeated major teams, ranking first and third in national ratings, would participate. The team with the best offensive record in the country would meet the team with the best defense. For the second time in three years a former head coach of one of the institutions would match wits with a former assistant. These factors provided the background for a flood of articles—comparisons and speculations about what would happen on January 2—in the major newspapers of the country.

The Sooner squad practiced until a day or two before Christmas, and were dismissed to spend Christmas at home, with instructions to be back in Norman for departure for Miami on Monday, December 26.

Mrs. Cross, Braden, and I flew with the squad and received the traditional Miami reception at the airport. Transportation was provided by a fleet of thirty new white Buick automobiles, each decorated with an Orange Bowl decal. The fleet made its way with police escort to the Bal Harbour Hotel. The welcome at the hotel was also impressive: a band in the lobby greeted the squad with "Boomer Sooner," followed by "Oklahoma!"

Unlike the 1954 game, which had been played in the afternoon, the 1956 contest was scheduled for the evening. The weather was good, and the sky was clear the night of the game. But the prospects for an Oklahoma victory were not so bright during the first two quarters. The huge Maryland defensive line and alert secondary smothered the OU offense, and the Sooners were unable to mount a sustained drive.

On offense the Terrapins threatened to score early in the game, when their halfback, Ed Vereb, took the ball behind his own 24-yard line, exploded through his right tackle into the clear, and traveled 64 yards to the OU 10 before Jay O'Neal managed

262

to trip him with a desperate diving tackle. But on the next play Wayne Greenlee slipped through the line and hit quarterback Frank Tamburello so hard that he dropped the ball. The fumble was recovered by OU end Don Stiller, and the first quarter went scoreless.

Rugged defensive play by both teams blunted offensive efforts during most of the second quarter, until less than three minutes remained in the first half. Then Maryland came up with a beautifully executed trick play in which Vereb received the ball, faked a pass, appeared to find his receivers covered, waited in apparent frustration as defensive linemen converged on him, and then took off around left end, where a convoy of blockers escorted him untouched across the goal line, with two minutes and forty seconds left in the half. Maryland missed the try for extra point.

After receiving the kickoff, the fast-breaking Sooners dominated the apparently tiring Terrapins in a drive that carried to the Maryland 25-yard line, but the half ended with OU trailing 0–6.

The complexion of the game changed dramatically with the start of the third quarter. The Sooners' rapid play during the final moments of the first half apparently gave the coaching staff some clue to what must be done to win the game. Obviously the Sooners were no match physically for the Maryland defense, and the logical solution to the problem was to run offensive plays so fast that the opponents would not have time to call defensive signals. As a result, the record breaking crowd of 76,561, and millions of television viewers, had the experience of seeing the OU quarterback call three plays in each huddle for several series of downs and in several instances operate so rapidly that the three plays were executed in less than a minute's time. Thinking back over the game, I recalled that after each play the eager Sooners were back at the line of scrimmage ready to go before all the Terrapin linemen had regained their feet. In an effort to slow the tempo, Maryland tacklers would lie on the ball carrier as long as possible after the whistle had blown, and I still remember Tommy McDonald kicking frantically to free himself from a tackler so that he could get into position for the next play.

This aggressive effort paid off early in the third quarter when McDonald returned a punt to the Maryland 46-yard line; from there OU scored in seven rapidly executed plays. The try for extra point was good, and OU led for the first time, 7–6, with 5:49 gone in the quarter.

Probably thinking that his first team was a bit worn down from such concentrated effort, Wilkinson sent in the alternate unit. The alternates accepted their responsibility in good fashion and to the delight of the Oklahomans directed much of their attack between the opposing tackles where, during the regular season, Maryland had appeared to be toughest. The alternates produced OU's second touchdown with only a little more than a minute gone in the fourth quarter, and with a successful try for point the score stood 14–6 in favor of Oklahoma.

Although the momentum of the game had turned definitely in OU's favor, the big, obviously tiring Maryland team was still determined to make a fight of it. Their reserve quarterback, Lynn Beightol, directed the offense after the ensuing kickoff and managed to move the ball to the OU 30-yard line. There he decided that a flat pass would be in order. That was a mistake that led to a third OU touchdown; Carl Dodd intercepted the pass on his own 18-yard line, and with the help of several enthusiastic blockers went all the way to the Maryland goal line. (Meece and Bryan, in their *Thirteen Years of Winning Oklahoma Football,* quote columnist Bob Considine as saying that "if his [Dodd's] forebears had run that fast in the Oklahoma run, he'd own half the state.") Dodd, perhaps winded from his 82-yard sprint, missed the try for extra point, but the happy Oklahomans could not have cared less.

The Sooners were definitely in charge throughout the remainder of the game and in the waning moments seemed on the verge of scoring again. But a pass interception prevented this, and the Terrapins were saved from what many would have considered a really humiliating defeat. The final score was 20–6.

During the jubilation in the Sooner dressing room after the game Wilkinson was reported to say, "That's the most satisfying victory we've ever had." Tatum, questioned in the Terp dressing room, told the reporters, "Oklahoma is definitely the best football team in the country. I've never seen a team with all the equipment this one has." When Wilkinson was told of Tatum's evaluation, he said, "I don't know if we're the best. But we haven't been beaten yet."

During the following days it appeared that the nation's sports writers agreed with Tatum that OU did indeed have the best football team in the nation. The Florida press was especially extravagant in its praise of the Sooners. Jimmy Burns, sports editor of the *Miami Herald,* wrote:

Displaying more speed than any football team ever seen here, Oklahoma Sooners Monday galloped away from Maryland, 20 to 6, after spotting the Terps a touchdown in the second quarter of the 22nd Orange Bowl classic.

It was a glorious comeback for the speed merchants from the west. They reacted like true champions to the challenges of the Atlantic Coast Conference's best team and extended records which have made Oklahoma one of the powers of football.

This was their 30th consecutive victory, and the ease with which it was scored once the Sooner machine shifted into high gear makes mockery of the claim Oklahoma prospered because of a weak schedule.

Oklahoma's emphasis on blinding speed ranged from darting into and out of the huddle to Carl Dodd's 82 yard sprint with an intercepted pass for the Sooner's final touchdown. This run along the southern boundary was the most spectacular of the day and made a telling impact, not only on the fans, but the Terps, too.

It was a well-earned victory which left one believing that for duration of the Big Seven-Atlantic Coast pact with the Orange Bowl, you might as well become reconciled to Oklahoma winning every other year.

With bowl activities now past, the OU campus returned to normal early in January. Preparations for final examinations and the winter sports program got underway. Football was put to rest—except, of course, for recruiting, planning for spring practice, and occasional conversation over coffee.

During January the rumor that Jim Tatum was being wooed by his alma mater for the head coaching job at North Carolina proved valid. Big Jim had indeed signed a contract to return to his old school, at an annual salary of fifteen thousand dollars. North Carolina would open the 1956 season with the University of Oklahoma late in September, and so Tatum- and Wilkinson-coached teams would play two consecutive games.

Jubilant Sooners, with Coaches Jones and Wilkinson kneeling in center, celebrate their defeat of the Maryland Terrapins in the 1956 Orange Bowl classic. Courtesy Sports Information Department.

The possibility that Wilkinson might make a coaching change had not been discussed seriously by the news media for about two years, not since the University of Minnesota had invited him to succeed Wes Fesler. Early in 1956, however, Wilkinson spoke at a football banquet in San Diego, California, and after his appearance Jack Murphy, sports editor of the *San Diego Union,* undertook a sort of one-man campaign to bring him and the University of Southern California together. Murphy apparently had had a rather lengthy talk with Wilkinson in San Diego, and in one of his columns he raised the possibility that Wilkinson might succeed Jess Hill, who was moving from the head coaching

To the victor of the OU-Maryland match went the massive Orange Bowl Trophy. Courtesy Sports Information Department.

position to the athletic directorship at Southern Cal at the end of the 1956 season. Murphy wrote:

On the surface of things this doesn't make much sense. Wilkinson has everything going for him at Oklahoma, including schedule, recruiting, staff and admiration from fans which borders on idolatry.

This is the logical view. But, to soil a phrase, one man's logic may be another man's poison.

At thirty-nine, Bud Wilkinson doesn't especially crave security. If anything, he's probably a little bored by his success with the Sooners. Having lost but eight games in nine seasons as the head coach, his principal opponent is his own record. Year after year he competes with his own success. . . . Listening to the things he says—and the things he doesn't say—the impression is strong that he hankers for a new challenge.

"If I ever make a change, it would be mostly for two reasons, salary and an opportunity to meet a new challenge." he said.

"In this respect, a football coach is just like anybody else. A coach has to be alert to opportunities to improve himself. Naturally, I'm happy at Oklahoma, and I'm not looking for another job.

"But the hypothetical question is asked if I would be interested if offered exactly the same position, with all conditions perfect.

267

"Now that's a purely hypothetical situation and perfection is difficult to obtain, but I'd have to say, yes, I would be quite willing to listen."

Murphy went on to say:

Possibly, Wilkinson hasn't been seriously considered because of the wide-spread notion he is wedded to Oklahoma till the end of time. I'll admit that I shared this thinking until yesterday.

But the Oklahoma coach is in the position of a beautiful girl who sits home by the telephone because everyone assumes she was dated for the big dance weeks ago.

After reading Murphy's column, I asked Wilkinson bluntly if he was negotiating with Southern California. He assured me that he was happy at the University of Oklahoma and planned to honor his contract with the school. However, I got the impression that he might have enjoyed receiving offers from other institutions and had missed them during the past two years. Perhaps, though he did not realize it, his remarks to Murphy had been intended to enlist the interest of other schools. One can never tell about such things.

During January, somewhat critical comments about the cost of the OU athletic program appeared in the news media. It was pointed out that the university had not given a public accounting of its athletic expenditures for several years. In response to this prompting, I asked Kenneth Farris to release a report concerning the actual and projected income and expenditures for the fiscal year 1955–56. The figures revealed that athletics would involve income and expenditures in excess of one million dollars that year. The bulk of the income—$821,502.80—came from football receipts, with OU's portion of the income from the Nebraska game and the Orange Bowl still to be received. But there was also appreciable income from other sources, including $17,383.00 from radio and television, $11,017.25 from the sale of football programs, $9,914.14 from golf-course fees, $9,192.62 from the sale of football-program advertising, and $15,637.89 in profits from the concessions. There would also be revenue from the remaining basketball, baseball, and wrestling events.

Expenses for the year, budgeted at $1,071,519.45, included the $105,000.00 annual payment on the stadium bonds, $260,000.00

paid to visiting schools in all sports, $21,830.00 to finance the intramural-sports program, $125,650.00 for the expenses of the football team, $70,000.00 for coach's salaries, $59,680.00 for eighty athletic scholarships, and various other items, including the expenses of other varsity teams, advertising, officials, ticket sales and printing, and the operation of the press box.

The cost of maintaining and equipping a single football player was broken down as follows: game uniform, $107.87; practice uniform, $86.72; board and room, $405.00; books, $38.00; tuition, $168.00; and incidentals, $15.00. A single football scholarship accordingly totaled $746.00.

In his release Farris emphasized that the athletic program was self-sustaining and that any deficits must be covered by surplus funds built up through the years. The department had never received support from the university's general budget. The report apparently satisfied those who had been concerned about athletic expenditures.

The university received word late in January that the institution would receive a second national football-championship award for 1955; the Grantland Rice trophy, sponsored by *Look* magazine and awarded by vote of the Football Writers of America. Grantland Rice had been a prominent sports writer for the *New York Herald Tribune,* and *Look* magazine, and he had produced a syndicated column that sold widely throughout the country. After the death of Walter Camp, who had picked the All-America Football Teams for *Look* from 1898 to 1925, Rice took over the responsibility and made the selections for many years. In recognition of his distinguished career *Look* created the Grantland Rice Award in his honor.

The first Rice trophy went to the UCLA Bruins in 1954, although Ohio State University had won the Associated Press poll that year and received the O'Donnell Trophy. Curiously enough, the Football Writers had voted the Oklahoma Sooners the best football team in the land even before their impressive win over Maryland in the 1956 Orange Bowl, although perhaps that was not surprising in view of the fact that the Sooners were picked first by practically every poll in the country that year.

Daniel Mich, the executive editor of *Look,* and Tim Cohane, the sports editor, brought the trophy to Norman for presentation on February 22, at a brief ceremony in Holmberg Hall. The trophy, a gold-plated stylized football mounted at an angle on a quadrangular mahogany base, with an appropriate inscription, was presented to me by Mich at the meeting that afternoon and became the permanent possession of the University of Oklahoma.

The Sooners were the almost unanimous choice of the pre-season prophets to go through the 1956 season undefeated. There appeared to be excellent reasons for this prophecy. Twenty-eight lettermen none of whom had ever played in a losing intercollegiate football game, were returning. In that number were five splendid athletes who were definite candidates for All-America honors: Jerry Tubbs, center; Tommy McDonald, halfback; Ed Gray, tackle; Jimmy Harris, quarterback; and Clendon Thomas, halfback. Enthusiasm for the coming season was not dampened by the alumni win over the varsity, 10–0, at the end of spring practice.

Additional cause for optimism was Wilkinson's glittering nine-year record as head football coach at OU. During that period his teams had won eighty games, lost seven, and tied three, for the best winning percentage in the country. Five major bowl appearances had produced four wins and one loss. Associated Press polls had ranked his teams in the top ten for eight of the nine years he had been head coach at OU. In seven of the nine seasons his teams had placed in the top five of the nation. He had established a modern record of thirty-one consecutive football wins and appeared about to break his own record. No other coach or team in the nation had done nearly as well. It was only natural that success of this kind should produce stress on Wilkinson, his staff, the football team, and the fans. As the 1956 season approached, Oklahoma was in competition with its own winning record.

The perceptible effects of the pressure on Wilkinson were preoccupation and restlessness in conversation. He frequently expressed doubt that his brilliant record could be maintained, that it was really worthwhile in any event, or that it would be a source of satisfaction in retrospect after his coaching career

The Grantland Rice Trophy, sponsored by *Look* magazine, was awarded to the University of Oklahoma by vote of the Football Writers of America. The trophy was presented at a ceremony in Holmberg Hall on the university campus, February, 1956. Courtesy Sports Information Department.

had ended. He spoke of doing other things—perhaps a career in counseling or business, or even politics. He was critical of the bureaucracy and waste in the political world, especially at the national level. I had an uneasy feeling that it would be difficult to hold him at the university if an interesting opportunity should develop elsewhere. He would occasionally remind me that his contract at OU was binding only with respect to coaching intercollegiate football and that he was free to consider other possibilities.

CHAPTER 20

The O'Donnell Trophy
1956–57

JIM TATUM brought a powerful, talented, well-coached North Carolina squad to Norman for the opening of the 1956 season on September 29. The sixty thousand spectators, sweltering in 90-degree weather, welcomed a brisk southerly wind that at times gusted to 30 miles an hour. During the first 24 1/2 minutes of the game, the Sooners, though impressive for brief periods, were unable to develop a scoring drive and gave little promise of repeating as national champions. But then, in the remaining 6 minutes, 30 seconds, both the first and the second units suddenly found themselves and produced three touchdowns in rapid succession, going into halftime with a 21–0 advantage.

A determined North Carolina team held pretty well during the third quarter, and neither team scored. But in the fourth quarter the OU team exploded once again, producing two additional touchdowns. The try for point after the fifth touchdown was unsuccessful, and the score was 34–0. Wilkinson then put in his reserves, who managed to come up with a safety when they tackled a North Carolina ball carrier behind his own goal line. Fifty-nine of the sixty OU players who suited up for the game saw action. Jakie Sandefer, a sophomore halfback, had a twisted ankle and did not play.

The victory was the thirty-first consecutive win for the Sooners and tied Oklahoma's previous winning streak of thirty-one games. But the win was a costly one: first-string left tackle Wayne Greenlee and first-string left guard Ken Northcutt were taken from the game with broken ankles.

The next three games turned out to be more or less warmup affairs for the long-awaited renewal of competition with Notre Dame—the last team to defeat Oklahoma back in 1953. The Sooners defeated Kansas State 66–0, on Homecoming Day at Norman, October 6, despite the noticeable lesser depth in the line caused by the loss of Greenlee and Northcutt. Texas, waiting

273

hopefully for revenge after losing seven of the last eight games to the powerhouse from the north, fell 45–0 on October 13. The University of Kansas proved a little more difficult at Lawrence the following weekend, scoring twice on the Sooners, but the outcome, never really in doubt, was Oklahoma 34, Kansas 12.

Curiously enough, although Oklahoma had had no perceptible difficulty defeating Kansas, many fans were disturbed because the Jayhawks had been able to score two touchdowns. Perhaps they had been spoiled a bit; OU had held its regular season opponents scoreless in the last seven games. I received several letters asking what had gone wrong with OU football. Had "Bud and Gomer," because of complacency, failed to prepare the team properly for the game? Was the administration cooperating with the athletic program? What did I propose to do to remedy the situation?

This discontent spread to members of the student body. Joan Emerson, the wife of tackle Tom Emerson, writing in the November issue of *Sooner* magazine, reported that members of the squad had heard such comments as: "I sure was disappointed in the game today, Tom." "What happened to you boys today, just get tired?" "Weren't you up for the game?" Such reactions were disquieting to me and to others on the campus because they indicated that football enthusiasts no longer had the game in proper perspective. They were placing disproportionate emphasis on the importance of not just winning but winning by overwhelming margins. I began to think that it might be wholesome if OU lost a game or two.

The unhappy fans were mollified to some extent the following Saturday when their supposedly faltering team met Notre Dame. The Sooner squad, with its coaches and a sizable contingent of Oklahoma fans, journeyed to South Bend for the contest, hoping to win over the institution that had earned the highest place in the country's football tradition—the only team that had been able to defeat OU in the past fifty-four games.

Another all-time record crowd, 60,128, assembled in the Notre Dame stadium. For the few Oklahomans it was a happy occasion; for backers of the Irish it surely was a most disappointing one. The Sooners scored 26 points the first half and 14 the second, winning by a score of 40–0. Oklahoma dominated the game so completely that Wilkinson was able to play all forty members of the traveling squad.

Afterward in the dressing room the jubilant Sooner squad interrupted their festivities long enough to present Wilkinson with the game ball. The coach later commented, "Nothing that has ever happened gave me more pleasure."

But a study of the statistics indicated that the score was not a reliable measurement of the strength of the two teams. Notre Dame won the battle of first downs, 16 to 12. In total offense Oklahoma outgained the Irish by only 235 yards to 218. The real difference in the ball game was the deadly Oklahoma defense that blunted all Notre Dame scoring thrusts and produced two pass interceptions and a blocked punt that were converted into touchdowns. Under only very slightly different circumstances there might have been a difference of only a touchdown or two in the outcome. No doubt the coaches understood this very well, but it was difficult to get the idea across to the players the following week, as preparations were made to meet the University of Colorado at Boulder.

The Colorado Buffalos, not handicapped by having defeated Notre Dame 40–0 the previous Saturday, were well prepared and determined to end OU's winning streak. As game time approached, forty-seven thousand enthusiastic fans gathered in the newly enlarged Colorado stadium and waited expectantly for the kickoff; some of the Oklahomans were shivering in the 33-degree weather.

During the first half it appeared that the Sooners could do nothing right. On their first possession Colorado recovered a blocked quick kick in the end zone for a touchdown, and the try for extra point was good. Later in the quarter a pass from Jimmy Harris to Tommy McDonald produced an OU touchdown and six points for OU, but the try for extra point failed. A few plays later McDonald received a Colorado punt and ran it back 75 yards for a touchdown, but the beautiful play was nullified by a penalty. During the rest of the half a promising OU drive ended in a fumble, while Colorado drove twice for touchdowns but failed to convert either time. The half ended with Colorado leading, 6–19; it appeared that the great OU team might be only thirty minutes away from an ignominious end of its record-breaking winning streak.

I had been watching the game with Regent Dick Grisso in the OU section. As the players left the field, Grisso turned to me and asked, "Can we possibly pull out of this situation?" I told him that I wasn't sure but that I planned to visit the dressing room to see what happened between halves.

I got to the dressing room too late to hear everything, but I learned later that Wilkinson momentarily "lost his cool" over his team's first-half performance and spoke rather harsh words about their failure to forget Notre Dame and prepare adequately for Colorado. But by the time I arrived, he had recovered his poise and was speaking earnestly and I thought somewhat apologetically about the coaches' failure to analyze quickly the Colorado offense. The half was nearly over, he said, before they realized that the OU linebackers had been playing too close to the line of scrimmage, thus permitting the Coloradans to run trap plays with unusual success. Speaking very calmly, he suggested that the players put the first half out of their minds and start a new ball game when play resumed. The linebackers were to move back one yard, and instructions were given about some other defensive adjustments. As the half-time period drew to a close and the team filed out of the dressing room, Wilkinson said to them, "Here's one man who thinks you can win."

The second half may not have been a new ball game, but it certainly was a different ball game. Sensing victory, the frenzied Colorado crowd began roaring when the teams returned to the field, and the noise was continuous almost to the end of the game. But the Sooners, evidently settled by the half-time session, received Colorado's kickoff and with savage blocking slashed and ripped the Colorado defense for 80 yards and a touchdown without giving up the ball. Early in the drive they found themselves with a fourth down and 2 yards to go on their own 28-yard line— surely a punting situation. But, without hesitation, Jimmy Harris decided to try for a first down. He gave the ball to Clendon Thomas, who bucked straight ahead for 3 yards. The starting and alternate teams collaborated during the rest of the half, effectively containing the Colorado offense while scoring two

276

additional OU touchdowns. The final score was 27–19. Disaster had been averted, and the OU team had demonstrated its ability to play well when the chips were down.

After the Colorado scare Oklahoma had no difficulty whatever with the remaining games of the schedule. They defeated Iowa State 44–0; Missouri fell, 67–4; Nebraska, coached by Pete Elliott, a former OU aide, was overwhelmed, 54–6; and Oklahoma A&M was submerged, 53–0, for the second year in a row. In none of the games did Wilkinson make a deliberate attempt to run up a lopsided score, although there were occasional hints from other states that he had done so in pursuit of another national championship. Each weekend, after the outcome was no longer in doubt, he substituted freely, using every available player. During the waning minutes of the Oklahoma A&M game, he may have humiliated his opponents needlessly by fielding an all-senior team and using left tackle Ed Gray at right halfback to score the final touchdown from the 2-yard line.

The Sooners of 1956 were the best team in the country. In the minds of many they were the best team the country had ever produced. On November 27, Elmer T. Peterson, distinguished political analyst for the *Daily Oklahoman* wrote on the editorial page:

> It is reasonably safe to assume that the Sooners will finish the season without a defeat. At any rate, the writer would like to give the opinion, after more than fifty years of observation and a slight amount of playing, that this is positively the finest football team ever put together. It might even be considered the best team of all time, so far as it is humanly possible to form such an estimate.
>
> Whether it can be excelled, even at Oklahoma University, next year or in succeeding years, is open to question. The 1956 edition seems to be a team of no weak spots, in short, an ideal organization, as perfectly integrated as human frailty will permit. Its smoothly meshed coordination of blocking and running is almost poetic in its rhythmic quality. In scrimmage defense tactics the linemen, line backers and ends are ruthlessly sure, and the pass defense would be hard to improve.

The statistics of the season supported Peterson's appraisal. The forty consecutive victories established a new all-time record in American football, breaking the former record of thirty-nine established by the University of Washington in 1914. The rushing average of 391 yards for the ten games broke the old national record of 378.3 yards set by the Texas School of Mines in 1948. A total of 222 first downs for the season was also apparently a new all-time national record; the old mark of 220 was set by Arizona State at Tempe in 1950. At the end of the 1956 season Sooner football teams had scored in 116 consecutive games, and during that season they scored 466 points, an average of 46.6 points a game. They outscored their Big Seven rivals by a ratio of 48.7 to 8.5, and all their opponents by a ratio of 46.6 to 5.1.

In view of all this it was not surprising that the Sooners were voted the best in the land for a second consecutive year. Because it was their third national championship the O'Donnell Memorial Trophy was permanently retired to the OU trophy case. The *Look* magazine people agreed with the polling, and once again Daniel Mich and Tim Cohane came to Norman to deliver the Grantland Rice National Championship Trophy.

Although the brilliant record of 1956 was due largely to team effort, certain individuals were outstanding. Center Jerry Tubbs not only was named outstanding lineman of the year but also won the Walter Camp Memorial Trophy, given to the outstanding football player in the United States. Tommy McDonald, halfback, won the Maxwell Trophy and the *Sporting News* Trophy as the outstanding college player of the year. Tubbs, McDonald, Bill Krisher, and Ed Gray were named to several All-America teams. Clendon Thomas, halfback from Oklahoma City, though missing All-America honors, won the major college scoring championship of 1956 with 108 points.

Oklahoma narrowly missed having a second Heisman Trophy winner that year. Apparently only the presence of McDonald and Tubbs on the same team prevented it, because the two split the vote of those who favored an Oklahoma candidate. Paul Hornung, of Notre Dame, won the coveted award, although McDonald led in the first-place voting, with 205 votes to 197 for Hornung. Tubbs received 121 first-place votes, an excellent showing, especially since voting preference had always been for offensive backs. Hornung was the winner because he received 162 runner-up votes to McDonald's 122.

Missing the Heisman Trophy was a disappointment to OU partisans, but on the whole 1956 had been a very good year for Okla-

The 1956 team. FIRST ROW (FRONT ROW), LEFT TO RIGHT: Don Stiller, Dale Sherrod, John Bell, Bob Timberlake, Jerry Tubbs, Ed Gray, Delbert Long, Don Nelson, Chuck Bowman, Bill Krisher, Wayne Greenlee, Joe Oujesky, Byron Searcy, David Baker, Bill Brown. SECOND ROW: Joe Rector, Bob Harrison, B. W. Scott, Hugh Ballard, John Pellow, Dale Depue, Dick Evans, Steve Jennings, Carl Dodd, Jakie Sandefer, George Talbott, Doyle Jennings, Benton Ladd, Mickey Johnson, Carl Buck, Roland Powell. THIRD ROW: David Rolle, Jay O'Neal, Robert Derrick, Bill Harris, Kenny Crossland, Ernie Day, Billy Pricer, Jimmy Harris, Tommy McDonald, Lyle Burris, Lynn Burris, Dick Gwinn, Lonnie Holland, Ken Fitch, Keith Lewallen, Benton O'Neal, John Ederer. FOURTH ROW: Dennit Morris, Clendon Thomas, Bob Martin, Ken Northcutt, Tom Emerson, Cloyd Shilling, Victor Hayes, Fred Hood, Jim Lawrence, Ross Coyle, J. Henry Broyles, Jr., Dick Corbitt. Courtesy Sports Information Department.

homa fans. Most would agree that it represented the zenith in Wilkinson's coaching career.

Wilkinson and OU's contingent of All-America players journeyed to New York early in December for a three-day get-together of All-America selections from across the country. During his stay in the big city reporters asked Wilkinson about rumors that he was negotiating seriously for jobs at Southern California and at Texas. At a session on Saturday evening, December 8, he was asked when he planned to go to Texas to take over his new coaching responsibilities there. Thinking the question was a joke, he replied, "Well, not before Monday." The news stories that developed from his flippant reply probably startled Texans as much as they did Oklahomans. Sports pages throughout the Southwest once again were littered with speculation that Oklahoma would lose its great coach, and the stories persisted for several days despite Wilkinson's denials that he had any intention of moving.

But Oklahomans close to the athletic program at OU did not appear greatly concerned by the prospect of losing one of the most successful coaches in the history of football. There were rumors of positive steps that had been taken to keep him on the job. The most impressive of these centered on the activities of Oklahoma's United States Senator Robert S. Kerr. Kerr, impressed by the favorable publicity that Wilkinson had given the state—and, according to some, perhaps concerned also with the possibility that Wilkinson might develop United States Senate aspirations—reportedly undertook a campaign designed to keep him in the coaching profession at Oklahoma. The plan, as explained to me by Paul Brown, a prominent member of the Touchdown Club, involved the solicitation of several wealthy Oklahomans for a gift of $3,000 each, to be placed in a fund for Wilkinson's benefit and, to a lesser extent, Gomer Jones's. The limit of each gift was set at $3,000 to avoid federal or state gift tax.

This fund-raising effort, launched sometime in the early 1950's, produced a sum of $250,000. Of that amount $200,000 was pledged to Wilkinson and $50,000 to Jones. There were varying accounts of the conditions accompanying these efforts to ensure the finan-

280

cial security of the two coaches—and thereby retain their services—and Brown did not tell me whether the money was actually
paid to them or was held in trust. But he did say that the arrangement included an agreement that the coaches would continue
at OU for some specified time.

In addition to the windfall Kerr and his friends provided, there
were reports of substantial gifts of oil properties and royalties.
According to Brown, a few members of the Touchdown Club
paid for the $40,000 house occupied by the Wilkinson family in
Norman.

When asked about these benefactions at a meeting in St. Louis,
a story released by the Associated Press quoted Wilkinson as
saying, "I think the rumor is foolish in every respect." Without
actually denying the existence of the fund, he did deny that he
had oil wells and a large income from that source. It was clear,
however, that Wilkinson's denial of special benefits did little to
dampen the assurance of the most prominent members of the
Touchdown Club that he would continue coaching at OU. Unlike
times in the past, I did not receive any inquiries from those
members about what was being done to ensure that the university
would not lose its coach.

The spring practice sessions gave some indication of probable
Sooner success in football in 1957. A census of the squad that
reported for the workouts revealed that eighteen lettermen had
completed their eligibility at the end of the preceding season,
including such outstanding performers as Jerry Tubbs, Tommy
McDonald, Ed Gray, Tom Emerson, Billy Pricer, Jimmy Harris,
Jay O'Neal, John Bell, Bob Timberlake, and Delbert Long. But
despite these losses a goodly number of excellent, experienced
athletes reported for the spring workouts. Conspicuous among
them were halfbacks Carl Dodd and Clendon Thomas; guards
Bill Krisher, Doyle Jennings, and Joe Oujesky; ends Don Stiller
and Joe Rector; and center Bob Harrison. Talented athletes were
available for most of the positions, but it was difficult to predict
who would play quarterback. David Baker, from Bartlesville;
Dale Sherrod, of Odessa, Texas; and Bennett Watts, of Breckenridge, Texas, were possibilities.

Perhaps the most interesting prospect from the freshman squad

Prentice Gautt, Oklahoma fullback, was the first black athlete to participate in intercollegiate football at the University of Oklahoma. Courtesy Sports Information Department.

was Prentice Gautt, a black halfback from Douglass High School in Oklahoma City. Although blacks had attended the university on a nonsegregated basis since 1950, and a black athlete named Buddy Hudson had lettered in basketball, no candidates for the football team had enrolled. Gautt had made an exceptional record in high school, and it was said that certain influential blacks arranged for him to attend OU on an experimental basis.

Wilkinson's staff for 1957 again included Gomer Jones, Sam Lyle, Ted Youngling, and Eddie Crowder. But Bill Canfield was no longer on the roster; he was replaced by Jay O'Neal and Gene Calame, who coached part time.

In mid-May, 1957, the faculty representatives of the Big Seven Conference got around once again to considering Oklahoma A&M College as a possible eighth member. This possibility had been under study for some time, but a majority of the faculty representatives had been reluctant to enlarge the conference. But at the meeting on May 16, in Lincoln, Nebraska, a motion to extend an invitation to Oklahoma A&M was passed, and the Big Seven became the Big Eight. Effective promotional effort by Earl Sneed, OU's representative to the conference, was largely responsible for this pleasant turn of events.

Dr. Oliver Wilham, president of Oklahoma A&M, accepted the invitation, given by telephone that day, and the conference set up a committee to work with the new member on scheduling the various sports.

It was agreed later that the new member would participate in all conference championship events during the 1957–58 school year except football and basketball. Participation in basketball would begin with the 1958–59 season, and football would be added as soon as all member schools could work A&M into their schedules. This was accomplished for the 1960 season.

CHAPTER 21

The End of the Winning Streak— The Orange Bowl

1957-58

WHEN the Sooners journeyed to Pittsburgh for the opening game of the 1957 season, some credence was given to Wilkinson's earlier expressed concern about the potency of his offense. With Carl Dodd and David Baker operating at quarterback, neither the starting nor the alternate team could develop a scoring drive during the entire contest. Although the final score was 26–0 in favor of Oklahoma, two of the touchdowns came after Pittsburgh fumbles near their goal line, and the other two resulted from a penalty against the Panthers and a deflected forward pass. The pass, thrown by Baker, hit the headgear of a Pitt defender and bounced in an arc toward the goal line, where OU's deep receiver pulled it in and went on to score.

Of historic significance is the fact that, for the first time since OU was founded, a black athlete represented the institution on the football field. Prentice Gautt was in the Pittsburgh game briefly; he carried the ball once for a 3-yard gain. He would play much more later, and many other blacks would contribute their talent to OU's football tradition.

In the following three games Oklahoma's offense looked somewhat better. Iowa State was defeated 40–14 at Norman; Texas, where Darrell Royal was in his first year as head coach, was somewhat stronger than the previous year, but was decisively whipped, 21–7, at Dallas; and Kansas, handicapped by an outbreak of Asian flu in the squad, was trounced 47–0 at Norman.

There was an interesting development after the Kansas game. For several years Wilkinson and his staff had taken the squad to the Skirvin Hotel in Oklahoma City to spend the night preceding each home game. The idea was to get the athletes away from noisy campus life and control their environment as closely as possible during the final hours before kickoff. The addition of Prentice Gautt to the OU squad in the fall of 1957 resulted in a change of hotels. Gautt was with the squad at the Skirvin the night before the Iowa State and Kansas games, but protests from hotel patrons led the management to inform OU officials that he would not be permitted to stay there in the future. Fortunately, the team was able to get reservations at the Biltmore Hotel for the remaining home games on the schedule. The squad stayed at the Biltmore during the 1958 and 1959 seasons. When Gautt's eligibility ended, they moved back to the Skirvin.

The attitude of the Skirvin management came as a surprise. In Texas, because of state law, Gautt was not permitted to stay with his teammates at the Worth Hotel in Fort Worth the night before any of the Texas games but stayed in another hotel down the street. He was permitted to rejoin his teammates at the Worth for breakfast the morning of each game, but he was restricted to a room that had been rented for the use of the coaches and trainer. But there was no such law in Oklahoma, and several people were critical of the Skirvin's attitude and resented the squad's return to the Skirvin after Gautt graduated.

The Colorado Buffaloes, again coached by Dal Ward, made their biennial trip to Oklahoma with every intention of ending the OU winning streak. It was Dad's Day at the university and the largest crowd in Big Seven history, 61,700, assembled for the occasion. In an excellent, close game marked by superb defensive play, Colorado had the lead at the beginning of the fourth quarter, 7–13. But the Sooner starting team received the kickoff after the second Colorado touchdown and marched across the goal line without giving up the ball. Carl Dodd booted the extra point, and OU won, 14–13. The statistics of the game were as close as the score, and the breaks were even. Each team earned one touchdown, and each scored a touchdown on a break. The difference was that Bill Krisher spoiled a Colorado try for extra point by charging through the line and shoving a Colorado man in the path of the ball.

The Colorado win brought Oklahoma's string of victories to forty-five—as one OU enthusiast put it, "Just five short of half a hundred." The tension of the long winning streak had grown weekly on the campus and was especially noticeable following the narrow win over Colorado. The football squad obviously felt the pressure, and the mood of the coaching staff seemed constantly grim. Wilkinson appeared preoccupied, finding it difficult to concentrate on matters under casual conversation. He was unable to relax and was bothered by insomnia. It was reported that he occasionally visited the training room in the middle of the night seeking relaxation on a vibrating table there—that he had been found asleep on the table at least once when the training room was opened for business the following morning.

The question whether Oklahoma could go through another season still unbeaten, and lengthen its string of victories to fifty was obviously taking its toll on everyone in the football program, and I became thoroughly convinced that OU needed to lose a football game and perhaps thus get the sport back in proper perspective. I made this suggestion in a speech to a local group during the fall, but it was not well received. Several indignant notes and a few telegrams of protest came to my office.

After the narrow win over Colorado the Sooners went to Kansas at Manhattan on November 2. The outcome was an enormous disappointment to OU fans: their favorite team won by a score of only 13–0. That the game was the one hundredth victory of Wilkinson's coaching career and his forty-sixth consecutive win seemed completely overshadowed by the relatively small winning margin. I again had several letters and telegrams of inquiry asking what had happened to the team. "Have Bud and Gomer lost their touch?" "Have they become fat and lazy?" There were occasional pointed suggestions that my attitude about the desirability of losing a game might have affected the team's morale.

The situation eased a bit the following week, when Oklahoma decisively defeated a very good Missouri team at Columbia, 39–14. This win clinched a berth at the Orange Bowl, and Wilkinson described the game as OU's "best performance of the season."

Notre Dame was next on the schedule, at Norman on November 16—Oklahoma's fiftieth anniversary of statehood. In his newsletter, Wilkinson wrote about OU's prospects:

As always in football, a squad can't stand still. Last week's game was a big one and this week's against Notre Dame is even bigger. The Irish have lost 2 games but have defeated Purdue, Indiana, Army and Pittsburgh. Last year Notre Dame held our fine offensive team to only 147 net yards rushing. We realize the rugged quality of the Irish play backed by their fine coaching and great tradition. We face our hardest game of the season this Saturday.

Wilkinson's appraisal turned out to be a realistic one.

Notre Dame's second appearance on the OU campus had been long awaited by OU partisans. All the tickets to the contest had been sold six months before the game, and many fans had bought season tickets for the first time to be sure they would be able to see the Fighting Irish in action. Countless others were looking forward to watching the game in color on national television. Governor Raymond Gary proclaimed November 16 University of Oklahoma Day, as a tribute to the progress made by the institution during its sixty-five years.

The Notre Dame official party arrived in Oklahoma City on Friday and came to Norman on Saturday morning in time for a pregame lunch in the Student Union Building. Father Hesburgh was not with the party but was represented by Father Edmund Joyce, vice-president in charge of campus activities. Father Joyce accepted my invitation to sit in the president's box, but the rest of the Notre Dame party joined their fellow fans in the east wing of the stadium.

The weather was ideal for football—scattered clouds, 58 degrees at game time, and a gentle breeze from the north. The turf was in excellent condition despite heavy rains during the week; it had been protected by a canvas tarp.

Notre Dame won the toss and chose to receive. Oklahoma had a little difficulty kicking off. Although there did not appear to be much wind, the football toppled over twice before the kicker could get to it, and finally was held in place by an OU player.

The action that followed was described as a "flaming defensive dual" by John Cronley, writing for the *Daily Oklahoman,* and sports writers were practically unanimous in proclaiming it a defensive classic. Twice the Oklahoma defense stopped the Fighting Irish within six yards of a touchdown—on one occasion only inches from the goal line. Notre Dame was even more successful in coping with the Sooner offense, which some thought had been a bit erratic at times during the season. For three quarters the struggle went on, with neither team able to score, but unbiased spectators could see clearly that Notre Dame had the better football team, both on offense and on defense. The Notre Dame quarterback, Bob Williams, certainly had one of his better days, and Nick Pietrosante at fullback battered the Sooner line in a manner not seen on Owen Field in many years.

Shortly after the beginning of the final quarter, I began to suspect, from the time spent on OU's half of the field, that the Sooners would lose the game. I turned to Father Joyce and said: "Father, we are not getting anywhere with this football game. Obviously it's going to end in a tie. Why don't we just declare a tie right now, stop the game, and let this record-breaking crowd of sixty thousand get an early start home?" The good Father looked at me thoughtfully for a moment, but with a twinkle in his eye, and then replied, "No, I'd rather lose a football game than have it end in a tie." I said, "OK, then, we'll keep on playing."

With less than thirteen minutes left in the final quarter, Notre Dame received the ball on its own 20-yard line after an OU punt dropped in the end zone. Then, in a series of nineteen plays, mostly through the center of OU's line, they rammed· the ball to the OU 3, where it was fourth down and goal to go. Apparently convinced that the next play would be a repetition of what had worked so well during the drive, the Sooner defenders jammed the center of the line, expecting Pietrosante to come there with the ball. Instead Williams took the snap, retreated briefly, and then pitched wide to halfback Dick Lynch, who scampered round right end untouched into the northeast zone for a touchdown. A successful try for point made the score 0–7, with about a minute and a half left.

OU returned the kickoff to its own 39-yard line. Here a passing attack was launched which gave the Sooners a first down on the Irish 24, but an intercepted pass on the next play ended the Sooner threat, and OU's winning streak was ended at forty-seven games—ended by the same team to which it had bowed last.

At game's end the jubilant Notre Dame fans poured onto the field to show with enthusiastic handshaking and backslapping their appreciation of their team's effort. The somewhat dazed Oklahoma partisans sat in silence for a moment while the dismal truth permeated their consciousness and then rose spontaneously to a sustained standing ovation. There were various interpre-

OU and Notre Dame in the waning moments of the close, well-played game at Norman, 1957. Courtesy Sports Information Department.

tations of the ovation. Some regarded it as an expression of appreciation of OU's splendid record and assurance of continued support. Others thought that the demonstration was, in part at least, a tribute to the great Notre Dame effort. Father Joyce chose the latter interpretation and said that I could well be proud of the fans' generous behavior.

He and I walked down to the sidelines and slowly made our way across the playing field through the swirling crowd to the Notre Dame dressing room under the east stand. We congratulated an obviously pleased but very gracious Coach Terry Brennan, who complimented the OU team on its hard play and sportsmanship. His football team was somewhat less restrained in expressing pleasure at their upset victory. They happily reminded each other that they had gone into the game as three-touchdown underdogs and agreed that they had avenged the humiliating loss suffered at the hands of OU the preceding year. Later Nick Pietrosante was quoted as saying that "we did it for the Catholics of Oklahoma." Many Oklahoma Catholics took a dim view of his remark, denying that they had sought benefit of that kind.

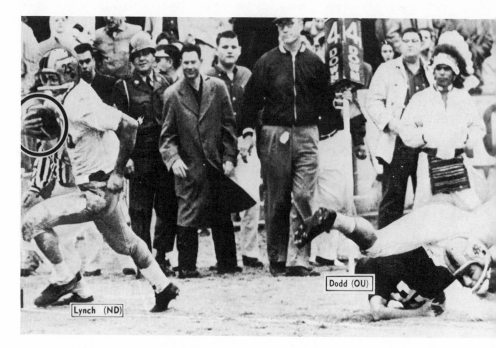

Dick Lynch, Notre Dame halfback, ran the touchdown that broke OU's forty-seven-game winning streak. Notre Dame won, 7–0, in the game, played at Norman, November 16, 1957.

As Father Joyce and I left the dressing room, I found myself becoming increasingly philosophical about the loss. Notre Dame's young coach, Terry Brennan, had desperately needed a victory. His 1956 season had been a disastrous one—one of the worst, if not the worst, in Notre Dame history. His team had lost two games in 1957, and a third loss to Oklahoma might have signaled the beginning of the end of his career as head coach at his alma mater. And, I reflected, OU really needed a loss, even if it was Statehood Day.

Father Joyce and I walked across the south end of the stadium to visit the OU dressing room. The atmosphere there was somber, and the players were somewhat depressed, but several members of the squad had begun to talk about putting the loss in proper perspective and making plans for the rest of the season.

Father Joyce and I walked down the hall to where Wilkinson

290

was talking with several sports writers. When he saw Father Joyce, he excused himself and came with extended hand, saying, "Father, I want to congratulate you and your fine football team. OU played as well as it could every minute of the game. We're lucky we didn't lose by two or three touchdowns instead of one."

After Father Joyce had made an appropriate response, Wilkinson returned to his conference with the writers. Father Joyce turned to me and said, "I am amazed. I've never before heard a losing coach, and I have visited with many of them, say that his team played as well as it could. Almost invariably they try to explain what went wrong to cause their defeat."

As we walked home across the campus, Father Joyce mentioned Wilkinson's good attitude two or three times, and as we paused in front of the house before entering the front door, he put his arm around my shoulder and said, "Isn't it too bad when you have two such fine teams, two such fine coaches and two such fine schools, that both can't win the same afternoon?" I replied, "Yes, Father, it is too bad, but probably a game that could be won by both teams wouldn't attract sixty thousand spectators. Of course, it would be possible to have two good teams tie, but *you* don't like tie games."

By and large the Oklahoma fans accepted the loss to Notre Dame without a great deal of grumbling. Literally stacks of letters and telegrams expressing appreciation and support arrived on Wilkinson's desk the following week. But there were a few almost unbelievable expressions of discontent and criticism. One such, a letter to the editor, appeared in the *Oklahoma City Times* on November 22:

> Saturday's defeat of the Big Red by Notre Dame emphasizes the need for a move that has now become inevitable—kicking Coach Wilkinson upstairs to the position of athletic director.
>
> . . . the truth is that this man can be outcoached, as proved by Bear Bryant and Terry Brennan. His day, like that of his mentor, Faurot, has passed its zenith.
>
> Today's football requires a dynamic type of coaching, that is beyond the now outdated Golden Boy of Oklahoma.
>
> Plentiful material, including important contributions from neighboring Texas; a pushover schedule; and a phenomenal run of luck have built a bubble reputation for the likable Minnesotan.

His record this year is a monumental reflection on his limitations—the same limitations that make ex-Sooners a drug on the pro football market.

And so it goes. As has been said, its time for a change. Let's get a young hero able to cope with modern football before the great publicity value of our football team goes into a shadow.

The King is dead! Long live the King!

Admittedly, this letter did not represent widespread public opinion, but I've always been impressed by the large number of "spectator athletes" who, disappointed by their own performance in life, appear to live in a fantasy world of achievement while watching great athletes in action and resent having their dream world interrupted by even a single loss.

The coaching staff and squad spent little time grieving over the loss. They settled down to prepare for the rest of their 1957 schedule—specifically for the University of Nebraska, where Bill Jennings, former aide to Wilkinson, had succeeded Pete Elliott as head football coach. They whipped the Cornhuskers in Lincoln decisively, 32–7, after a mild scare in the first quarter, when Nebraska scored the first touchdown.

The only remaining opponent on the Oklahoma schedule was Oklahoma State University (formerly Oklahoma A&M College). Defeated only twice during the season, and then by very narrow margins, the Cowboys appeared to have one of their best teams in recent years. Scouting reports had indicated that they might be the toughest team on OU's 1957 schedule, with the possible exceptions of Texas and Notre Dame. But in Norman on November 30, after being held to a 6–0 score during most of the first half, the Sooners exploded for 14 points in less than a minute just before half time and then during the second half rolled on to an easy 53–6 win.

Despite the loss to Notre Dame, the season certainly could be regarded as an outstanding success. In the national polls the Sooners placed fourth behind Auburn, Ohio State, and Michigan State. They had set a new victory skein of forty-seven games, and they had established a new national record for scoring in consecutive games (123) before being shut out by Notre Dame. They also set a national record for the number of rushing plays in a season—679. Clendon Thomas and Bill Krisher were named to several All-America teams.

Duke University was selected as the opponent for Wilkinson's third appearance at the Orange Bowl on January 1, 1958. The North Carolina Blue Devils, champions of the Atlantic Coast Conference, had lost only twice during the season, to Georgia Tech and North Carolina.

The Oklahoma squad, with coaches and the official party, including Mrs. Cross, Braden, and me, flew to Miami on December 26 in two chartered planes and checked into the Bal Harbour Hotel. We had as our guest for the game Dr. A. H. Glasure, pastor of the First Presbyterian Church at St. Petersburg, Florida. I had met Dr. Glasure on a trip to the Middle East the preceding summer, and a warm friendship had developed.

The kickoff was at 1:45 P.M. on New Year's Day. Mrs. Cross, Braden, Dr. Glasure, and I arrived at the stadium a little before noon, found our seats high in the stands under the upper deck, and watched the pregame activities—twirlers from Miami high schools, nine bands, and a huge American flag formed by 192 Miami girls carrying red, white, and blue pompoms. The flag was impressive, stretching the entire distance between the 35-yard lines.

The Sooners won the New Year's classic by the comfortable margin of 48-21. However, the two teams were much more evenly matched than the score indicated. Duke moved the ball well on the ground, outrushing the Sooners 231 to 165 yards. They scored their three touchdowns as a result of sustained drives. They held their opponents to a total of six first rushing downs. At the end of the third quarter they were behind only 21-14, and two of the Oklahoma touchdowns had followed an intercepted pass and a bad snap from the center.

But Oklahoma broke open the game in the fourth period with a 27-point splurge, which broke the Orange Bowl record for the most points scored in any one quarter (the previous record had been set in 1943 by the University of Alabama, with 22 points). But OU's four touchdowns came after two fumbles, a blocked punt, and an intercepted pass.

As the two teams made their way to their dressing rooms, the

293

Sooner cheerleaders managed to elicit a final roar from the OU section of the stadium. Hearing it, a Duke player with an unusual sense of humor was reported to have said, "Good Lord, don't tell me they've scored again!" Later, in a press conference, the obviously pleased Wilkinson said, "As of today, these boys are as good as any team we've had at Oklahoma." Probably most Duke partisans would have agreed.

Oklahoma fans, drifting home from their junket to Florida, were startled the following week to read in *True* magazine that the University of Oklahoma had been accused of administering drugs, perhaps amphetamines, to its football players during games. The article, by one Neal Wilkinson (no relation to Bud Wilkinson) stated: "Speaking of football teams, during the 1956 season when Oklahoma was increasing its sensational victory streak, several physicians observed Oklahoma players being sprayed in the nostrils with an atomizer. And, during a televised game, a closeup showed Oklahoma spray jobs to the nation." The author went on to suggest that, when this kind of thing happens in a horse race, the case goes to court. Oklahoma, the article charged, was not alone in this practice; there was considerable evidence that the practice was widespread in the country.

The *True* article understandably received considerable attention in newspapers of the country before Ken Rawlinson was able to get the facts before the public. When questioned, he indignantly denied that drugs were administered to his charges. Asked to explain the spraying that had been observed on television, Rawlinson reported that oil of peppermint was used and that it was sprayed, not into the nostrils, but into the mouths of the players to relieve "cottonmouth," caused by lack of saliva. The effect, he said, was the same as when a player chewed gum, but the desirable results came faster. Use of the oil of peppermint was optional with the players, not a requirement. He ended the interview on a note of finality: "We breed a brand of players at OU who don't need stimulants." Rawlinson's explanation was accepted by most loyal Oklahoma fans, but it was reported that fans of the opposing teams, who had felt the brunt of OU's prowess during the past several years, were skeptical, preferring to believe that Wilkinson's success had been drug-induced rather

The 1957 team. FIRST ROW (FRONT ROW), LEFT TO RIGHT: Prentice Gautt, Delmas Thorne, George Talbott, Bill Krisher, Benton Ladd, Don Stiller, Clendon Thomas, Dennit Morris, Doyle Jennings, Waroo McDaniel, Benton O'Neal, Dick Carpenter, Buddy Oujesky, Byron Searcy, David Baker, Jerry Thompson. SECOND ROW: Bob Harrison, Jim Davis, Ben Wells, John Pellow, Brewster Hobby, Dick Evans, Jere Durham, Jared Rowe, Steve Jennings, Carl Dodd, Ken Northcutt, Bobby Boyd, Jackie Holt, Jakie Sandefer, B. W. Scott, Ross Coyle, Bob Morford, Billy Jack Moore, Dick Gwinn, Jim Bowen (student manager). THIRD ROW: Dale Sherrod, David Rolle, Joe Rector, Gerry Marchbank, Lee Horne, Gary Baer, Cloyd Shilling, Dick Corbitt, Jim Lawrence, Mickey Johnson, Glenn Sears, Bennett Watts, Jerry Payne, Mickey Jackson, Gilmer Lewis, Lester Bradley, Chuck Bowman, Don Nelson, Bill Levonitis. Courtesy Sports Information Department.

than based upon a combination of superior athletes and superior coaching.

Neal Wilkinson's reference to court cases may have given some of the OU players—or an attorney—an idea. In any event, Dennis Morris, OU fullback, sued the magazine (Fawcett Publications) and won a judgment of $75,000 in damages. The case was appealed, and finally the United States Supreme Court awarded Morris $92,573—damages plus interest. Two other group suits initiated by athletes were settled out of court for substantial amounts, providing a satisfactory end to the episode.

National forecasters, perhaps out of habit, picked OU to finish high in the national ratings for 1958—among the top five teams. The *Saturday Evening Post* came up with the most optimistic prediction: OU would be the national champion. But Wilkinson was characteristically evasive when asked about the prospects. He did say that "we hope to be a little more dangerous offensively than we were last season. We cannot possibly be as strong defensively. We lack experience, particularly in the line."

Wilkinson's cautious optimism about the offense may have stemmed from the work he and his staff had done on what they called a "new multiple offense." The plan involved, at least in part, what some writers dubbed a "sputter huddle." After the quarterback had called the signal in the huddle, the center and widely split ends would go to the line of scrimmage. Then the interior linemen would jump to the line, either in normal formation or all four to the right or left of the center. One halfback might act as a flanker, a potential pass receiver. The other might line up five yards behind the strong side tackle, while the fullback moved in behind the strong side guard. Through the use of the "sputter shift" the formation could be kept a secret from the defense until the last possible moment. From the formation the quarterback had all the options he had under the regular split-T; he could pass, hand off on either the strong or the weak side, or keep the ball himself.

Another innovation awaiting football fans in the fall was a new conversion rule, which provided that two points could be earned after a touchdown if the ball was taken across the goal line by rushing or passing rather than being kicked from placement.

Spring practice was enlivened early in March when former

President Harry S Truman visited the practice field and spent some time with the coaches and squad. Of course, it was not the former president's interest in athletics alone that brought him to Norman. He was here by invitation of the Young Democratic Club of the University of Oklahoma. The occasion was a national testimonial dinner in honor of the twenty-fifth anniversary of Franklin Delano Roosevelt's presidency. It was scheduled for the Union Ballroom on the evening of March 4, 1958. Both Mr. Truman and Mrs. Eleanor Roosevelt had been invited to be speakers for the occasion, and both accepted.

The memorial dinner was a great success, and it served as a prelude to other political activities later in the year, activities involving a general election that was to have a significant impact on Wilkinson's future. Under state law Governor Raymond Gary was not eligible to succeed himself. Eight Democratic hopefuls finally announced their intentions to compete for their party's nomination for governor. Among them was J. Howard Edmondson, who had a degree in law from the University of Oklahoma and was serving as Tulsa county attorney. Another candidate was W. P. ("Bill") Atkinson, who had founded and developed Midwest City. Although the remaining six were seasoned politicians, it was generally conceded early in the campaign that Atkinson would win in the primary. Edmondson, because of his youth and relatively limited political experience, was thought by political pundits to have no chance for victory. Many predicted that the most he could possibly get out of the campaign was political experience.

But Edmondson and his young supporters were imaginative and innovative. They selected as campaign slogan the "Big Red E." The "Big Red" part of the slogan referred to Edmondson's red hair but also signified that he had graduated from an institution whose "Big Red" football team had won three national championships. The "E" in the slogan stood not only for Edmondson but for "energy, effort, and efficiency." Though campaigning on a shoestring, Edmondson's group managed to publish a campaign newspaper, the *Prairie Fire News,* which was distributed widely. Campaign headquarters was an automobile trailer with a big red "E" painted on each side.

As the campaign proceeded, it gradually became apparent that

297

Edmondson might well be the man to beat in the primary. His supporters managed to raise enough money to buy some television time, and the young candidate proved to have a captivating television personality. He was definitely superior to all other candidates in that respect, but even so he was given very little chance of winning the nomination. Then, on election day, to the astonishment of practically everyone, he received the largest number of votes of any candidate—108,000, to 107,000 for Atkinson. The other six candidates trailed far behind. Three weeks later, after a period of intensive campaigning, Edmondson defeated Atkinson in the runoff by a margin of nearly 200,000 votes. His Republican opponent for the general election in November was Phil Ferguson. Edmondson's momentum carried him to victory by a margin of more than 300,000 votes.

At the celebration that followed this stunning political success, older politicians were conspicuous by their absence. The newly elected governor, at thirty-three the youngest in the nation and the youngest in Oklahoma history, was surrounded by youthful admirers, and the executive offices of the State Capitol Building shortly were to be occupied by a group known as the "Crewcuts." The significance of all of this in the affairs of Bud Wilkinson and the University of Oklahoma was not to become apparent until many months later, when the "crewcuts" began making preliminary plans for a successor to Edmondson in the governor's office.

CHAPTER 22

The 1958 Season—The Orange Bowl—
Bad Press at Miami

1958-59

ALTHOUGH Notre Dame had ended Oklahoma's record-breaking winning streak at forty-seven games, the Sooners were still regarded as the top team of the midlands when the season opened in 1958. There were impressive statistics to support this ranking. Teams coached by the Wilkinson-Jones combination in regular season play had won ninety-nine games, lost eight, and tied three for a fantastic 0.925 percentage of wins. Their record stood at 5-1 in bowl competition. They had won national championships in 1950, 1955, and 1956, and had been voted among the top ten by the Associated Press for ten consecutive years.

The coaches had been on the whole pleased with spring practice. They liked the spirit displayed by the squad, and they were favorably impressed by David Baker and Bobby Boyd at quarterback and Bob Harrison at center. Harrison, they thought, was probably the best offensive center in OU's history, and the second-best defensively.

The 1958 season's opener was with West Virginia at Owen Field the last Saturday in September. Box-seat guests for the day included Elvis J. Stahr, Jr., then chancellor of the University of Pittsburgh but to assume the presidency of West Virginia on February 1, 1959. Another guest was James Garner, the film and television star, who was visiting his family in Norman.

The game gave fans their first opportunity to see OU's much-publicized new offense. With David Baker and Bobby Boyd handling quarterback chores, the first two teams displayed what one sports writer described as a "weird assortment of flankers and spread formations" and established a university passing record of 264 yards. Although beset by fumbles and other misadventures, Prentice Gautt played outstanding ball, OU won handily, 47-14, and the entire squad of fifty-eight suited players saw action. The offense apparently impressed a University of Oregon scout. When he was asked what he thought of it, he was quoted as saying,

299

Prentice Gautt levels his fourth would-be tackler on a twenty-seven-yard touchdown run that led the way to a win over West Virginia in 1958. Courtesy Sports Information Department.

"They'll never believe me back home; they'll never believe me. Len Casanova [Oregon's head coach] will swear I was drunk."

The Oregon scout must have turned in an effective report, because, when his team came to Norman the following Saturday, the Sooners' offense was stifled. OU managed to win, 6–0, only because of an Oregon fumble. Oregon's president, Dr. O. Meredith Wilson, came with the team to see the action. He was an interesting, sensitive person, who later became president of the University of Minnesota. He and I became so interested in discussing mutual problems that we missed much of the action during the second half, when OU was striving to hold on to their slender six-point lead.

The following week Wilkinson warned in his newsletter:

Texas, our opponent Saturday at Dallas, is as good or better defensively than Oregon. Against West Virginia, the element of surprise aided our offense tremendously. Last week Oregon had us well scouted, and we did not move the ball well. Texas will have us scouted even better. Our problem is to improve our overall blocking and ball handling so that we can present a semblance of offense against what will be a truly tough defensive opponent.

As it turned out, both teams demonstrated considerable defensive capability in the Cotton Bowl that weekend. Ten minutes of the game had elapsed before either opponent earned a first down. Thereafter Oklahoma won the rushing game, amassing 201 yards to Texas' 57. But Texas displayed greater finesse in its aerial attack, netting 153 yards to the Sooners' 62. Texas scored the first touchdown, and, taking advantage of the new two-point conversion rule, used a rushing play successfully in establishing an eight-point lead during the second period.

OU managed to score a touchdown during the third quarter, but an incompleted pass on the try for extra points left the Longhorns ahead, 8–6. Things seemed fairly well in hand for the Sooners a few minutes later, when OU scored a second touchdown and followed with a two-point conversion that gave them a lead of 14–8. But in the final quarter the Longhorns launched a 75-yard drive, liberally spiced with fantastic aerial receptions, and crossed the OU goal line with only 3 minutes, 10 seconds left. The try for extra point was good, and the one-point lead it produced stood for the remainder of the game. However, Texas fans did experience a few moments of uneasiness when, in the waning moments, Bobby Boyd circled left end and proceeded to the Texas 26-yard line, where he found only one man between him and the goal line. Unfortunately for OU, one man was enough; he abruptly ended Boyd's journey.

Thus, in his second year as head coach at Texas, Darrell Royal, former OU quarterback, brought an end to the Longhorn's six-year drought in the annual Cotton Bowl hassle. I went to his dressing room to offer my congratulations, but though the facility was filled with jubilant players, fans and assistant coaches, the head coach was nowhere in sight. I finally found an assistant coach who thought he had seen Royal leave the dressing room and suggested that perhaps he had gone out behind the building

A grim Gomer Jones watches the play as Wilkinson looks to the bench for a replacement, 1958 season.

to be alone for a few minutes. Following this lead, I went outside and found Royal leaning against the back of the building. His face was colorless, except for a sort of greenish-blue tint around his mouth. He was obviously ill; it was apparent that he had lost at least part of his lunch.

When I congratulated him on his victory, he mustered a wan smile, acknowledged that he was glad to win, but said that it somehow "just didn't seem right to beat Mr. Wilkinson." He explained apologetically that the tension of playing against his old coach whom he admired so much, combined with sweating out his team's final 78-yard touchdown drive and OU's threat in the final moments of the game, had caused him to become ill. When I apologized for intruding on his privacy, he waved the apology aside and thanked me for coming to see him.

I then made my way to the OU dressing room, where Wilkinson and some of the OU players were being interviewed by sports writers. Wilkinson was complimentary of the Texas team. He remarked that "their fourth quarter drive was as fine a finish as I've ever seen." Quarterback Bobby Boyd, when asked whether he thought Texas had earned the victory, replied: "Sure, they earned it, or they wouldn't have got it. They came 74 yards. If you can't stop a team in 74 yards, you don't deserve to win."

In the final paragraph of his football letter the next week, Wilkinson said: "I hope people realize now that while we are a reasonably good college team, we can be beaten any Saturday we play. It probably will happen again at Kansas this week." Wilkinson's unusually wary statement may have been related to the fact that, for the second weekend in a row, he would be facing one of his former players as a coaching adversary. Jack Mitchell, who had preceded Darrell Royal as quarterback at OU, had moved from the head coaching position at the University of Arkansas to take charge of the football fortunes at the University of Kansas. However, in his first game against his former mentor he was able to do only slightly better than his predecessor had done the year before, losing by a score of 43–0 in a game played at Lawrence.

The remaining games of the 1958 season provided little by way of challenge to OU's supremacy in the conference. Colorado made the best showing against the OU powerhouse, losing by 23–7. Oklahoma State, soon to become a member of the conference and coached by Cliff Speegle, provided the stiffest competition of the last half of the schedule, holding the traditional rivals to a narrow 6–0 victory.

It was the twelfth consecutive conference championship won by teams coached by the Wilkinson-Jones combination. In only one year, the 1947 season, was the championship shared with another team. The Sooners placed fifth in national ratings in 1958, behind Louisiana State University, Iowa, Army, and Auburn. They led the nation in defense, permitting their opponents an average of only 4.9 points a game. The opposing teams were collectively outscored by an average of 30 to 5.5. OU's great center Bob Harrison was named to most All-America teams. As the result of this superb record the Orange Bowl officials asked the conference to waive its regulation prohibiting a member team from playing at Miami two years in a row and allow OU to participate in the bowl's Twenty-fifth Anniversary celebration, scheduled for New Year's Day, 1959. The conference and the university agreed to this request, and OU accepted the invitation to play there against Syracuse.

During the latter part of the season Wilkinson had been disturbed by reports that his quarterback, David Baker, had been irregular in class attendance. He had several talks with the young man, who kept assuring him that he would get his scholastic affairs in order and attend classes. However, about the time the coaches and squad started their preparations for the Orange Bowl game, Wilkinson learned that Baker had not attended any of his classes for a long time—that his absences from all classes had already exceeded the number permitted under university regulations. Although under conference rules Baker's eligibility would extend to the end of the autumn semester, Wilkinson decided that it would be unethical to allow him to play in the Orange Bowl game. This decision came as a jolt to the coaching staff, the squad, and the fans. Baker was not only the best quarterback available but one of the best defensive backs in the country. It appeared that his loss would seriously weaken OU's chances for a fourth victory at Miami.

Many fans protested Wilkinson's action. The most interesting and dramatic protest came by telephone from a group of fans at Ada, Oklahoma. A few years earlier, after a series of frivolous phone calls to my home in the middle of the night, Mrs. Cross and I had asked the university switchboard operator not to ring the house after 10:30 P.M. It was arranged that incoming calls that might be emergencies would be screened by John Kuhlman, superintendent of buildings and grounds.

One night about the middle of December, 1958, the phone rang at about 11:30 P.M. The OU operator reported that I had a call from Ada, Oklahoma, about an automobile accident involving Bud Wilkinson—that he was seriously injured and had been taken to a hospital at Ada. I hurriedly accepted the call, but when I got on the line I found myself talking to a man who was apparently drunk. He said that he was calling on behalf of a group of loyal football fans at Ada. They wanted to protest the university's decision not to let David Baker play in the bowl game. I spent a few minutes listening to a recital of reasons why the boy should be restored to the eligibility list, a recital interspersed with expressions of hope that university officials, especially the president, would finally come to their senses. With some truculence, my caller said that OU had absolutely no chance to win without Baker. If he did not play I, and I alone, would be responsible for OU's loss. I finally managed to cut off the conversation and, though somewhat shaken, get back to sleep.

Wilkinson was unmoved by the protests and pressure. He spent his time taking stock of the remaining quarterbacks, Bobby Boyd, Bob Cornell, Bob Page, and Benton O'Neal. He soon settled on Cornell as the most likely prospect for New Year's Day. He worked constantly with Cornell during the few practice periods before the game and had lengthy sessions with him in the office. By the time the team checked into the Ivanhoe Hotel at Miami Beach the day after Christmas, he seemed reasonably satisfied with the results of his intense efforts. But many diehard fans were still convinced that Baker, technically eligible to participate, should be with the team.

New Year's Day was warm and muggy, 80 degrees, when we made our way to the Orange Bowl that afternoon. Mrs. Cross, Braden, and I were seated high in the stands on the side of the field opposite the box seats, with a clear view of the box area.

During previous years other occupants of the boxes had complained that they were unable to see the football games because reserve players along the sidelines blocked their view. There had been pointed criticism of the OU reserves occupying the sidelines during the game with Duke the preceding year. The Orange Bowl officials decided that a solution was needed for the 1959 contest. Their solution, unbelievably, was to dig a trench on each side of the football field and require the opposing teams to sit on the ground with their feet and legs in the trenches.

It had always been Wilkinson's policy to keep his reserves kneeling on one knee along the sidelines so that the entire squad could keep track of what was going on and be available for immediate substitution. He used to tell his boys, "When you're on the sideline, think football, be playing the game all the way."

In an effort to be cooperative the OU players used the trench briefly at the beginning of the Syracuse game, but they soon found that from that position they could not see what was happening on the field. Wilkinson then moved them out of the trench and put them in their usual formation along the sidelines. This incensed the dignitaries in the box seats and others seated along the sidelines at ground level, who became vociferous in their criticism of the OU squad. They booed throughout the game and threw ice cubes, pop bottles, and other objects at the players, and a few even went to the sideline to protest. During the game the police were intermittently busy escorting belligerent fans back to their seats.

The Sooner football staff and the squad, at least outwardly unperturbed by all of this, quickly got down to the business of the day, winning the football game. Bob Cornell, seemingly unconcerned about his suddenly acquired quarterbacking responsibilities, directed the Sooner offense with poise and precision. The first time OU had possession, Cornell pitched to Prentice Gautt for a sweep around right end that netted 10 yards, placing the ball on the Syracuse 42-yard line. On the second down Cornell again lateraled to Gautt, who this time went around left end 42 yards for a touchdown, giving the Sooners a 6-point lead with 2 1/2 minutes gone. A fine block by Jerry Thompson cleared Gautt past the line of scrimmage, and Joe Rector removed a Syracuse safety from his path. The Big Red then went on to win decisively, 21–6, although the huge Syracuse team managed to outrush the Sooners, 239 yards to 153.

Speed and quickness made the difference. After the game Ben

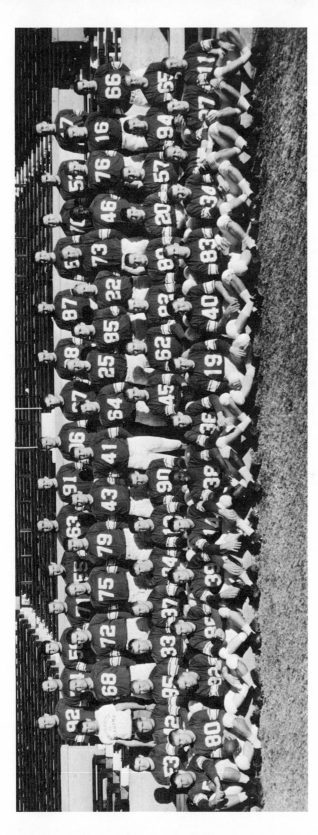

The 1958 team. FIRST ROW (FRONT ROW), LEFT TO RIGHT: Bob Harrison, Joe Rector, Brewster Hobby, Dick Evans, Elton Salmon, Bob Cornell, Prentice Gautt, Jim Steward, Benton O'Neal, Wahoo McDaniel, Jere Durham, Jackie Holt, Lester Bradley, Jakie Sandefer, John Pellow. SECOND ROW: Jim Davis, Dale Keadle, Max Morris, Dick Carpenter, Bill Levonitis, Ross Coyle, Jared Rowe, Steve Jennings, Ronnie Hartline, Larry Munnerlyn, Stan Ward, Jerry Tillery, Bill Noble, Bill Winblood, Brent Morford, Ronald Smith. THIRD ROW: Darrell Ray (manager), Vernon Lang, Marshall York, Travis Columbus, Walt Metcalfe, Glenn Sears, David Rolle, Billy Jack Moore, Bobby Boyd, Jimmy Feagan, Jimmy Carpenter, Gilmer Lewis, Wallace Johnson, Dean Emerson, Lee Horne, Jerry Thompson. FOURTH ROW: Jim Lawrence, Dick Corbitt, Mickey Johnson, Ben Wells, Jerry Payne, Cloyd Shilling, Bill Brown, Jim Steard, Bob Morford, Bob Yingling, Mickey Jackson, Bill Watts, Dick Gwinn, Robert Scholl, Bob Page. Courtesy Sports Information Department.

Schwartzwalder, the Syracuse coach, said: "We couldn't convince our kids they had to play wide on defense. Before the game they couldn't believe Oklahoma had that much speed. But they believe it now." Wilkinson, typically generous in winning, commented: "If we played Syracuse again tomorrow, I wouldn't be surprised if they beat us. They're that good. I, for one, am satisfied."

Miami newspapers were caustically critical of Wilkinson and the OU football team. The behavior of the Sooner squad was compared unfavorably with that of the "well-disciplined" Syracuse reserves, who stayed in their dugout throughout the game. The fact that Oklahoma won the football game was given minimum attention. Sports writers seemed to take the view that Oklahoma was not as good as in the past and that the team play was erratic and spotty. But Jack Bell, writing for the *Miami Herald,* did give some credit where credit was due:

The best player on the field was Oklahoma's Prentice Gautt, the mighty Negro fullback. His touchdown run that put the Sooners on top was his most spectacular effort. But he reeled off several other long gains and his defense play was the mostes'. As a linebacker he was everywhere when needed. The Syracuse boys said plenty about Oklahoma's linebackers.

As I reflected on the over-all picture during the return flight to Norman on January 3, it occurred to me that the OU football team had been making too many appearances in the Orange Bowl —that the Miamians and Oklahomans were getting bored with each other. Accordingly I recommended to the university regents that OU not return to the Orange Bowl when we were next eligible to do so. Under conference rules the team could not return in 1960 after the 1959 season but would be eligible in 1961 if we won the conference championship in 1960. The contract between the Orange Bowl and the conference had only two years to run, and the recommendation meant in effect that OU would not return to Miami at all unless the contract was renewed.

The regents gave unanimous approval to the recommendation, and Earl Sneed, faculty representative to the conference, was instructed to inform the conference of the action. Unfortunately word of what we had decided leaked to the newspapers and received considerable publicity. This piqued the faculty representatives of the conference, who, at their meeting in February, voted to rebuke the University of Oklahoma for what they called its "unilateral handling" of a problem that really involved the jurisdiction of the conference. This action of the faculty representatives seemed a bit unnecessary but was perhaps understandable. Jealousy, and even resentment, of Oklahoma's program was widespread in the conference. Moreover, the trips to Miami that the faculty representatives and their wives from each Big Eight institution had enjoyed at conference expense had been pleasant experiences during the several years the contract with the Orange Bowl association had been in force, and possibly the representatives were concerned that Oklahoma's attitude might result in failure to renew the contract.

Early in January, 1959, controversy over the reappointment of Quintin Little to the Board of Regents erupted in the state senate. Little, an enthusiastic supporter of OU football and a figure of considerable political importance in the state, had completed his seven-year term on the board the spring of 1958. Governor Gary reappointed him to the board, but, because the legislature was not in session at the time of the reappointment, the senate had not confirmed it. Incoming Governor Edmondson made it clear to all concerned that he did not favor Little's reappointment, and a movement arose in the senate to block his confirmation. Not wanting to test the new governor's strength in the senate, Little sent his resignation to the outgoing governor, Raymond Gary. Governor Edmondson did not immediately appoint anyone to succeed Little, but he appointed Julian A. Rothbaum, of Tulsa, to succeed Joe McBride, whose term expired in 1959.

Early in 1959 I gave a luncheon talk to the directors of the Oklahoma City Chamber of Commerce. Before my appearance I had been told that there had again been some question about the cost of athletics at the University of Oklahoma, especially the drain on the budget necessary to maintain a championship football team. I was pleased to include in my report to the chamber that in 1958 the athletic department had contributed $385,000 to the university for various campus projects having nothing to do with athletics. Perhaps the largest of these was the university's share of paving Brooks Street from the campus to Highway 77.

CHAPTER 23

A Big Ten Disaster—Wilkinson's First Conference Loss—More Trouble with NCAA
1959-60

WILKINSON began preparations for the 1959 season with a changed and somewhat reduced coaching staff. Clive Bush, Gene Calame, and Jay O'Neal left the university for other jobs, and Bob Blaik, son of Red Blaik, the coach at West Point, was the only replacement Wilkinson hired. Gomer Jones, Eddie Crowder, J. D. Roberts, and Rudy Feldman were back.

It was obvious during the spring and summer that Wilkinson was not enthusiastic about prospects for 1959. While he had always been careful and conservative in evaluating his teams in the past (largely for the psychological benefit of his squad and the fans), those who knew him well soon realized that his pessimism about 1959 was genuine. Several factors seemed to be involved in his concern. First, the team did not have the depth of material that had characterized the great teams of the past. Since the two-year suspension imposed on Oklahoma football in 1955, it may have been more difficult to recruit quality athletes to replace those completing their eligibility each year.

But it appeared also that his interest in coaching may have started to wane. Perhaps the strain of the long winning streak, followed by the relief he must have experienced when Notre Dame ended it, may have caused him to wonder what was left for him to accomplish in collegiate coaching. During one of our several talks during the spring and summer of 1959 he repeated his doubt that football coaching would bring him much satisfaction in later years. He wondered if he might not have made a more important contribution in some other kind of work.

He had always been interested in politics, and he often expressed his concern about political trends in the country, especially at the national level. He was conservative by nature, and he strongly disapproved of the Keynesian philosophy that characterized federal spending. He did not mention having personal political ambitions of any kind, but it was obvious from his remarks that he had given some thought to the possibility that he might one day have such interests.

As the summer passed, tangible reasons for Wilkinson's concern over his football team emerged. Jimmy Carpenter, of Abilene, Texas, whom Wilkinson regarded as his best all-around halfback, had pulled a muscle playing baseball in the spring. The injury stubbornly refused to heal, and Carpenter's availability for the early part of the new season was in doubt. Prentice Gautt, perhaps the best fullback in the conference, had undergone knee surgery following the 1958 season, and only time would tell whether he would regain his former effectiveness. In addition, there had been extensive losses from the 1958 squad through graduation or completion of eligibility. From the first two teams eight of the fourteen linemen would not be back, nor would three of the eight backs.

In July, Wilkinson was shocked and depressed by news from North Carolina that Jim Tatum had died suddenly from a virus infection.

The football schedule for 1959 included, for the first time during Wilkinson's career at OU, a Big Ten institution. The opening game was with Northwestern University at Evanston. The Northwestern Wildcats, coached by Ara Parseghian, had been the Cinderella team of the Big Ten in 1958. They had defeated Michigan decisively, beat Ohio State, and then lost to Iowa's Rose Bowl champions by a narrow margin, 20–26. While their over-all record was a modest 5–4, practically all the players on the first three teams would be back. Followers of football were much interested in seeing how Oklahoma would fare against Big Ten competition; there had been talk that Oklahoma's great success in football had been due to relatively weak competition.

The Sooners took off for Evanston by chartered plane on Thursday. Stormy weather made the flight rough, and several members of the squad had upset stomachs when they arrived in Evanston. To provide a relaxing evening for the squad, an early dinner followed by a floor show was scheduled at the Chez Paree night club, and the Oklahomans looked forward to a pleasant evening. But in a matter of minutes after eating dinner, several members of the squad became violently ill, complaining of stomach pains and nausea. Finally all but a small number were returned to the hotel in considerable distress. A few were hospitalized briefly. It was learned later that those who did not become ill had not eaten salads with their dinners.

The incident was widely publicized, of course, with most writers speculating on the question of whether the food had been deliberately treated to produce illness and thus handicap the team in the game the following Saturday. There was much talk about extensive investigations being made and tests to be run on the contents of the players' stomachs. But nothing definite came of it all, because the containers with the stomach contents mysteriously disappeared.

After resting on Friday and Saturday mornings, the team took the field against Northwestern Saturday afternoon, but in a driving rain that continued during most of the afternoon.

Wilkinson's first encounter with the Big Ten was a nightmare for the OU fans who saw the game at Evanston and for the thousands who saw it on television. The Wildcats humiliated the great Sooner team by a score of 45–13, the worst defeat ever administered to a Wilkinson-coached squad.

Analysis of the game showed surprising statistics: OU had earned fifteen first downs as against eight for Northwestern and had gained a total of 306 yards to 283 for Northwestern. But the Sooners had fumbled twelve times to their opponents' two, losing the ball on five of the twelve occasions.

In addition to fumbling, the Sooner players committed several other errors that might have been related to their gastronomic upset. An interesting example of the squad's lack of alertness came on the third play of the game, when quarterback Bobby Boyd threw a beautiful pass to Brewster Hobby, who was downed on the Northwestern 25-yard line after a gain of 50 yards. Unfortunately, OU had a couple of ineligible receivers downfield during the play, and after the penalty yards were stepped off, the ball rested on the OU 8-yard line instead of the Northwestern 25. Only moments later, when Boyd called a quick kick by Wahoo McDaniel, the center snap struck an OU player's leg, the kick was blocked, and Northwestern recovered the ball on the OU 9-yard line.

The Sooner squad's misery did not end with the game. Flying home that evening, they once again ran into foul weather, and the plane had to detour a long way to avoid high winds.

Despite their poor showing against the Wildcats, the bookies had the Sooners posted as a 27-point favorite over Colorado the following week, an indication that the gambling world believed the poor showing at Evanston had been due to illness caused by food poisoning.

Wilkinson offered no excuses for the Northwestern loss. In his football letter he said:

We made many mistakes and an alert Northwestern squad made deadly capital of our errors with their hard hitting play. . . . We must work hard in practice to eliminate our errors and correct our poor tackling. We hope to play better next Saturday.

The team did do better the following Saturday, defeating Colorado at Norman, 42–12. But after the game Wilkinson expressed concern about the injuries his rather thin squad had sustained in the first two games. Jimmy Carpenter, starting left halfback, had been lost for the season. Brewster Hobby, starting right halfback, was injured and probably could be used only sparingly against Texas. Bob Scholl, alternate center, and Bob Page, reserve quarterback, seemed out of the picture for ten days to two weeks.

Texas had got off to a splendid start for the season. The Longhorns had defeated Nebraska, Maryland, and California and had held all three opponents scoreless. The squad apparently had great speed, excellent personnel, and sound coaching.

But the Sooners journeyed to Dallas that weekend with the hope that they could maintain the momentum they had generated during the Colorado game. It appeared that the hope was justified during the first quarter, when Oklahoma scored 12 points while holding Texas scoreless, but 12 points was to be their total for the afternoon. The Texans, on the other hand, used the last three quarters of the game to contain Oklahoma's offense and score 19 points of their own making the final score 12–19. When I made my usual visit to the Texas dressing room following the game, I found Darrell Royal in much better condition than he had been after the game the year before. He was happy and poised while receiving the compliments of his well-wishers. As I left the dress-

313

ing room I had a feeling that it might be some time before OU would win another game in the Cotton Bowl.

Despite the loss Wilkinson was pleased by his team's playing. He said that it was "by far" the best team effort of the season. He went on: "I believe our men discovered how well they can play if every man does make a supreme effort. This is what it takes to win in football—and in all other areas of life."

The next week, after winning handily from Missouri at Columbia on the Tiger's Homecoming weekend by a score of 23–0, the Sooners returned to Norman to prepare for the University of Kansas, coached by Jack Mitchell, the former OU quarterback. Oklahoma managed to win the game, but only because a Kansas try for two points after a touchdown failed, leaving the score 7–6. Perhaps the outstanding feature of the game was a magnificent 94-yard punt by left halfback John Hadl, who later was to become one of professional football's outstanding quarterbacks. Wilkinson later said that it was the longest kick he had ever seen in competition.

Next on the schedule was the University of Nebraska, at Lincoln, on October 31. Bill Jennings, Wilkinson's former assistant, was the Cornhuskers' coach, and his team had at least one outstanding victory to its credit, a 32–12 win over the University of Minnesota.

Interest in the Oklahoma-Nebraska tilt was heightened because Wilkinson and Jennings were thought not to be on the best of terms. Jennings had left his assistant coaching job at the University of Oklahoma a few years before under what I sensed had been somewhat strained conditions. After taking over at Nebraska, he had accused Wilkinson of trying to recruit an outstanding athlete from Nebraska. Wilkinson had denied the accusation. The game would be played on Homecoming Day at the Cornhusker school, and all the Nebraskans would be remembering how their team had been humiliated at Norman the year before.

The game turned out to be a memorable one. After receiving the opening kickoff on their 18-yard line, the Sooners drove to a touchdown in nine plays and converted successfully. But apparently that was more prosperity than they could stand, for the team seemed to relax and take things for granted.

314

A series of Sooner errors characterized the remainder of the game. The first of these occurred with a Nebraska punt that sailed to the OU 6-yard line. Instead of letting the ball bounce across the goal line, the safety signaled for a fair catch and then ran with the ball. Penalized half the distance of the goal line, the Sooners put the ball in play on their own 3 instead of their 20. Later poor blocking enabled Nebraska to field a partly blocked quick kick and run it back for a touchdown. Poor tackling permitted the Cornhuskers to return a punt 61 yards to the OU 4-yard line. Three men, playing safety, failed to field a Nebraska punt; it dropped dead on the OU 4-yard line.

Taking advantage of these errors, and playing a superb kicking game, the Cornhuskers managed to win by a score of 21–25.

The exuberant Nebraska crowd had much to cheer about. It was the first time in seventy-five consecutive conference games that the University of Oklahoma had been defeated. It was the first time that a Wilkinson-coached team had been defeated in the conference. Perhaps the era of Oklahoma's domination of the conference was ending.

I had not made the trip to Lincoln with the team, but I read the unpleasant details of the game the next morning in the *Sunday Oklahoman*. As my wife came into the breakfast nook to refill my coffee cup, I remarked, "Well, OU has finally been whipped in the conference." To this she replied, "Yes, but do you realize that the last time we lost a conference game, we didn't have that boy?" and she pointed to our thirteen-year-old son Braden. She added, "You will be welcome if you visit the Nebraska campus during the coming year." I was a little surprised at how well she kept up with football, but I pointed out one small error in her statement. We really "had" Braden the last time we lost to a conference team back in 1946 — to Kansas by a score of 13–16 — but he wasn't born until six days after the game.

Wilkinson's football letter of the following week began with the following somber paragraphs:

Although our assistant coaches are doing a fine job, it must be that I am not. If I were, our team would not continue to make the same type of basic mechanical errors so repeatedly in every game.

It's difficult to explain how and why such things happen but I have always believed they were controllable if the team had the morale and discipline which results from proper leadership. I will try to do a better job of coaching in our four remaining games.

Wilkinson did all right as far as the four remaining games were concerned. Only the game with West Point was close. Played at Norman in 28-degree weather, the Sooners won a thriller from Army, 27–20. However, Army made 24 first downs to Oklahoma's 13 and outgained the Sooners 388 yards to 201. But the Army backs fumbled to Oklahoma on three occasions, a handicap that a brilliant aerial game, netting 297 yards, could not overcome.

Despite the loss to Nebraska, Oklahoma won the conference championship outright, and Wilkinson's poorest season was good enough for his team to finish fifteenth in the nation. One All-American was named that year from the OU squad: Jerry Thompson, a guard from Ada, Oklahoma.

During the calendar year 1959, and perhaps during most of 1958, Oklahoma football had once again been the subject of an investigation by the National Collegiate Athletic Association. It started in 1957, shortly after Bill Jennings was appointed head football coach at the University of Nebraska. In May of that year Wilkinson thought that he had reason to question the eligibility of a couple of athletes who had received grants-in-aid from the Cornhusker school. Accordingly, he sent a letter of inquiry to Bill Orwig, Nebraska's athletic director. Orwig did not reply, and Wilkinson then asked Dean Earl Sneed, OU's faculty representative, to look into the matter. In July, Sneed wrote to Earl Fullbrook, faculty representative at Nebraska, requesting information.

A few days later Sneed received a long-distance call from Jennings during which Jennings said that if Oklahoma made a formal complaint to the NCAA about the athletes in question it would be necessary for him to reveal information concerning matters at Oklahoma that had not come to light at the time the NCAA committee visited the OU campus in December, 1954.

Wilkinson and Sneed talked with me about the problem in August, 1957, and I suggested that they tell the whole story to Earl Fullbrook, Nebraska's faculty representative. They did so, and Sneed made a complete report to Fullbrook in October.

316

The 1959 team. FIRST ROW (FRONT ROW), LEFT TO RIGHT: Max Morris, Paul Vaughan, Lester Bradley, Prentice Gautt, Mike McClellan, Gilmer Lewis, Bobby Boyd, Jerry Pettibone, Jackie Holt, Wahoo McDaniel, Elton Salmon, Brewster Hobby, Jerry Tillery, Jerry Thompson. SECOND ROW: Jim Davis, Ronnie Hartline, Mickey Jackson, Henry Wells, Bill Levonitis, Dick Carpenter, Jim Byerly, Phil Lohmann, Jared Rowe, Johnny French, Billy Meacham, Tom Cox, Tommy Raley, Bennett Watts, Bill Winblood, Bill Watts. THIRD ROW: Marshall York, Paul Benien, Glenn Cunningham, Dale Wallace, Ronnie Dombek, Frank Smith, Bill White, Ronny Payne, Karl Milstead, Billy Jack Moore, Bob Page, Bob Scholl, Vernon Lang, Bob Morford, Ben Fellows, Brent Morford. FOURTH ROW: Bobby Wyatt, Walt Metcalfe, Jerry Payne, Dennis Ward, Jim McCoy, Sam Davis, Dale Pernini, Wallace Johnson, Bob Cornell, Dale Keadle, Bob Yingling, Darrell Ray (manager). Courtesy Sports Information Department.

Sneed also suggested that if Jennings had information of interest to the NCAA he should present it immediately.

In the spring of 1958 the OU Department of Intercollegiate Athletics received a phone call, a letter, and a visit from a Nebraska high-school athlete named Monte Kiffen, who expressed an interest in attending the University of Oklahoma. Later, by invitation from the boy's parents, OU coaches visited with the family at his home. After the visit Wilkinson said that he had encouraged the boy to attend the University of Nebraska.

Later Wilkinson received a letter from Jennings in which he said that if Kiffen enrolled at Oklahoma it would be necessary for him, Jennings, to give information to the NCAA which he had withheld at the time of the investigation in 1954.

Wilkinson brought the letter to my office, with a reply that he had prepared. In the reply he suggested that if Jennings had information that had been withheld from the NCAA at the time of the OU investigation, he should immediately give the information to the NCAA, whether or not Kiffen enrolled at Oklahoma. Wilkinson thought that a copy of his reply should be sent to Chancellor Hardin at the University of Nebraska, and to Walter Byers, executive secretary of the NCAA. I agreed, and the letters went out on May 13, 1958. Later in the year I received a letter from Byers, asking about a fund that he said had been used for the recruitment of athletes from 1952 through 1954, handled by Arthur L. Wood, an accountant in Oklahoma City.

I immediately got in touch with Wood, who admitted freely that he had, indeed, handled such a fund and had made disbursements from it at the direction of Bill Jennings, then assistant coach. The fund, he said, had been discontinued in 1954, when Jennings resigned from the University of Oklahoma to accept a public-relations job with an oil-drilling company.

Wood went on to explain that, during the latter part of 1953, he had personally contributed funds for Jennings to use in transporting prospective athletes to the Norman campus. The practice was continued after the 1953 season, and gradually the demand for money to be used in this way became greater than Wood felt he could supply from his own resources. He asked some of his friends to contribute, and he acted as custodian and disburser of the monies collected until Jennings left the university. He said that the amount of money involved was not more than six thousand dollars.

I passed this information on to Walter Byers, and later Byers asked Wood if representatives of the NCAA could examine the records of the fund — bank statements and canceled checks — on a confidential basis. Wood refused, contending that, as an accountant, he could not reveal the confidential records of his clients. He said that to do so would be a violation of professional ethics and also of a federal statute that might result in a one-thousand-dollar fine and/or one year's imprisonment for him.

Wood's explanation did not satisfy the NCAA, and early in January, 1960, the organization placed the University of Oklahoma on indefinite suspension, with the added provision that the football team could not appear in postseason games or on television.

When he announced the suspension, Byers said that the investigation could be reopened and the action reconsidered whenever Wood was willing to let the NCAA explore his records of the fund. But Wood apparently was not about to do so. Despite requests of the university and pressure from Oklahoma fans, he was adamant in his refusal to disclose the records of his clients. Byers made it clear that nothing could be done until Wood changed his mind. The likelihood of this happening decreased when Wood decided to move to Nevada.

Unquestionably, this second probationary period during a single decade was a major factor in what was to be a decline in the quality of OU football. The recruitment of exceptional athletes became more difficult, and the morale of those already on the campus seemed to be affected. Nevertheless, Wilkinson and his staff recruited vigorously during the early months of 1960 and made their customary preparations for the new season.

In the summer of 1960 there was some talk of scheduling a series of football games with the University of Hawaii. For a time it seemed an attractive possibility. The president of the University of Hawaii was Dr. Laurence Snyder, who until 1958 had been dean of the Graduate College of the University of Oklahoma. OU could be sure of a cordial welcome in Honolulu.

It was proposed that the first game would be played there after the close of the 1960 season and that Hawaii would come to the mainland for a game the following year. Wilkinson thought such an arrangement would be desirable, since Oklahoma was prohibited from playing in NCAA postseason contests. After a tentative agreement with Hawaii had been worked out, OU petitioned the faculty representatives of the conference for permission to play, because conference regulations limited each school to a ten-game schedule.

But the conference quite properly refused to approve a proposal that might give the University of Oklahoma a recruiting advantage during a probationary period, and, when the faculty representatives met during the summer, the petition was denied by a vote of five to three. According to information that leaked from the meeting, opposition to the Hawaii series was led by Iowa State University and OU's sister institution at Stillwater. The news brought a storm of protest from OU fans and sports writers sympathetic to the university. There was a surge of sentiment in favor of withdrawing from the conference.

John Cronley, sports editor of the *Oklahoma City Times,* led off with a column under the headline "It's Time for Sooners to Leave the Big Eight." He outlined several reasons why he thought a change would be beneficial and suggested ultimately scheduling football games with "Army, Navy, Notre Dame, Pittsburgh, Penn State, Syracuse, Air Force Academy, plus a team from the Big Ten, a Southwestern Conference team and one from the west coast." He saw no difficulty concerning schedules in other sports if the university should leave the conference.

The regents, in session on June 9, were almost unanimous in expressing belief that ties with the conference should be severed. T. R. Benedum, president of the board, was quoted in various newspapers as supporting the move to separate. But Earl Sneed, faculty representative to the conference, attended the board meeting and cooled matters by suggesting that "several ramifications would have to be considered in connection with a proposal that OU drop out of the conference." It was decided that Benedum would appoint a committee to make a study of the matter and report back to the board at an early meeting. The committee consisted of Glenn Northcutt, Willis, chairman; Leonard Savage, Oklahoma City; and Julian Rothbaum, Tulsa. In announcing the formation of the committee, the regents reported that they had taken the action in recognition of "an overwhelming sentiment throughout the state."

The question was debated extensively in the newspapers during the next few days, along with reports that Wilkinson was seriously considering leaving the university because of his disgust with the treatment received from the conference. But as time went on, tempers cooled, the furor subsided, and the regents decided to stay in the conference.

CHAPTER 24

A 3-6-1 Season—The Physical Fitness Program—Wilkinson for Governor?

1960-61

WITH the opening of the 1960 football season Oklahoma State University became eligible to contend for the conference championship, having finally been able to include all seven of the conference teams in its schedule.

The Sooners' first event of the 1960 season was a return game with Northwestern, to be played in Norman. A total of 61,500 fans, mostly Oklahoma sympathizers, crowded into the stadium, hoping to see evidence that the "food-poisoning incident" at Evanston the preceding year had been a major factor in the humiliating loss to the Wildcats. The game was closer than the year before, but it was not in the books for the Sooners to win. Still in contention at the beginning of the fourth quarter, with the score 3–12, the OU team fumbled and lost the ball the first two times it came into possession. The final score was 3–19. In his football letter the following week, Wilkinson wrote:

> Northwestern has an excellent football team. However, the big disappointment of the game was our lack of mental and physical toughness in the fourth quarter—after playing quite well for forty five minutes.
>
> To be an excellent football team, you must play physically tough at all times. . . . Northwestern outfought and outoughed us in the crucial fourth quarter.

The team managed to defeat Pittsburgh at Norman by the narrow margin of 15–14. But the rest of the season was something of a nightmare. Darrell Royal's Longhorns overwhelmed their rivals from the north by a score of 0–24. The game with Kansas ended in a 13–13 tie. A 49–7 victory over Kansas State the following week gave Sooner fans the hope that the good old days might be returning, but in the remaining games the Sooners lost to Colorado, 0–7, for the first time since 1912; lost to Iowa State, 6–10, for the first time since 1928; and lost to Missouri, 19–41, for the first time since 1945.

322

Despite the three disastrous weekends, Sooner fans still had hopes for a victory over Nebraska that would compensate in part for the 1959 loss. But the Cornhuskers, coming to Norman with victories over Army and Texas, played sixty minutes of sound football, winning 14–17. In his newsletter Wilkinson said:

It is the coach's primary responsibility to develop in his squad a will to win, an attitude that results in their giving sixty minutes of total, all out effort by every man.

We have had this in other years. However, we do not have it this season. This is the weakness of our team. As the coach I must admit that I feel that I have failed since I have not been able to impart this continual tenacious fighting spirit of our men.

There was some improvement in the squad's "will to win" the following week. They wound up the season with an impressive 17–6 win over Oklahoma State, and in the process originated sixty-five rushing plays without losing the ball a single time through a fumble. They yielded only one pass interception. It was the first time during the season that the team had not made costly errors. As Wilkinson put it in his newsletter, "It was very gratifying to play this, our best football of the season, in our final game."

The season, with three wins, six losses, and one tie, was Wilkinson's poorest in collegiate coaching, and the team wound up fifth in conference standing. For the first time in his career no member of his squad received All-America recognition.

Wilkinson's morale, somewhat restored by his team's performance against Oklahoma State University, received an additional boost early in January, 1961, when the NCAA announced at its annual meeting at Pittsburgh that Oklahoma's indefinite suspension from the association's activities had been lifted. Art Wood, then living at Reno, Nevada, had, by showing a portion of his records, convinced NCAA officials that no record had been kept of the funds he had handled for Bill Jennings and that university officials had not been involved in handling the money.

Other events took place early in January that were to have an influence on Wilkinson's career. Governor Howard Edmondson appointed two new regents to the OU board. Eph Monroe, a peppery, personable attorney from Clinton, was named to fill the unexpired term of Quinton Little, who had resigned the preceding year. Dr. Mark R. Johnson, an Oklahoma City physician, whom I had known as an undergraduate student at OU, was named to succeed Dick Grisso, whose term expired in 1960. The new regents assumed their responsibilities at the January meeting of the board.

In February, 1961, Wilkinson participated in a national conference on physical fitness called by President John F. Kennedy in Washington, D.C. The theme of the conference was the formalization of a national physical-fitness program that would begin in the elementary schools. During the course of the conference Wilkinson was invited to visit the President at the White House. Later it was rumored that he would become the national director of the new program. Wilkinson denied that any formal offer had been made to him but did admit that he had made some suggestions to the President about the program.

In March, President Kennedy invited Wilkinson to return to Washington for further discussion. The invitation brought him to my office to discuss what his answer should be in the event the President offered him a post of some kind in the new program. We agreed that I would poll the regents by telephone and ask for prior approval of any reasonable arrangement that might be worked out with the President. The regents gave unanimous approval to my request but stressed that no commitments should be made that would interfere with Wilkinson's coaching responsibilities.

After the second trip to Washington, President Kennedy announced that Wilkinson would serve as a special consultant to the President on physical fitness—that he would immediately begin conferring with government agencies, private organizations, and groups outside the government with the objective of formulating a youth fitness program "to meet the demonstrated need for action in this field."

Wilkinson worked vigorously on his new assignment, although he did not permit it to interfere with his duties at the university. In several trips to Washington he became rather well acquainted with the President's brothers, Robert and Edward, as well as the President, and he reported enjoying these experiences very much. He conferred with several government agencies and private organizations in an effort to get a clear picture of what might be

324

The 1960 team. FIRST ROW (FRONT ROW), LEFT TO RIGHT: Bobby Wyatt, Billy Meacham, John Tatum, Jimmy Payne, Bennett Watts, Jerry Tillery, Phil Lohmann, Jimmy Carpenter, Mike McClellan, Max Morris, Mel Sandersfeld, Paul Lea, Monte Deere, Bud Dempsey, Jerry Pettibone, Bill Pannell, Jim Hensley (student trainer). SECOND ROW: Duane Cook, Tom Cox, Karl Milstead, Ronny Payne, Billy White, Leon Cross, Wayne Lee, Marshall York, Ronnie Hartline, Gary Wylie, Elton Salmon, H. O. Estes, Vernon Lang, Bill Winblood, James Parker, Ralph Maxfield, John Clapp, Jimmy Mihlhauser, Dale Keadle. THIRD ROW: Dale Perini, Glenn Cunningham, Jim McCoy, Bob Cornell, Eddie Wood, Jim Byerly, Claude Hamon, Sam Davis, Dennis Ward, Larry Pannell, John Black, Frank Smith, Paul Resler, Paul Benien, Dean Bass, Don Roberts, John Porterfield, John Hornung. Courtesy Sports Information Department.

accomplished. But when he returned to Norman after such conferences, he always seemed depressed by his meetings with the various groups. He reported that those with whom he talked had been more inclined to discuss the congressional appropriations needed to finance the project than to discuss the project itself. They spoke in terms of millions of dollars. Wilkinson's idea was that a successful program could be launched with relatively little federal money. He thought it would be necessary only to develop and publicize a plan that would be implemented at the local level through the use of local personnel. He was critical of many agencies of the federal government that he thought had been wasteful of federal funds, and he was emphatic that the citizens should make an effort to reduce the waste in Washington. For the first time he mentioned that he might be interested in entering politics. He suggested one day, partly in jest, that he might change his registration to the Republican party and run for the United States Senate sometime.

T. R. Benedum's term as regent expired in the spring of 1961, and in July, Governor Edmondson appointed Jim Davidson, of Tulsa, to succeed him. Thus in a period of less than three years Edmondson had appointed four of the seven members of the board. That the governor had, in such a short time, in effect gained control of the board gave me some concern; his appointees were appearing so rapidly that I had no time to introduce them to their new responsibilities—or so it seemed to me. It turned out that my concern was justified, because I soon found myself in difficulty with three of the new board members.

The difficulty arose during the summer of 1961, when the regents became concerned about the traffic situation on the university campus. The parking lots were filled to overflowing, and the advisability of forbidding students to have cars at the university came in for close scrutiny. At the board's August meeting it was decided that a committee consisting of Regents Northcutt (chairman), Rothbaum, and Davidson should study the possibility of banning or restricting students' cars. If the committee could come up with a recommendation quickly, the board would be polled by telephone to approve a policy for the coming school year.

The committee struggled with its problem for several weeks

326

before it finally recommended on January 4, 1962, that a no-car rule for freshmen at OU be put into effect in September, 1962—with some exceptions, such as married students, disabled students, and commuters. I advised strongly against the recommendation, because I foresaw all kinds of difficulties in policing freshmen's automobiles. But despite my objections the rule was passed with one dissenting vote, Regent Monroe's.

The new rule was made public the following day. After reading about it in the morning paper, Wilkinson called my office to express concern, saying that he thought it would have an adverse effect on his recruiting. As an example, he and his staff had been trying to attract an unusually promising quarterback from Wichita Falls, Texas. The boy was to receive a new automobile for graduation that spring, and there would be no possibility, Wilkinson said, of persuading him to enroll at the University of Oklahoma unless he could have the car with him.

I told Wilkinson that I had already made myself unpopular with some of the regents by opposing the rule, and I was not inclined to bring up the matter again. I told him also that Northcutt had been chairman of the committee that had recommended the rule and perhaps he might care to talk to him.

Wilkinson followed my suggestion, and within a matter of hours I had a phone call from Northcutt, asking that I poll the regents by telephone about rescinding their action. When I conducted the poll, I found that a majority of the regents had changed their minds about the rule, but I did not receive a unanimous vote. Because it was a rule of the board that business could be conducted by telephone only through unanimous vote, it was necessary to take up the matter again at the board meeting on January 9. At that time Regent Johnson moved that the result of the telephone poll be ignored but that the action taken at the meeting on January 4 establishing a no-car rule be rescinded. The motion passed. Johnson, Monroe, and Davidson seemed embarrassed and somewhat resentful that a regulation passed by the board should be rescinded so quickly upon the request of a football coach. From their conversation I got the impression that they thought I had used Wilkinson to get the rule changed because I did not like it myself.

During the summer and early fall of 1961 there was a widespread rumor that Wilkinson would seek the Democratic nomination for governor of Oklahoma during the 1962 campaigns. Wilkinson disclaimed any interest in making the race, but many thought he would change his mind after the 1961 football season. Actually, Governor Edmondson, and at least one of his appointees to the OU board thought that Wilkinson could be persuaded to run and could win. The board member approached Wilkinson with the proposal that he should take a leave of absence to make the race. If he was successful, he would be governor, and the Edmondson administration could, in effect, be perpetuated. If he should lose, he could return to the university as head football coach and director of athletics. The fact that the university had a specific policy that any of its employees who ran for major public office must resign from the institution apparently was not given serious consideration by the governor or his representatives on the board. Wilkinson discussed the regent's proposal with me, and, while he seemed to have little or no interest in it, he was curious whether it would be possible for him to take a leave of absence and run for public office. I assured him that, in my opinion, it would not be possible, and he said he thought that it should not be possible.

One troublesome problem soon emerged for the Edmondson group. Earl Sneed, dean of the College of Law and faculty representative to the conference, was reported to be considering the race for governor himself. This naturally worried those who were supporting Wilkinson, because if the two were in the race, the OU vote would be split instead of going almost solidly for Wilkinson.

To solve this dilemma, Governor Edmondson approached Sneed with the suggestion that he might want to consider becoming president of the university instead of running for governor. When Sneed asked what was to happen to the incumbent, the governor supposedly replied that, while the current president would be removed, he would not be hurt financially—that a chancellorship would be provided for him. Sneed apparently gave no serious consideration to the governor's proposal, but he soon announced that he would not become a candidate for governor. I think that Wilkinson never gave serious thought to making the race.

328

CHAPTER 25

Wilkinson Rebuilds—Back to the Orange Bowl

1961–63

THE first half of the 1961 football season was an unbelievable disaster for the OU squad and its coaching staff, not to mention the thousands of fans who had taken such pride in the team's exploits in the past. The opening game was with Notre Dame at South Bend. The Big Red was defeated there on a hot, windy day, 6–19. Losses to Iowa State, Texas, Kansas, and Colorado followed in discouraging succession.

With the season half gone and no win recorded, Wilkinson made a significant speech to a group in Oklahoma City. There, after analyzing the first half of the season, he made an unprecedented prediction: his team would win the remaining games on the schedule. On the five following Saturdays, skeptical fans watched his prediction come true. Although by rather narrow margins, the Sooners defeated Kansas State; Missouri; Army, in Yankee Stadium in New York; Nebraska; and Oklahoma State.

Though they won only half their games, the Sooners finally placed fourth in conference standing, and fans generally conceded that Wilkinson and his staff had turned in one of their best coaching efforts. Darrell Royal commented that the 1961 season was Wilkinson's finest performance, going from 0–5 to 5–5. There were simply not enough good athletes to get the job done as well as Oklahomans would have liked. For the second year in a row no member of the squad received All-America recognition.

During the summer of 1962 Wilkinson was approached by officials of Stanford University who were looking for a head coach of football. They told him that the contract of Jack Curtice, whose football teams had not measured up to the expectations of the Stanford alumni, would not be renewed and that the job was Wilkinson's if he wanted it. Wilkinson appeared to have much greater interest in the Stanford offer than he had shown in any of the others he had discussed with me. He wondered if a move to Stanford, with the academic excellence for which the

329

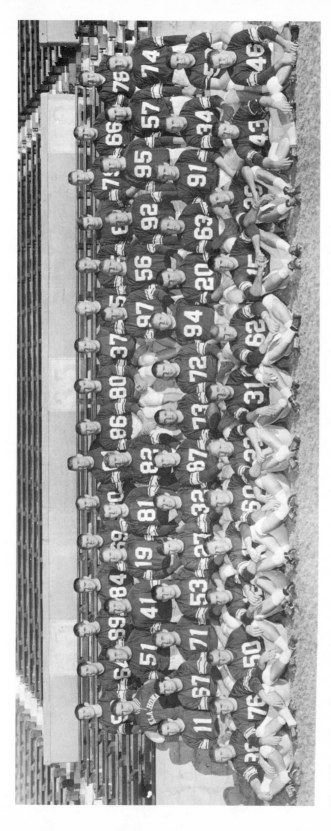

The 1961 team. FIRST ROW: Paul Lea, George Jarman, John Tatum, Monte Deere, Bob Page, Jimmy Gilstrap, Jimmy Carpenter, Mike McClellan, Larry Vermillion, Bill Van Burkleo, Virgil Boll, Bud Dempsey, Phil Lohmann. SECOND ROW: Chris Clapp, Doyle Ivester, Leon Cross, Wendell Robinson, Pat Hogan, Jackie Cowan, James Parker, Billy White, Duane Cook, Larry Pannell, Jerry Pettibone, Karl Milstead, Richard Inman, Geary Taylor, Bobby Wyatt. THIRD ROW: Jim Hensley (student manager), Dan Jordan, Richard Beattie, Billy Meacham, John Benien, John Porterfield, Jerry Cogburn, Bill Pannell, Ralph Maxfield, Nick Oakley, Thomas Farris, Bennie Shields. FOURTH ROW: Dave Southard, Claude Hamon, Jim Jackson, Dale Perini, Sam Davis, Jim McCoy, Dennis Ward, Ronny Payne, Paul Benien, Gary Wylie, Melvin Sandersfeld, Wayne Lee, Tom Cox, George Stokes, Jerry Hayden. Jimmy Payne. Courtesy Sports Information Department.

institution was noted, and perhaps less rugged competition for good athletes, might provide the stimulation needed to give him a fresh interest in coaching, an interest that he admitted was waning at OU. I did not make much effort to dissuade him during the three or four sessions we had; he decided on his own to decline the Stanford position, possibly because he was giving increasing thought to entering politics in Oklahoma—of registering as a Republican to run for the United States Senate. On the other hand, as John Cronley suggested in the *Oklahoma City Times,* he may have been influenced by the fact that an impressive number of his top twenty-five players of the 1961 season would be back for the 1962 campaign, thus giving him an opportunity to wind up his coaching career in somewhat more impressive fashion.

It was difficult in early 1962 to assess the potential of the team that would be in action that fall. The coaching staff, consisting of Gomer Jones, Eddie Crowder, Rudy Feldman, Bob Ward, Jay O'Neal, and George Dickson, seemed adequate. The squad had performed well during spring practice and had wound up the session with a 47–24 victory over a star-studded but somewhat disorganized alumni team. Speculative stories before the season opened included the names of tackles Dennis Ward, Duane Cook, Ralph Neely, and Butch Metcalf; guards Jimmy Gilstrap, Leon Cross, and Ed McQuarters; centers Wayne Lee and Johnny Tatum; end Glen Condren; quarterbacks Monte Deere, Norman Smith, and Ronny Fletcher; halfbacks Gary Wylie, Paul Lea, Virgil Boll, and Charlie Mayhue; and fullbacks Jim Grisham and Alvin Lear. Unheralded at the time was Joe Don Looney, a fullback who had transferred from Cameron Junior College and would have a brief but impressive career in OU football.

The opener of the 1962 season was with the University of Syracuse, a perennial power in the East. Played at Norman, it was a typical opening game, outstanding for rugged defensive play and costly offensive errors by both teams. There was no scoring until, with fifty-four seconds left in the first half, Syracuse kicked a 35-yard field goal for 3 points.

The half-time period featured what was perhaps the most impressive ceremony in the history of OU football. Before the kickoff the university had, as usual, raised its 5-by-7-foot American flag to the top of the flagpole at the south end of the stadium. Colonel Richmond Thweatt, commanding officer of the university ROTC unit, who had observed this ceremony on many past occasions, had decided that the flag was entirely too small for the purpose. Accordingly, he arranged for the military corps to present the institution with a new, much larger flag. The presentation ceremony was scheduled for the half-time period at the OU-Syracuse game.

The crowd milling about the stadium at half time that day suddenly realized that something out of the ordinary was in the offing when the small flag was lowered slowly from the flagpole. But as the small flag descended, another was rising in the relatively quiet air, its folds hugged the pole for more than half its length. As the crowd watched, the usual stadium noises diminished to a murmur. Then, as the new flag reached the top of the pole, a perfectly timed gentle breeze caught its folds, and it lazily extended to nearly full flight—its brilliantly colored red, white, and blue silk, 20 by 36 feet, shining in the bright sunlight. After the hushed crowd had gazed for a few moments in awe, the OU band sounded off with "The Stars and Stripes Forever." It was an emotional experience impossible to describe adequately. Now a "garrison" flag, the largest official flag the country flies, waved gracefully at the south end of the stadium. For days afterward, many who had been there spoke of the shivering thrills, moist eyes, and small catches in throats. As one young man put it at dinner after the game, "Boy, that was something!"

After the flag ceremony, the second half seemed an anticlimax, but there were stirring moments near the end of the game. Fierce defensive play and occasional offensive errors prevented either team from scoring during most of the half, and late in the fourth quarter it appeared that Syracuse would win by the narrow margin of 0–3. Then, with 2 minutes, 57 seconds left to play, OU got the ball on its own 27-yard line—a discouraging prospect. Three plays later the Sooners had advanced to their 40-yard line, with 2 minutes, 21 seconds left. Then came the big moment of the day, at least as far as OU fans were concerned. Quarterback Monte Deere pitched to Joe Don Looney, who had started around

The presentation of the new thirty-eight-foot garrison flag provided a thrilling moment during half-time ceremonies at the OU-Syracuse game, 1962.

left end. Tackle Dennis Ward removed the defensive end from the play. Left end John Flynn blocked the line backer, and Looney moved into the secondary. Moments later two Syracuse tacklers hit him simultaneously, and it appeared that he would go down. But he somehow stumbled from their clutches and found himself free in open field. He went down the east side of the stadium, accompanied by the roar of fifty thousand fans, and completed his 60-yard run for the game's winning touchdown. Wilkinson was to describe the run as "the finest exhibition of power ball carrying" he had seen in many years. Looney, the transfer from Cameron College, had not started in the game. He was only one of four fullbacks who played that day.

OU was host to Notre Dame the following week and lost in a rugged defensive battle, 7–13. Notre Dame's quarterback was Daryle Lamonica, who later became prominent as a professional quarterback. For OU fans probably the most interesting play of the game came in the fourth quarter, when the Sooners moved 71 yards to a first down on the Notre Dame 3-yard line. However, Notre Dame managed to shut off the drive approximately 2 feet from the end zone. A touchdown followed by a successful try for point would have given OU a win. As Wilkinson said, "Such are the narrow margins which separate success from failure."

Two weeks later the Sooners lost another close game to Texas by a score of 6–9. A fumble enabled Texas to score a field goal. A second fumble was recovered by Texas in the OU end zone for a touchdown. But in losing the Sooners showed considerable promise. In his newsletter, Wilkinson wrote:

> I have never been more proud of an Oklahoma team than I was Saturday against Texas.
>
> Our squad carried the fight to an excellent opponent. Without a single letup, we fought as hard as is humanly possible through the whole sixty minutes. We scored on two successive long, rather fortunate forward passes, but fumbled twice deep in our own territory.
>
> These two fumbles nullified the great effort our squad made against a fine opponent.

Wilkinson's squad won all the games remaining on the schedule, five of them by wide margins. The closest games were with Kansas (13–7) and Missouri (13–0). At the end of the season the Sooners were champions of their conference and the Associated Press ranked them eighth in the nation. Three members of the squad received All-America recognition: Leon Cross, a guard from Hobbs, New Mexico; Wayne Lee, center from Ada, Oklahoma; and Joe Don Looney, halfback from Fort Worth, Texas. A bid from the Orange Bowl to play in the New Year's classic there against fifth-ranked Alabama was accepted.

The coach of the Alabama Crimson Tide was Paul ("Bear") Bryant, who was bringing his alma mater to perennial national prominence in football. The Sooners had met a Bryant-coached team before—the Kentucky squad that ended Oklahoma's first long winning streak (thirty-one games) in the 1950 Sugar Bowl. His quarterback at Alabama was Joe Namath, who later became the most publicized quarterback in professional football while playing with the New York Jets. Lee Roy Jordan, a line backer of All-America quality, was another standout on his squad; he achieved outstanding success in later years with the Dallas Cowboys.

Pregame festivities on New Year's Day were marred by sad news from Washington, D.C. Oklahoma's Senator Robert S. Kerr, who had been hospitalized on December 18 by what his doctors reported was a medium-severe heart attack, had died that morning. News of his death had come to many Oklahomans by the time the crowd assembled at the Orange Bowl in the early afternoon. As we awaited the kickoff, Governor Edmondson came to where I was sitting with Mrs. Cross and Braden to ask if I had heard the news—if I thought it was really true that the senator had died. When I assured him that I thought it was indeed true, he left, apparently much shaken.

The game with Alabama was a shambles. The problem may have started in the Sooner dressing room a few minutes before the team went onto the field. President Kennedy had agreed to drop by for a visit with his friend Bud Wilkinson and to wish the Big Red team good luck. The visit later caused speculation about the impact that the presidential visit had on a football squad about to start an Orange Bowl contest—to what extent it might have influenced the team's ability to concentrate.

In any event, the Sooners obviously were not up to their usual form. Twice during the first quarter, they launched drives that reached the Alabama 10-yard line only to fumble to the Crimson Tide. A drive late in the game carried to the Alabama 20-yard line but failed as had all other offensive attempts. A major obstacle to OU's efforts was Alabama's Lee Roy Jordan, who made thirty-one tackles that afternoon.

President John F. Kennedy came to the Oklahoma dressing room just before the 1963 Orange Bowl game with Alabama. Wilkinson said, "Gentlemen, I'd like to present the President of the United States." President Kennedy said, "Well, fellows, as you know, Bud is head of our physical-fitness program. So I thought I'd drop by to see somebody who was physically fit." In leaving, Kennedy wished the team well, but Alabama won the game. Photo by Ned Hockman. Courtesy Department of Intercollegiate Athletics.

Defensively the Sooners were able to cope well with the Alabama rushing attack, but not with the passing genius of Joe Namath. The final score was 0–17.

The performance of the Oklahoma rooting section was about as flat as that of the football team. Perhaps word of Senator Kerr's passing was a factor in the crowd's reaction. According to the *Daily Oklahoman* the "cheering section was so quiet that the gaily clad cheerleaders could be heard discussing what on earth they might do to get the fans to yell."

Only the OU band, performing at half time to the music of currently popular songs, behaved in normal fashion. And even the band had bad luck: during their six-minute stint President Kennedy and his party on the Oklahoma side of the bowl chose to rise and stretch their legs. The crowd rose en masse to get a better view of the President and those with him. Someone shouted,

"There's Peter Lawford!" The band, oblivious to what was happening, played on and at the end of the performance received at least a measure of the applause it deserved.

Oklahomans returning from Miami found the local newspapers rife with speculation about who would succeed Senator Kerr. It was, of course, the responsibility of the governor of Oklahoma to appoint someone. Governor Edmondson's term was to expire, on January 14, when he would be succeeded by Governor-elect Henry Bellmon, the first Republican to reach that high office since statehood. Had Senator Kerr died after January 14, responsibility for naming his successor would have been Governor Bellmon's, and a Republican senator certainly would have been named. But Governor Edmondson retained the privilege by a thirteen-day margin.

Edmondson had at least two alternatives. He could appoint his brother, Congressman Ed Edmondson, to the post. Or he could resign the governorship and have Lieutenant Governor George Nigh succeed him as governor, with the understanding that Nigh would name him to fill Kerr's unexpired term. Although four years of Kerr's six-year term remained, the appointment of his successor would be effective only until Oklahoma voters had a chance to express themselves at the next primary and general elections in 1964.

Out of respect for Senator Kerr and his family, Edmondson and his associates refused to comment on the possibilities before the funeral ceremonies, but it was the consensus of political writers that the governor would resign and arrange to have himself named to the Senate. Such proved to be the case, and early in January, George Nigh became the sixth governor with whom I would work during my tenure as president of the university.

Rumors about Wilkinson's future were also circulating in early January. One of these termed him a prospect for the next gubernatorial election. Another rumor had it that he would become a candidate for the United States Senate at the next general election, either as a Democrat or as a Republican. But Wilkinson had gone to a meeting in Los Angeles a few days after the Orange Bowl game, and this trip caused many writers to revive the speculation that he was seriously considering a move to Stanford.

337

When asked about this in Los Angeles, he did little to clarify the situation when he replied: "To say I'm not interested in the Stanford position would be inaccurate. To say I am interested also would be inaccurate. And any comment I would make has to be damaging to my position." At Stanford, President J. Wallace Sterling was similarly unhelpful. When asked about the prospect of hiring Wilkinson for the head coaching position there, he replied, "No comment—on Wilkinson or anyone else."

While I had a feeling that Wilkinson would not coach much longer at Oklahoma, I had no clue to what he might finally decide to do. He had been noncommital when I suggested that if he wanted to retire from coaching he might continue with the athletic directorship and in addition help the university in its fundraising activities. In any event, I thought the prospect of this lessened somewhat when Edmondson resigned the governorship to become senator, because the possibility that Wilkinson might be Edmondson's opponent at the next general election could cause tension between him and the Edmondson appointees on the OU board.

In May, 1963, Wilkinson was spotlighted in the news for alleged political activities—for attempting to use political influence with Governor Bellmon. It had to do with the appointment of a member of the Board of Regents. Early in March the governor had appointed John Houchin to succeed Dave Morgan on the board. But he took no action to name a successor to Leonard Savage, whose term had expired the previous spring, an omission that some interpreted to mean that Savage would remain on the board and that in due time the governor would send his name to the senate for confirmation.

But Quintin Little, whose service on the board had been interrupted by Governor Edmondson, emerged as a possibility to succeed Savage. According to Senator Tom Tipps from Little's district, thirty-nine members of the state senate had signed a petition asking the governor to name Little. The most interesting reason given for this was that Little had been unusually successful in recruiting football talent for OU. One state senator pointed out that OU had not won a football game from Texas since Little left the board.

338

The 1962 team. FIRST ROW (FRONT ROW), LEFT TO RIGHT: Paul Lea, Charles Mayhue, Jimmy Payne, Norman Smith, George Jarman, Larry Vermillion, Wayne Lee (co-captain), Leon Cross (co-captain), Teddy Dodson, Bert Gravitt, Bud Dempsey, Joe Don Looney, Bill Hill, Rick McCurdy. SECOND ROW: David Voiles, John Running, Richard Boudreaux, Jackie Cowan, John Flynn, Johnny Tatum, Duane Cook, Monte Deere, Jimmy Gilstrap, Dan Jordan, Geary Taylor, Jerry Hayden, Larry Pannell, Pat Hogan. THIRD ROW: Dale Pontius, Jim Jackson, Melvin Sandersfeld, Ron Harmon, John Garrett, Jim Gard, Ed McQuarters, Charles Pearce, Glen Condren, Bobby Page, Bennie Shields, Bill Pannell, Ronnie Fletcher, James Parker, Billy Joe Woods (student manager). FOURTH ROW: Ralph Neely, Alvin Lear, John Porterfield, Wes Skidgel, Virgil Boll, John Benien, Greg Burns, Newt Burton, Butch Metcalf, Dennis Ward, Ronnie Horn, Jim Grisham, Lance Rentzel, Gary Wylie, George Stokes, Allen Bumgarner. Courtesy Sports Information Department.

Bob Breeden, senate Republican minority leader, apparently had not thought that Little should be reappointed to the board; at least his name was not on the petition that was delivered to the governor. But Wilkinson very much wanted Little to be reappointed. He came to me and asked if it would be proper for him to intercede with Senator Breeden on Little's behalf. I told him I had no objection to his telling the senator that Little would be acceptable to the OU administration. Wilkinson delivered the message to Breeden, and Governor Bellmon announced Little's appointment a few days later. This action produced some resentment in the senate. Cleeta John Rogers, chairman of the senate's Committee on Higher Education, scheduled a meeting of the committee to discuss the governor's nomination. However, the senate, in what was reported to be a somewhat stormy executive session, voted to confirm Little's appointment without recommendation from its committee.

Little's appointment prompted considerable editorial commentary, and Wilkinson was widely criticized for using political pressure to get his friend back on the board. It was generally agreed that a football coach should not have a voice in naming a member of the governing board of the state university.

The Edmondson appointees on the OU board took a dim view of Wilkinson's role in the appointment and were critical of me for not advising him against making his views known to Senator Breeden.

During the summer of 1963 many Oklahomans became concerned that Wilkinson would resign his positions at Oklahoma after the 1963 football season and run for the United States Senate as a Republican contender. Queried by reporters about the possibility that he would become a candidate, Wilkinson said, not quite accurately, that he had not thought about running for the Senate. He was quoted as follows:

I haven't thought a thing about it. This is like people talking to me about running for governor.

There is no way you can answer questions like these. I have been trying for years, but I haven't found a way yet.

I can't control what is said in the newspapers. However, I never have articulated any political philosophy to my knowledge. The only thing

I am interested in right now is OU's football schedule for the next season.

Despite his denial the Oklahoma delegation in Washington was convinced that he would make the race and that, with Barry Goldwater on the presidential ticket, his chances for election might be very good.

Wilkinson's Last Season—"Seven Against the Country"—Coach Gomer Jones

1963-64

WILKINSON's immediate responsibility was the 1963 season. There was optimism on campus and around the state. Sports writers seemed to hold the unanimous opinion that OU would finish the season in the top ten. *Playboy* magazine evaluated OU as the third best team in the nation.

But the schedule was a formidable one. It included Clemson College, the favorite to win the Atlantic Coast Conference championship, and Southern California, the nation's number-one team the year before. Four of the teams on the schedule had played in bowls after the 1962 season: Southern California, Texas, Nebraska, and Missouri.

A more than adequate group of linemen was on hand. After spring practice the probable starting line was John Garrett at center, John Flynn and Rick McCurdy at end, Ralph Neely and Glen Condren at tackle, and Ed McQuarters and Newt Burton at guard. In the backfield Joe Don Looney, All-America the preceding season, was back. Several other competent halfbacks were available, including Virgil Boll, Larry Shields, Jackie Cowan, and Lance Rentzel. Jim Grisham had proved capable of handling the fullback chores very well.

There was some uncertainty about the quarterback spot. Mike Ringer, John Hammond, and Tom Pannell were possibilities, but after spring practice and preseason drills Ringer was selected to handle those duties in the opening game with Clemson at Norman.

Oklahoma won over Clemson, 31–14, in a game marred by many Oklahoma errors. That his team was able to win despite the errors pleased Wilkinson, who commented, "We played poorly for the first twenty minutes of the game, making more errors than a team can usually ever commit and still maintain a chance to win." He said that the chances against Southern California the following week would depend on the extent to which errors could be eliminated. One benefit of the Clemson game, not realized at the time, was that the game had been played in debilitating heat—90 degrees at kickoff.

At Los Angeles the temperature at kickoff time was 105 degrees on the playing field, heat for which the Sooners were better prepared than the Trojans. Playing in the stifling heat, they were able to upset the national champions 17–12 and, in the process, won the statistical battle by a substantial margin, except in yards gained in passing. It was a good team effort, without individual stars, although Looney's 19-yard run for OU's first touchdown brought him to the attention of the sweltering fans in the coliseum and the several million watching by television. The key to the victory was the ability of the defense to contain the Southern California offense and thereby keep possession of the ball most of the game.

Victory over Southern California boosted OU to first place in the national rankings the following week. But during that same week Mike Ringer, who had seemed on his way to becoming one of OU's better quarterbacks of the Wilkinson regime, accidentally shoved his elbow into the blades of an electric fan and was out for the rest of the season. Fortunately Oklahoma had an open date that weekend, and so Wilkinson had a little time to pick a new starting quarterback before the annual fracas with Texas in the Cotton Bowl. He selected Bobby Page.

There had been rumors of unrest and lack of morale during the week preceding the Texas game. Most of these involved All-America Looney, who allegedly had been lackadasical in practice and even negligent in attendance. Questioned about this, he was reported to have replied that he was in shape and did not need the practice—that if he could get a little blocking during the game he would get the job done.

Whatever the cause, something was decidedly wrong when the Sooners took the field against Texas on October 12. With only a few exceptions the squad seemed lacking in fire and determination. Blocking and tackling were indecisive and ineffective. Looney, who had performed so brilliantly during the first two games when there was unified team effort, gained only 3 yards the entire game. Some suggested that the offensive line, displeased by Looney's alleged disparaging appraisal of their importance, may have decided to let him find out how well he could perform without effective blocking.

By contrast the University of Texas (which was later voted national champion) played superbly and won the game 7–28. As Wilkinson put it, "They were well prepared, and they played like champions." His opinion of his own team's performance was somewhat different:

I have been coaching at Oklahoma sixteen years but never can I recall an Oklahoma team playing with as little fire and determination as we did against Texas Saturday. We were unaggressive, we lacked real effort, we were totally flat.

Contrary to public opinion, we are not and have never been a great team. We are far too slow, we lack quickness to too great a degree to be a great team. But we have more ability than we showed in the Cotton Bowl Saturday. In such circumstances, coaching is obviously a major factor. As a coach, I feel I have failed to properly prepare our men for the job at hand. I can assure you I tried. Yet I failed to get through.

After consultation with members of his staff and key members of the squad, Wilkinson announced that Looney would be dropped from the squad. The decision surely was made with regret, because Looney had the physical potential to become an outstanding player: a beautifully developed physique, with extraordinary coordination and speed for a man of his size.

The defeat by Texas toppled Oklahoma from its lofty position in the national ratings, but there was still the possibility of a Big Eight championship. After a squeaker with Kansas (21–18), the Big Red won handily from Kansas State, Colorado, Iowa State, and Missouri before meeting Nebraska at Lincoln on November 23.

Nebraska loomed as a formidable obstacle. Bob Devaney was completing his second year as coach of the Cornhuskers. His record for the season was 6–0 in conference competition, and 8–1 over all. It had been predicted the summer before that OU and Nebraska would fight it out for the conference championship when the two teams met in the fall.

The OU team and official party flew to Lincoln on Friday morning, November 22. After lunch I took a brief walk, and when I returned to the hotel, the desk clerk told me that President

Kennedy had been shot and seriously injured in Dallas that morning. Late in the afternoon we were shocked to learn that the President had not survived.

With a presidential assassination on Friday, what should be done about a football game scheduled for the following day? There were many opinions and much advice. Regents of the University of Nebraska had arrived in Lincoln for the game along with thousands of other fans. The regents went into session, and word finally came from the president's office that the Nebraskans thought the game should be played as scheduled. After discussing the matter thoroughly with Wilkinson and a few members of the team and making a phone call to Governor Bellmon for advice (the governor left it up to the university), it was finally decided that the deceased President and the members of his family, if they could be reached for their opinion, would want the country's activities to go on in reasonably normal fashion in the days before the funeral. The Nebraska officials were notified that Oklahoma would play.

The weather was bleak and cheerless the next day. The mood of the capacity crowd in the stadium was somber—in keeping with the weather and the tragedy of the day before. None of the festivity usually associated with a football game was in evidence. Following a prayer and a few moments of silence in honor of the dead President, the game got under way with only restrained expressions of enthusiasm from the crowd.

OU made a great many offensive errors that day, permitting Nebraska to take possession of the ball on six occasions—five of them on the Oklahoma side of the 50-yard line. But despite such unfavorable field position, the OU defense played so well that Nebraska was held to a single field goal, from the OU 18-yard line, during the first half.

In the third quarter OU fumbled to Nebraska on three occasions, on its own 15-, 31-, and 32-yard lines; the Cornhuskers turned two of these mishaps into touchdowns. In the fourth quarter Nebraska was able to intercept two Sooner passes, one of which was returned to the OU 15-yard line and the other to the 20. To climax a bad afternoon, OU fumbled during a kickoff return to Nebraska on the Sooner 31-yard line.

In the meantime, Nebraska played an excellent game and, capitalizing on the OU mishaps, led 7–29 with approximately five minutes left to play in the fourth quarter. Finally, managing to eliminate errors, the Sooners scored twice in the final five minutes but at the game's end were defeated 20–29. The Cornhuskers had won a conference championship and a trip to the Orange Bowl, but the team and its followers showed little enthusiasm in winning. The huge crowd drifted quietly from the stadium.

When we returned to Norman, my office and the athletic office received a fair amount of criticism for having played the game. But we thought that we had made the right decision, considering all the circumstances. The overwhelming problem of making refunds to ticketholders was avoided. We learned that several other institutions that did cancel were plagued by this problem for several years.

OU completed its 1963 season with a relatively easy 34–10 victory over OSU in a game played at Norman before a relatively small crowd of 47,000. Although placing second in the Big Eight conference, the Sooners were rated eighth in the nation by the UPI and tenth by the AP. Fullback Jim Grisham and tackle Ralph Neely made the first All-America team.

A few days after the season ended, Wilkinson came to my office. He told me that he was undecided about whether to make the race for the United States Senate but that he had decided to resign from his coaching position. He said he was no longer able to get himself into the "proper frame of mind" to prepare for a football game and therefore was unable to get his staff ready. If he and the staff were not ready, it followed that the squad would not be ready. He said that he would present his resignation as coach within the next few weeks but that, temporarily at least, he would like to retain the title of athletic director.

It was not until the middle of the second week in January that Wilkinson came to my office and announced that he was resigning as head football coach. He said that he was preparing a statement that he would like to present to the regents and explain in person the reasons for his action. I arranged a meeting of the board for Saturday morning, January 11. There Wilkinson submitted the following statement:

346

I am announcing my resignation as football coach. I had hoped I could, at this time, end all speculation that has surrounded my future plans. Circumstances beyond my control have made this impossible.

However, I recognize my primary responsibility and obligation to the university. In order that our football program, particularly recruiting and spring practice, may move ahead without a break, it is best that I resign. Our new coach must have a fair and equal start with our competition.

At this time, I plan to continue as Athletic Director and devote my energies to the advancement of all sports at the university. It remains my goal to have all our intercollegiate athletic teams continually contend for conference and national honors.

With regard to the political speculation, it would be neither proper nor accurate to say I am not considering the senate race. Frankly, I am. But I would like to state with all candor, that my resignation is not motivated by politics.

My brother's recent illness and death have added to my responsibilities to his widow and my mother. I must help them reorganize his business and settle his affairs. Also, the much needed National Physical Fitness program continues as an increasing obligation.

In moments of reflection, I have often considered this date of retirement from active coaching. I have reached the decision with reluctance. Obviously, I will always owe a debt of gratitude to the players, coaches, faculty and loyal fans of Oklahoma football who have made these years good beyond anything I deserve. These relationships of mutual trust and respect are the very factors which make it unfair for me to continue coaching at a time when it would be difficult to devote my undivided attention to our team and the university.

Wilkinson assured the board that the recruitment program was ahead of where it had been the preceding year, because recruiting had not been interrupted by a bowl game. He recommended that Gomer Jones be named to succeed him as head football coach and suggested that prompt action would be helpful so that recruiting and plans for spring practice could proceed without interruption.

After his statement, in response to questions from reporters, he admitted his interest in politics. He said, "I feel the experience I have had in Washington is one of the things that has led me to seriously consider it." But more persistent inquiry brought from him only the cautious response, "I don't mean to say I will run for the senate, and I don't mean to say I won't."

Wilkinson's resignation, though not a surprise to those who had attended the board meeting, had a somber effect on all

After a brilliant career in football coaching, Bud Wilkinson resigns to run for the United States Senate in 1964. Courtesy *Oklahoman and Times.*

present. After all, it was the end of an era—an era in which one of the most successful coaches in college football had established a legendary reign at OU, with a record of 145 wins, 29 losses, and 4 ties in regular season play (a most impressive 83.3 per cent winning record) and a major-bowl record of 6–2. He had compiled an all-time national record for consecutive wins: 47 games. His teams had won thirteen conference championships outright and tied for a fourteenth during his seventeen years with the university.

He had been inducted into the Oklahoma Hall of Fame, and he had received the highest honor the university could give, the Distinguished Service Citation. He had received an award from B'nai B'rith for his advancement of Americanism and citizenship. He had received a citation from the National Brotherhood of Christians and Jews for his contributions to interracial relationships through his work in the church, in athletics, and in civic affairs. He had served as president of the National Football Coaches' Association. He had accomplished the objective the university had in mind for the OU football team when he came to the university back in the 1940's: to give the state a program of which all citizens could be proud, to dispel the "grapes of wrath" image.

After the morning session, the regents recessed for lunch and then resumed their meeting at 1:00 P.M. in the office of Dean Sneed, chairman of the Athletic Council and OU's representative to the Big Eight Conference. Other members of the Athletic Council had been asked to attend the meeting to confer about procedures to be followed in hiring a new coach. After a brief discussion it was decided that the regents' Committee on Athletics—Quintin Little, John Houchin, and Eph Monroe—would represent the board in working with the Athletic Council in the search. Names of several prospects were mentioned, including an impressive list of successful coaches who had played under Wilkinson: Jim Owens, Jack Mitchell, Eddie Crowder, Darrell Royal, Buck McPhail, and Jay O'Neal. But as the meeting neared an end, Wilkinson again made an unqualified recommendation of Gomer Jones for the job and emphasized his hope that a decision could be reached soon so that no recruiting time would be lost.

After the board adjourned, it became clear from informal discussions that some of the regents thought Wilkinson should have resigned both as coach and as director of athletics. Then, one regent pointed out, it would have been possible to offer the athletic directorship as well as the head coaching job, which, he believed, practically any coach in the country would be happy to have. There was a hint of suspicion that Wilkinson really planned to run for the Senate but had retained the athletic directorship temporarily only to help Jones get the job.

As soon as Wilkinson's resignation was announced, members of the football squad went into action to choose his successor. On Sunday morning, January 12, a petition asking that Gomer Jones be named was circulated among the athletes, and all but two or three of those who had played the past season and would be back the coming year signed it. Word of the petition got out, and several members of the press asked me Monday morning what I would do about it. I replied that if the petition came to my office I would endorse it and pass it on to the regents. News of the squad's petition and my comment were widely publicized in the media; this brought unfavorable reaction from some of the regents, who thought that I should have made no mention of my choice of coach at that time.

The following Wednesday, January 15, the regents met with four representatives from the football squad to discuss the petition. Spokesman for the athletes was co-captain Newt Burton, who had played guard on the 1963 squad. Because I was out of favor with some of the regents, Glenn Northcutt, president of the board, suggested that it might be better if I did not attend the meeting; but I was told later that the discussion had lasted for about an hour and ended without any indication from the regents about what they planned to do.

The same day Jack Taylor, president of the Alumni Association, reported to the public that the Executive Board of the association had been canvassed and that "a very strong majority are in favor of Gomer Jones for head coach." Letters and telegrams began to arrive at my office from a number of alumni and other fans who strongly supported Jones for the coaching job.

In a statement handed to the press after the meeting with the football players, Regent Northcutt announced that the board would meet the following Sunday, January 19, to consider the names of several prospects, perhaps as many as fifteen. In the statement also was a comment that the board probably would

350

not reach a decision for a couple of weeks. That remark caused much discussion about the strategy of the regents. Local rumor had it that the board would deliberately withhold a decision until after February 1, 1964, the deadline for changing party registration in Oklahoma. In this way it would be possible for the regents to force Wilkinson's hand. If he wanted to run for the Senate on the Republican ticket, it would be necessary for him to change his registration before February 1, thus revealing his intentions. Such action might justify a request for his resignation as athletic director.

In the meantime, Wilkinson had flown to Washington, presumably to talk with President Lyndon B. Johnson about his future as physical-fitness consultant. According to the newspapers he was scheduled to meet with the President the weekend of January 18. But after he arrived in Washington, he received word that the regents would not name Jones, at least not immediately, as his successor but instead would spend some time considering other prospects for the position. Interpreting this as an effort on the part of the board to pressure him into reaching a decision about his candidacy for the Senate, Wilkinson passed up the meeting with the President and flew back to Oklahoma early Saturday morning. He said to the press, "I'm going to try to get Gomer Jones appointed football coach." He told the press that he thought a coach must be selected at once to avoid jeopardizing the recruiting program.

I had had no contact with Wilkinson since the day of his resignation. I knew of his trip to Washington only by reading about it in the newspapers. Accordingly, on Saturday afternoon, January 18, as I was driving to our weekend home at Hall Park, I was startled by a radio news report that Wilkinson had announced that he would resign as athletic director at a press conference he had called for 1:00 P.M. that afternoon. He told the assembled reporters that he would present his resignation to the regents at 1:00 P.M. on Sunday, at the time the board was to consider several prospects for the coaching job.

In announcing his intention to resign, Wilkinson was quoted as saying:

It has become increasingly apparent that political maneuvering on

351

the part of some regents has taken precedence over the early choice of a new coach.

So that these considerations can no longer play a part in the delay, I am resigning as athletic director. This action will free the regents from any further political involvement related to this selection.

I repeat again with all possible emphasis that Gomer Jones is unequivocally my recommendation to be the head football coach and athletic director. I hope with every fiber of my being that they do name Mr. Jones. I believe the University of Oklahoma football team has a better chance of winning with Mr. Jones than any other man. Gomer and I have been virtual partners for seventeen years.

I believe it is clear to all who are interested in the football program at the University of Oklahoma that the delay in naming a new head coach is unnecessary and damaging.

In making his announcement, Wilkinson made it clear that he was resigning only as athletic director and not as professor of physical education, and he did not disclose his intentions about the Senate race.

Wilkinson's Saturday press conference was evidently characterized by tension and emotion. Doug Todd, a staff writer, reported in the *Daily Oklahoman:*

No matter who the ultimate choice of the regents turns out to be, the events of this past week have taken their toll on the persons most closely involved. Wilkinson was something less than his usual smiling, gracious self at the press conference Saturday. Whether from anger at the regents' delays, impatience with reporters' questioning or just plain fatigue, Bud appeared tired, and at times, short tempered.

But perhaps the main reason for Wilkinson's emotional state was an article in a local paper in which some of the regents had been quoted as saying they were "fed up" with him and displeased with his political maneuvering and vacillation.

Sunday, January 19, was to be the day of decision. It was an unhappy situation, with the regents at odds with Wilkinson, me, the Athletic Council, the faculty, and a substantial segment of the public.

Because I was out of favor with some members of the board, I was not invited to attend the Sunday session at which Wilkinson's resignation was received, and prospects for the coaching job were interviewed. As a matter of fact, I was not even told of the meeting. I read about it in the papers, and I had no idea who might be coming for interviews. Reports in the Oklahoma City papers that I would attend the meeting and have a part in the interviewing were erroneous. My differences with the board apparently were pretty well known locally. Nick Seitz, sports editor for the *Norman Transcript,* wrote in the Sunday, January 19, edition:

> It has been said that some of the regents were holding off on the naming of a coach until they could force Wilkinson's hand on his political intentions, and that Jones was caught in the middle—with his qualifications for the job of secondary concern.
>
> But there would seem to be another angle to the crossfire. Some of the regents reportedly dislike Cross, and, according to generally reliable members of the university staff, don't want to see Cross get his way about anything.
>
> This source said he heard that the regents voted not to consider Jones for the coaching job even before Wilkinson resigned, after Cross told the regents that Wilkinson might resign as coach. Cross reportedly recommended Jones at that time.

Seitz's account was accurate to a point. I had told the regents that I expected Wilkinson to resign, and I had recommended Jones as his successor, but the regents had not voted not to consider Jones at that time. They had merely indicated displeasure with my recommendation.

The regents assembled at 1:00 P.M. on Sunday afternoon to cope with their complex problem. All the board members were present for the meeting, and as they proceeded to the football offices in the north end of the stadium where the meeting was scheduled, they were greeted by several individuals carrying signs endorsing Jones for the coaching job. Seeing them, one regent was quoted as saying, "It's seven against the country." After a brief session with Wilkinson the regents accepted his resignation and then went into executive session to interview four prospects for the coaching position: Coleman ("Buck") McPhail, an All-America fullback at Oklahoma in 1952 and then backfield coach at the University of Illinois; Sam Boghosian, line coach at the University of California at Los Angeles; Mike Corgan, backfield coach at the University of Nebraska; and Gomer Jones.

According to Volney Meece, staff writer for the *Daily Okla-*

"Seven against the country," the Board of Regents responsible for selecting a new head coach after the resignation of Bud Wilkinson. Clockwise from behind the table: Eph Monroe, Clinton; Julian Rothbaum, Tulsa; Mark Johnson, Oklahoma City; Glenn Northcutt, Willis (president); Jim Davidson, Tulsa; Quintin Little, Ardmore; John Houchin, Bartlesville; Emil Kraettli (secretary of the board), and President Cross.

homan, the meeting lasted for six hours and thirteen minutes. The regents then announced, to no one's surprise, that Gomer Jones would be the next head football coach at OU. Reporters waiting in the halls and stairways for the verdict agreed that their quarters looked like "a maternity ward waiting room."

That evening, Jones gave a short statement to the press:

I am happy the regents have appointed me, I thank them sincerely.

I also appreciate more than I can say, Bud Wilkinson's strong endorsement of me, also the support of President Cross, the Athletic Council, and the faculty of the university. The people of Oklahoma stood by me loyally, and I am very grateful for their support.

I am especially pleased and gratified that the football team backed me so solidly. I know this means that they will give a one hundred per cent effort.

354

We will continue to need the loyal help of the people of Oklahoma in our recruiting and in all other phases of our athletic program.

No minutes were kept of that long and memorable meeting, and my office never did receive official notice from the board that this action had been taken. But on January 24 I received a report from Earl Sneed, chairman of the Athletic Council, which read as follows:

At a meeting on 21 January 1964, the Athletic Council voted to make the following recommendations to you.

I. *Head Football Coach*

Mr. Gomer T. Jones has been selected as head football coach. The Council recommends that Mr. Jones be employed for a term of four years, effective the date of his appointment, 19 January, 1964. Compensation for Mr. Jones is set forth in relation to our recommendation for the athletic directorship.

II. *The Athletic Directorship*

The Council recommends that Mr. Gomer T. Jones be appointed athletic director, effective 1 March, 1964, for a period of four years. This would make Mr. Jones' contract as head football coach coincide with his contract as athletic director.

We recommend that Mr. Jones be paid a salary in his positions as head football coach and athletic director as follows:

Base salary	$18,000.00 —	this is to include the present $500 annuity for which payments are withheld monthly.
Expense allowance	$ 3,500.00	
Annuities	$ 1,900.00 —	this represents a $1,000 and $900 annuity now being paid annually by the Athletic Department.
Total	$23,400.00	

It was the unanimous concensus of the Council that the base salary of Mr. Jones be used in any publicity releases concerning the new contract and that there was no need to publicize the expense account. In other words, the Council felt that the compensation for Mr. Jones should be treated in the same manner as was the compensation for Mr. Wilkinson.

Gomer Jones, long-time assistant to Bud Wilkinson, was appointed head coach by the Board of Regents on January 19, 1964. Courtesy Sports Information Department.

The council recommends that as head football coach Mr. Jones refrain from receiving any remuneration whatsoever from the Touchdown Club. Mr. Jones agrees. As you know, Mr. Jones has been receiving a yearly supplement of approximately $2,500 from the Touchdown Club.

The major change in the compensation paid Mr. Jones under this recommendation would be in the base salary. He is now receiving $10,596, but in addition is receiving the $2,500 supplement from the Touchdown Club. His annuities would remain the same as before. Mr. Jones is now receiving $2,000 in expense money and we recommend an increase in this amount to $3,500.

Not knowing what, if any, arrangements had been made with Jones about the terms of his appointment, I decided to pass Sneed's report along to the regents, without comment, at their meeting on February 13.

The 1963 team. FIRST ROW (FRONT ROW), LEFT TO RIGHT: Bill Hill, Charley Mayhue, Robert Vardeman, Teddy Dodson, Jerald Gilbert, Bill Thomas, Bill Carlyle, John Garrett, Larry Vermillion, Jimmy Gilstrap, John Benien, Greg Burns, Lance Rentzel, Jerry Alfieri, Ronnie Horn. SECOND ROW: Dale Pontius, Jerry Goldsby, Ron Harmon, Allen Bumgardner, Ed McQuarters, Newt Burton, Don Kindley, Ed Hall, Glen Condren, Gary Williams, Mike Ringer, Jim Reynolds, Pat Hogan, Jackie Cowan, Charles Pearce, Vernon Burkett. THIRD ROW: Ralph Neely, Wes Skidgel, Larry Shields, Marion Bayles, Larry Brown, Ken Aboussie, Thurman Pitchlynn, Roger Rains, Butch Metcalf, Rick McCurdy, Norman Smith, David Voiles, Gordon Brown, Carl McAdams, Jim Doolittle. FOURTH ROW: Frank Dombek (student manager), John Porterfield, Nehemiah Flowers, Bennie Shields, Ronnie Frost, Coy Kersey, Jr., George Jarman, Jon Running, Bobby Page, John Hammond, Jim Grisham, Virgil Boll, Ronnie Fletcher, Tommy Pannell, Carl Schreiner, John Flynn. Courtesy Sports Information Department.

The regents discussed the recommendations contained in Sneed's report but ended by referring it to the board's Athletic Committee, consisting of Regents Little, Houchin, and Monroe, for further study and report to the board.

The regents did not get around to clarifying Jones's status until the April, 1964, meeting. Then they approved his appointment as head coach and athletic director at a salary of $18,000 a year for a four-year period. They made it a condition of the contract that the two positions were inseparable—thus ending, they thought, any possibility of confusion of the kind that arose when Wilkinson resigned as head coach but retained the athletic directorship.

But the details of Jones's contract took a bit longer. Eph Monroe, who succeeded Glenn Northcutt as president of the board, worked on the document with Jones and his attorney for weeks. Agreement finally was reached, and the contract was signed by Monroe, Jones, and Emil Kraettli on July 16, 1964. On that date Jones became the only employee of the university to hold a contract signed by the president of the Board of Regents.

CHAPTER 27

Wilkinson Runs for the Senate—
Jones Takes Charge

1964-65

As many expected he would, Wilkinson changed his political registration from Democrat to Republican late in January, 1964. Curiously enough, he made his announcement through Harold Keith, the university sports publicist. This brought him mild criticism from a local paper: a writer suggested that he had used Keith because he did not care to face questioning by the press. The writer emphasized that Wilkinson, who had always been good on his football fundamentals, should be aware of a political fundamental: those who run for office must be willing to face, unshielded, the public and the press. Perhaps in response, a few days later (February 5) Wilkinson announced at a press conference in Oklahoma City that he would become a candidate for a seat in the United States Senate, and he fielded all questions effectively. On the same day he resigned as adviser to the President's Council on Physical Fitness.

Wilkinson's candidacy was welcomed by Governor Bellmon, but not all members of the Republican party. Already announced as candidates in the primary election were Republicans Forest Beall, Tom Harris, and Tom Moore.

Howard Edmondson had made known his intention to run for the remainder of Senator Kerr's term at the coming election. Former Governor Raymond Gary and State Senator Fred Harris had also announced their intentions to run. Edmondson was given the edge to reach the general election on the Democratic ticket, and most political forecasters believed that Wilkinson would be the Republican candidate. An interesting race appeared to be shaping up between Wilkinson and the man who had first suggested (in 1960) that he enter politics as a Democratic candidate for the governorship of Oklahoma.

Another event of some interest took place that spring when, at a meeting in Stillwater, the faculty representatives to the conference voted "that the 'Big Eight Conference' be adopted as the official name of the organization, replacing the 'Missouri Valley Intercollegiate Athletic Conference.'"

Both Wilkinson and Jones met disappointment in their new roles. Wilkinson had little difficulty winning the Republican nomination for the Senate seat, defeating his opponents in the primary with relative ease. But he was not to face Howard Edmondson in the general election, as he and most of his friends had anticipated. Fred Harris, with bachelor's and law degrees from the university, won over Edmondson in the primary election. Oklahomans apparently had taken a dim view of the maneuvering that had placed Edmondson in the Senate after Senator Kerr's death. This was unfortunate for Wilkinson because doubtless he had expected to face a somewhat discredited candidate in the general election; instead he faced a popular young legislator who had a strong following not only in the OU family but throughout the state.

But Wilkinson campaigned vigorously for the general election, aided by one of his former athletes, Jackie Ging. Ging, a rising actor in the television and motion-picture industry in California, spent a great deal of time in Oklahoma helping with the campaign.

The university family, alumni and faculty, was widely split in support of the two candidates. The split was emphasized about the middle of October, when a political advertisement with headlines "OU Faculty and Staff Strongly Support Fred R. Harris for U.S. Senate," paid for and signed by 210 employees of the university, appeared in the Oklahoma City and Tulsa newspapers. The ad precipitated a storm of protest from Wilkinson's friends, who forcefully expressed their disapproval. I received a phone call early one morning from the president of an Oklahoma City bank who suggested that those who had signed the ad should be disciplined in some way—preferably fired. The advertisement, he said, was misleading because the 210 employees who had signed it constituted no more than 10 per cent of the university employees. My expressions of regret and efforts to be conciliatory were ineffective. My caller finally ended the conversation with the suggestion that, unless some positive action was taken to cure the wrong that had been done, the University of Oklahoma might be looking for a new president.

During the following days the advertisement was discussed, pro and con, in editorials and letters to editors. The excitement finally died down; it was apparently agreed that, while the employees of the university had the right to express their voting preferences, they had no right to claim that they were expressing the views of all employees of the institution.

Probably the advertisement had very little effect on the outcome of the election. Historically, the thinking of Oklahomans has not been affected greatly by the political opinions of employees of the University of Oklahoma. Wilkinson lost the election by a very narrow margin, perhaps because a slight majority of the voters thought Harris' legal and political background better preparation for the Senate seat than Wilkinson's spectacular coaching career.

Wilkinson's amazing record at the University of Oklahoma, even though much of it was due to the splendid help of Gomer Jones, made it difficult for Jones to succeed him. Oklahoma fans were accustomed to championship football nearly every season, and they were unwilling to accept anything else.

Prospects for the 1964 season had appeared good, with seven starters returning from the previous season, when the Sooners had been ranked tenth in the nation. But after a win over Maryland in the opening game, the Sooners were soundly trounced by Southern California the following week, 14–40. Texas then continued its domination of the series by defeating the Big Red 7–28, the same score as that of the 1963 game. Next came the University of Kansas in a game that for a time seemed to promise better things. Although the great Kansas back Gale Sayers returned the opening kickoff 93 yards for a touchdown, the Sooners were able to hold the Kansans in check during most of the remainder of the game, while scoring 14 points of their own. Then, with only seconds remaining in the game, Kansas scored on a 26-yard screen pass and, with no time remaining, converted for 2 points on a double reverse. The final score: Oklahoma 14, Kansas 15.

Oklahoma won the next three games on its schedule but only managed a 14–14 tie with Missouri in a game played at Norman. The tie gave an undisputed championship to Nebraska, even though the Cornhuskers still had to play Oklahoma; the Nebraskans were undefeated in conference play, while OU had lost one game and tied another. Though the Sooners defeated Nebraska by the rather convincing score of 17–7, the victory was meaningless as far as conference standings were concerned.

But the defeat of Nebraska and a win the following week over Oklahoma State University, with a 6–3–1 record for the season, brought OU a bid to the Gator Bowl with Florida State as the opponent. The Gator Bowl game turned out to be an ill-fated venture. Only hours before the kickoff four members of the squad were accused of signing undated contracts with professional football teams. Included were three members of the starting eleven: Jim Grisham, Lance Rentzel, and All-America tackle Ralph Neely and a fourth member of the squad, Wes Skidgel. After conferring with the players, Jones dismissed them from the squad, and reorganized his lineup as best he could.

OU fans, badly spoiled by the great wins of the preceding decade, considered the game a disaster. Florida State's brilliant passing attack, fueled by quarterback Steve Tensi and receiver Fred Beletnikoff, overwhelmed the crippled OU team. The score was 19–36 in favor of Florida State. In a postgame ceremony Beletnikoff and I believe one or more other members of the Florida State squad signed pro contracts on the football field.

Before the bowl game Jones had received considerable support for his prompt and forthright action in dropping from the squad the players who had signed pro contracts, but the reaction of the fans after the game was somewhat different. Eph Monroe, president of the OU Board of Regents, received about two hundred letters, telegrams, and long-distance calls complaining about the coaching situation in all sports at the university. Some of the communications hinted that OU coaches might be involved in moonlighting activities designed to recruit athletes for professional teams. After a discussion of this possibility at the regents' meeting in January, 1965, it was decided that the entire board should act as a committee to investigate the charge. It was agreed that the regents would make a special effort to determine whether any of the coaches had acted as scouts for professional football teams. Later the regents had a session with Jones and with other coaches, but nothing was uncovered that would justify further action. But there was speculation on the campus that Jones would have to revive football prestige at the university very promptly if he was to survive in the job.

The 1965 football season was, in the minds of Big Red partisans, equivalent to a national disaster. The team finished the season with a 3–7 record, defeating only Kansas, Kansas State, and Iowa State. Perhaps most frustrating of all was the 16–17 loss to Oklahoma State University, the first time that the Cowpokes had defeated the Sooners since 1945. The contest was bitterly fought on Owen Field. Ron Shotts, of Weatherford, played a superb game that day, rushing for 163 yards, many of which he gained after suffering a shoulder separation. With about three minutes to go, he kicked a field goal to give his team a 16–14 margin, but a minute and a half later Oklahoma State retaliated with a field goal that gave them the one-point margin of victory.

A few days later Jones resigned as head coach, but his fate in the position had been settled much earlier. About mid-November I was invited to meet with four members of the OU Touchdown Club in Oklahoma City. At the meeting they told me that unless Jones was replaced as coach the Touchdown Club would withdraw its support from the OU athletic program. I told them that I could have no part in removing Jones and thought that I should not have the responsibility of reporting the club's attitude to him. They agreed that members of the club would talk with him.

Later Jones told me that members of the Touchdown Club had talked with him, but he did not report that they had delivered an ultimatum, although I suspected that they had done so. He said that he had decided to resign, whereupon I assured him that, as far as I was concerned, he could continue with his coaching duties. In presenting his resignation to the regents, and in talking with reporters about it, Jones shrugged off the suggestion that he had been forced to resign because of threatened withdrawal of support by the Touchdown Club. He stated simply, "I just got tired of the criticism and of constantly reading and listening to all the untrue rumors concerning my position as head coach here." He was too much of a gentleman to say anything that might cause a rift in the relationship between the Touchdown Club and the university. In accepting his resignation, the regents revoked the provision in his contract that the positions of head coach and athletic director would be inseparable. After a brief discussion—so brief that I suspected the matter had been settled in advance—they voted to retain him as athletic director and enlist his aid in finding a new coach.

Although some considered him unsuccessful during his tenure as head coach at OU, Jones had in earlier years proved to be a great coach. On more than one occasion Wilkinson said that Jones was the greatest football teacher he had ever known. His players admired and respected him, and many of them regarded him as a sort of "father away from home." He continued to serve effectively as director of athletics until he was fatally stricken by a heart attack in the spring of 1971.

CHAPTER 28

Carrying on the Tradition—Jim Mackenzie, Chuck Fairbanks, Barry Switzer

1966 –

THE end of the Wilkinson-Jones coaching dynasty did not signal the end of great football at the university. After Jones resigned in 1965, university officials, including the Athletic Council, set out to find a coach who could keep the tradition going. They received a lot of unsolicited help from fans who thought that OU should be able to attract any coach in the nation merely by making an offer.

One such group, numbering several hundred people, promoted Darrell Royal for the position. The core of this group consisted of Royal's teammates in the years he played at OU. Many of his supporters had suggested his name when Wilkinson resigned. They had insisted that Royal wanted very much to "come back home" and that it would take only an offer to bring him.

With the resignation of Jones, Royal's fans renewed their efforts. In three or four days I received a three-inch stack of letters and telegrams. One said: "You goofed when Wilkinson resigned. For heaven's sake, don't goof again. Bring Royal back to coach at OU."

While Royal would have been a welcome solution to OU's coaching problem, I felt sure that he was not available. I had reliable information that he was receiving an income from all sources of about $50,000 a year at Texas and also had tenure as professor of physical education. But I knew also that his supporters would never believe that he would not come to Oklahoma unless he had an opportunity to turn down the offer. I asked Gomer Jones and the Athletic Council to join me in recommending to the regents that they offer Royal a six-year contract to take over the coaching duties at OU at a salary of $32,000 a year and that they announce the offer to the news media. The salary was higher than any OU coach had ever received, and it was certainly higher, I thought, than Royal's base salary at Texas. If he turned down an offer of that kind, those pushing him for the Oklahoma job would realize that he was not interested and

365

Jim Mackenzie, from the University of Arkansas, was selected by the OU regents to fill the head coaching job at OU in 1966. Courtesy Sports Information Department.

would then support the coach who was finally chosen for the job.

Jones and the Athletic Council joined me in making the recommendation to the regents, and, while they were somewhat hesitant to make public an offer to a prospective coach, they finally agreed to do so. The offer was widely reported in Oklahoma and Texas newspapers, and Royal, at least, was well pleased with the publicity. But, as I expected, it took him less than a week to decide that he was not interested, though he graciously expressed appreciation of the offer.

Jim Mackenzie, assistant to Frank Broyles at the University of Arkansas, was finally selected for the job. When Mackenzie reported for duty in the spring of 1966, he assembled what appeared to be an unusually competent team of assistant coaches, including Chuck Fairbanks, who had played football at Michigan State University, and Barry Switzer, who had played under Frank Broyles at Arkansas.

Mackenzie's relatively thin but well-disciplined squad won the first four games in 1966 and, to the delight of Oklahoma fans, ended the winning streak that the Texas Longhorns had enjoyed for eight seasons. Oklahoma was ranked tenth in the nation, the first national ranking the school had received for some time.

But of the six remaining games the Sooners were able to win only two (one was the Nebraska game) and, worst of all, lost for the second consecutive year to Oklahoma State University, again by a one-point margin.

Although producing a winning season by a very narrow margin, Mackenzie's program gave promise in the defeat of the two giants on the schedule, Texas and Nebraska. The Cornhuskers had dominated the conference since Oklahoma's decline, and despite their loss to Oklahoma they won the conference championship that year and a bid to the Sugar Bowl.

Mackenzie and his staff recruited vigorously for the following season and in 1967 worked enthusiastically on spring practice. But on April 28, Mackenzie died of a heart attack, shortly after returning home from a recruiting trip. His death brought temporary chaos to athletic affairs and a bewildering variety of suggestions about what to do. I had visited practice sessions on several occasions during the 1966 season and had been much

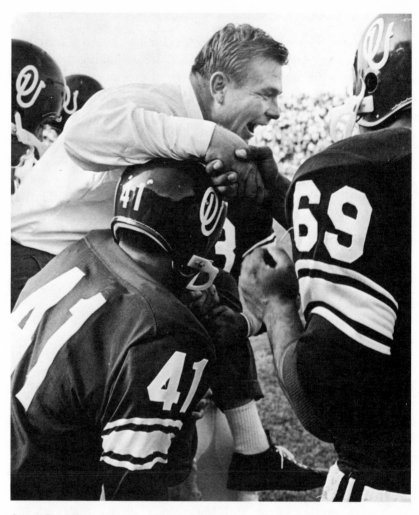

Coach Jim Mackenzie is carried to the dressing room by his victorious Sooners following an upset that ended an eight-season domination of OU by the Texas Longhorns. Courtesy Sports Information Department.

impressed by Chuck Fairbanks. I called James G. Davidson, president of the Board of Regents, and suggested that Fairbanks immediately be named Mackenzie's successor. But Davidson, who had been in touch with some of his fellow board members, thought that we should take whatever time was necessary to find a coach with an established national reputation. Later, conferring with

Chuck Fairbanks, an assistant to Mackenzie, became head coach after Mackenzie's untimely death in 1967. Courtesy Sports Information Department.

other members of the board, I found that all of them agreed that the university should be in no hurry to name a head coach. They suggested several coaches for consideration, including Pete Elliott, who had worked with Wilkinson at OU and later had coached at Nebraska, California, and Illinois.

With a man of Fairbanks' competence immediately available, it seemed to me extremely unwise to spend a month to six weeks hunting for an established coach, who would come in with a new coaching staff and start a new program. Several years earlier the regents had given me authority to fill vacant administrative posts when emergency situations developed. I decided that a head-coach vacancy during spring practice could be interpreted as an emergency and that I should exercise the authority given me by the board. I took moral support for this action from the fact that I had already announced my retirement from the presidency of OU effective June 30, 1968. After talking with Jones and Fairbanks and learning that Fairbanks would accept a somewhat shaky appointment of this kind, I announced to the news media that he had been named head coach by executive order, subject to the approval of the Board of Regents at the next meeting. Accordingly Fairbanks took over four days after Mackenzie's death.

To my surprise, when the regents assembled for their meeting in May, they reacted amiably to what I had done. But they made it plain that the appointment of Fairbanks was to be regarded as temporary and that I should immediately start looking for a coach with a national reputation. They approved a nine-month contract for Fairbanks, ending on January 31, 1968. After the meeting adjourned, one board member suggested that it was not too early to start looking for the "permanent coach."

But by the time Fairbanks' contract expired, OU had won a conference championship, was third in the nation in the final poll of the Associated Press, and had defeated Tennessee in the Orange Bowl. There was no difficulty getting his contract renewed.

Fairbanks continued as head coach through 1972. He had no losing years, but in 1969 and 1970 his winning margins were only 6–4. Although he and his staff had coached Steve Owens to a

Steve Owens became the second Sooner in OU's football history to win the Heisman Trophy, 1969. Courtesy Sports Information Department.

Barry Switzer became head coach in 1972. Courtesy Sports Information Department.

Heisman Trophy in 1969, the badly spoiled Oklahoma fans were not satisfied, and "Chuck Chuck" signs showed up on automobile bumpers, fraternity houses, and elsewhere.

But the 1971 and 1972 seasons restored Oklahoma to national prominence with a winning record of 21–1 in regular season play and with victories over Auburn and Penn State in the Sugar Bowl. After the 1972 season Fairbanks resigned to become head coach and general manager of the New England Patriots, and Barry Switzer, intense and personable offensive coach under Fairbanks, took over as head coach at OU.

Switzer inherited an impressive football squad—which, of course, he had helped recruit. A conspicuous component of his squad was the number of black athletes. Wilkinson had accepted Prentice Gautt back in 1956, but only a few talented blacks had followed Gautt to the OU campus in succeeding years. Since Mackenzie's time an aggressive effort had been made to recruit black athletes, and the effort paid off. The election of Glenn King as first black co-captain of the OU football team in 1971 doubtless had a favorable effect on the recruitment of blacks. Certainly the impact of such superb athletes as Granville Liggins, Eddie Hinton, Gregg Pruitt, Joe Washington, Rod Shoate, and the three Selmon brothers, to mention only a few, would be difficult to overemphasize. They, and the other talented blacks, working in reasonable harmony with the white members of the squad, were a major—perhaps decisive—factor in OU's return to national prominence in football.

At this writing Barry Switzer is head coach of football at the University of Oklahoma. After four seasons he enjoys the distinction of winning or sharing four conference championships, with two back-to-back national championships and an Orange Bowl victory to his credit. But he is in the unenviable position of knowing that he cannot continue to win national championships indefinitely, and Oklahoma football fans may have little tolerance for merely placing in the first ten teams of the country.

What have been the results of the great football tradition established at OU? Thinking back through the years and reflecting on the objective of the regents in 1946, when Tatum was hired—

to develop a sports program that would bolster the slumping morale of Oklahoma's citizens—I believe that that objective has been attained. Wilkinson's career can be compared with that of Will Rogers in its boost to state pride. Oklahoma football has been extremely effective in bringing the state to the attention of the rest of the nation.

But, critics sometimes ask, has football been a good thing for the University of Oklahoma? Frankly, I do not know. It was an important source of revenue to the university in the Wilkinson days, but in recent years, with seemingly uncontrollable rising operational costs, there have been budgetary deficits. During the late 1940's and through most of the 1950's postseason contests had a very distracting influence on the university's academic programs. But with the increasing sophistication of modern-day student bodies this effect has lessened markedly.

Thinking in terms of the basic purposes of higher education, many wonder whether athletic extravaganzas are relevant to the over-all mission of a university. Often I have been asked if it is necessary, or advisable, for a university to provide entertainment of such magnitude—entertainment reminiscent of the ancient Roman games scheduled periodically in the coliseums for the amusement of the masses. Should the largest, most expensive physical facilities on a campus be those used for athletics? Does this give at least a segment of the population the wrong impression of the function of an institution of higher learning and, as long as teams are winning, encourage the citizens to be satisfied with other campus programs that are less than first rate? These are questions that worry many thoughtful people. Regardless of the answers, big-time intercollegiate sports probably will continue their relationship to higher education. Popular demand will see to that.

It can be argued that a university should be a place where a student has an opportunity to develop to the fullest possible extent any potential—mental, physical, or both—that he or she may possess. Sports competition provides opportunities for that kind of growth.

If OU football has been extremely beneficial to the pride and image of the state as a whole, secondary benefits certainly have accrued to the university and will continue to do so. This alone may justify the sport's continued existence, especially if intercollegiate athletics can be kept within the over-all governance of the institution, with faculty, administration, and regents having appropriate roles—a very difficult goal to achieve, as many university presidents have found.

University presidents can't punt, though most of those in charge of football teams often wish that they could. They can only carry the ball and hope not to fumble. But now that I am president emeritus, with no further responsibility in such matters, I can look forward hopefully to enjoying great OU football for years to come.

Go Big Red!

Index